MW01097273

THIRD MIND

THIRD MIND

Creative Writing through Visual Art

Tonya Foster & Kristin Prevallet

EDITORS

TEACHERS & WRITERS
COLLABORATIVE

New York

THIRD MIND: Creative Writing through Visual Art

Library of Congress Cataloging-in-Publication Data

Third mind: creative writing through visual art / edited by Tonya Foster & Kristin Prevallet.
        p. cm.
Includes bibliographical references.
   ISBN 0-915924-94-3 (alk. paper)
  1. English language--Rhetoric--Study and teaching. 2. English language--Composition and exercises--Study and teaching. 3. Visual perception--Study and teaching. 4. Creative writing--Study and teaching. 5. Art--Study and teaching. 6. Art in education. I. Foster, Tonya, 1966– II. Prevallet, Kristin, 1966–.
     PE1404 .T483 2002
     808' .042'071--dc21

                             2002000352

Teachers & Writers Collaborative
5 Union Square West
New York, N.Y. 10003

Cover Design: Christina Davis
Cover Art: Mosaic by Ellen Driscoll, detail
from *As Above, So Below* (1993–99). © Ellen Driscoll.
Photograph by Mike Kamber.
Page Design: Christina Davis & Christopher Edgar

Printed by Philmark Lithographics, New York, N.Y. First printing.

Acknowledgments

The editors would like to thank Chris Edgar and Christina Davis for their patience and expertise in attending to the details surrounding this anthology. We would also like to thank Teachers & Writers Collaborative (where we were both employed as writers-in-residence for several years) and Cooper Union's Saturday Outreach Program. We are particularly grateful to Stephanie Hightower for her enthusiasm and vision, and to Marina Guitterez for opening the studios to us.

Many thanks to Matthew Sharpe, Catherine Barnett, and Nancy Larson Shapiro for their work on this project.

Teachers & Writers Books wishes to acknowledge the following institutions, galleries, and individuals for granting permission to reproduce the images that appear in the text: Erik Johnson, *An Allegory of Emotion(s)*, 2000. Courtesy of Erik Johnson. Wifredo Lam, *The Jungle*, 1943. Courtesy of The Museum of Modern Art Inter-American Fund. Photograph © 2002. The Museum of Modern Art, New York. Edward Lear, *View of Mt. Parnassus, 1849*. Collection of Edward Lear's watercolors. Courtesy of Gennadius Library, American School of Classical Studies, Athens. René Magritte, *Time Transfixed*, 1938. Joseph Winterbotham Collection, 1970.436 © The Art Institute of Chicago. All rights reserved. Additional permission was provided by the Artists Rights Society, New York. Joan Miró, *The Nightingale's Song at Midnight and the Morning Rain*. Private Collection, photograph courtesy of Acquavella Galleries, Inc. © Sussecio Miró /Artists Rights Society (ARS), New York /ADAAGP, Paris. Parmigianino, *Self-Portrait in a Convex Mirror*, 1523. Courtesy of Kunsthistoriches Museum, Vienna. Photograph © Erich Lessing / Art Resource, New York. Qi Bashi, *Scholar's Tools*, 1947. Courtesy of The Metropolitan Museum of Art. Mark Rothko, *Red, Brown, and Black*, 1958. Courtesy of The Museum of Modern Art. Simon Guggenheim Fund. Photograph © 2002 The Museum of Modern Art, New York. Nelson Savinon, *Study No. 30 for AMERIKA VI*, 1984–85. Courtesy of Trevor Winkfield. George Schneeman and Anne Waldman, *Homage to Allen G.*, 1997. Courtesy of Granary Books. Cy Twombly, *Untitled [Say Goodbye Catullus to the Shores of Asia Minor]*, detail, 1994. Courtesy of Cy Twombly Gallery, The Menil Collection, Houston. Gift of the Artist.

Special thanks to the following individuals for contributing photographs and artworks from the school projects that are featured in the text: Pamela Beal, Susan Karwoska, Holly Masturzo, Rosalind Pace, Tina Rotenberg, John and Julie Moulds Rybicki, Ezra Shales, Marcia Simon, Amy Trachtenberg, and Mary Whalen.

Teachers & Writers Books wishes to acknowledge the following publishers and individuals for granting permission to reprint poems that appear in the text: John Ashbery, "Pantoum," from *Some Trees* by John Ashbery. © 1956 by John Ashbery. Reprinted by permission of Georges Borchardt, Inc., on behalf of the author. Li Po, "Going to Visit Tai-T'ien Mountain's Master of the Way without Finding Him," "Ching-T'ing Mountian, Sitting Alone," "Gazing at the Lu Mountain Waterfall," and "Thoughts in Night Quiet," translated by David Hinton, from *The Selected Poems of Li Po*. © 1996 by David Hinton. Reprinted by permission of New Directions Publishing Corp. Robert Hayden, "Monet's 'Waterlilies,'" from *Angle of Ascent: New and Selected Poems by Robert Hayden*. © 1975, 1972, 1970, 1966 by Robert Hayden. Used by permission of Liveright Publishing Corporation. John Taggart, Section I from "Slow Song for Mark Rothko." Reprinted by permission of the author.

The essays by bell hooks and Michele Wallace in this volume were previously published. "Art Is for Everybody" by bell hooks is an excerpt from her book *Art on My Mind*. © 1995 by bell hooks. Reprinted by permission of The New Press. Michele Wallace's essay originally appeared in the exhibition catalogue, *Tim Rollins + K.O.S.* © 1989 Dia Art Foundation. Reprinted by permission of the author.

Teachers & Writers programs are made possible in part by grants from the New York City Department of Cultural Affairs and the National Endowment for the Arts, and with public funds from the New York State Council on the Arts, a State Agency. Teachers & Writers Collaborative is also grateful for support from the following foundations and corporations: AKC Fund, Axe-Houghton Foundation, The David and Minnie Berk Foundation, Bronx Borough President and City Council, The Bydale Foundation, The Cerimon Fund, the Chelsea Austin Foundation, The Saul Z. and Amy S. Cohen Family Foundation, Consolidated Edison, E.H.A. Foundation, Fleet Bank, Jenesis Group, The Janet Stone Jones Foundation, Low Wood Fund, Inc., Manhattan City Council Delegation, M & O Foundation, Morgan Stanley Dean Witter Foundation, NBC, New York Community Trust (Van Lier Fund), New York Times Company Foundation, Henry Nias Foundation, North Star Fund, The Open Society Institute, Queens Borough President and City Council, Joshua Ringel Memorial Fund, Maurice R. Robinson Fund, Rush Philanthropic Arts Foundation, St. Ann's School, The Scheide Fund, The Scherman Foundation, the Verizon Foundation, and the Wendling Foundation. T&W's 30th-Anniversary Endowed Residencies are supported by Marvin Hoffman and Rosellen Brown, the New World Foundation, Steven Schrader, Alison Wylegala (in memory of Sergio Guerrero), John Gilman (in memory of June Baker), and anonymous donors.

Contents

List of Illustrations

Introduction

Monet's "Waterlilies"

for Bill and Sonja

Today as the news from Selma and Saigon
poisons the air like fallout,
   I come again to see
the serene great picture that I love.

Here space and time exist in light
the eye like the eye of faith believes.
   The seen, the known
dissolve in iridescence, become
illusive flesh of light
    that was not, was, forever is.

O light beheld as through refracting tears.
Here is the aura of that world
   each of us has lost.
Here is the shadow of its joy.

—Robert Hayden

In "Monet's 'Waterlilies'" the poet looks into a serene, impressionist painting and, in the midst of waterlilies reflected on a pond, sees the looming shadow of the world around him. The effect of simultaneously being in two worlds inspires the poet to create something new—a poem that reflects both the painting and his engagement with the events of his own time. This is the power of bringing visual art and writing together. Contributor Terry Blackhawk writes in this book that "looking at a work of art is like looking into the act of creation." This "looking into" requires close and concentrated focus and a sensitivity to that moment in which the painting and the world meet each other halfway. The aim of this anthology is to unite these two powerful allies—creative writing and visual art—in the classroom.

Any student who tries *ekphrasis* (writing that takes its inspiration from visual art) becomes a participant in the kind of dialogue that has engaged writers and artists for centuries. Plato writes of it in *Phaedrus*, observing that paintings and poems, when put together, "seem to talk to you as if they were intelligent." Listening to works of art and participating in a conversation with them can produce exciting and shifting responses in each of us: poems, stories, self-portraits, essays, and other creative works are generated that "talk back" to the visual stimulus. This is what William Burroughs called the "third mind." The third mind, to cite contributor Anne Waldman, is a state in which "something new, or 'other,' emerges from the combination that would not have come about with a solo act."

As teachers of writing in Cooper Union's Saturday Outreach Program (intensive courses for high school students interested in careers in art), we regularly confront the problem of how to inspire students to write. Showing students a painting and telling them, "Write a description of all that you see," is only the first step in the process of getting them to understand what we mean when we say that "good writing shows, not tells." Tangible and colorful, with shapes and images to grab onto, visual art inspires students to write using details that are lively because what is emphasized is the "I" looking. Visual art allows students to immerse themselves in their own processes of reflection, which encourages them to generate unique responses to the world around them.

Unfortunately, for many of our students writing seems disconnected from their day-to-day lives, from the individual ways they have developed to make sense of the world. In school they are often asked to categorize the world in standard ways and to learn information that may seem unrelated to personal experience. This is, of course, necessary—structured writing enables students to enter a literate community. Intrinsic to childhood is a fervent desire to please and to grow up, and the eagerness to embrace adult ways of categorizing and naming things. Michael Theune observes in his essay "*Ut Pictura Poesis*" that "young people…are often more concerned about distancing themselves from their childlike aspects than they are about indulging them." This desire for maturity frequently means that greater attention is paid to external forms that evidence "adulthood" than to the students' particular visions.

All of these things are complicated by the fact that students often believe that their imaginations are limited to a set of mental images derived from Saturday morning cartoons, video games, and Hollywood movies. How, then, do we as writers and as teachers help students gain control of their own imaginations? How do we engage the unique potential of each student in ways that illuminate what Will Alexander in his essay "Igniting the Inward Prodigy" calls "interior sonority"? And, from there, how do we inspire students to see themselves as vital parts of a larger world?

Many teachers have found innovative ways to accomplish this. The essays in this book draw lines of connection between the written word, the light seen, and the life lived. They offer both practical and theoretical insights into how we as teachers can encourage students to see themselves as vitally connected to a multiplicity of other minds and ways of thinking.

These essays cover a broad range of perspectives—from the classroom teacher's to the arts administrator's to the writer's—as well as a wide range of artistic disciplines. Susan Karwoska's essay, for example, shows how to collect and incorporate students' memories into a quilt. Pamela Beal suggests practical ways to create interdisciplinary literature units for public school curricula—including making a papier-mâché giant to illustrate *The Epic of Gilgamesh*. Ezra Shales describes portraiture techniques that blend photography, drawing, and writing. John and Julie Moulds Rybicki use photography to encourage students to become engaged in representing their own worlds. Holly Masturzo introduces her students to the paintings of Cy Twombly—an abstract artist whose "scribbles" across the canvas replicate the gesture of writing—so they can recognize their own emotions in the lines they are drawing, the "feltness of that moment of creation." There are examples of ways to incorporate artwork from various cultures: Beth Zasloff, for example, uses Chinese brush painting to inspire students to "translate their visions into words on the page," and Debora Iyall (in Tina Rotenberg's essay) creates puppet shows based on Native American creation myths. Kathy Walsh-Piper's essay at the end of the anthology provides valuable information on the many writing programs that exist in art museums across the country.

This anthology also explores the larger social and political issues involved in introducing students to visual culture. As educators working with art, we need to be mindful of the social power of images and the possibility that canonical artworks do not necessarily represent our students' real worlds. As bell hooks writes in her essay "Art Is for Everybody," it is important to keep in mind that there is a "politics of seeing." Hooks explicitly discusses the effects of the "underrepresentation" of images that reflect the experiences of African Americans. "Identification with art is a process," hooks writes. "We look with the received understanding that art is necessarily a terrain of defamiliarization: it may take what we see/know and make us look at it in a new way." The motivation to write and to create comes in part from the incentive to respond to, and engage in dialogue with, the social, cultural, aesthetic, and economic contexts that surround us.

With these complexities in mind, we invite teachers to transform the classroom into what René Magritte so aptly titled one of his paintings—*The Listening Room*. In the painting, a green apple is surrounded by four walls. The apple may be, like Alice, on the verge of outgrowing the room. Or the apple may be of normal size, placed in a house that is inordinately small, shrinking around it. It is not one or the other, but both: the painting suggests multiple perspectives and multiple realities, simultaneously. "The Listening Room" is both the room in which we listen and the room that listens to us. It is also the classroom in which multiple minds are all working independently, absorbed by the moment of writing.

—Tonya Foster and Kristin Prevallet

Ekphrastic Poetry

Entering and Giving Voice to Works of Art

by Terry Blackhawk

*i*T WAS ONLY AFTER SEVERAL YEARS of using art to launch students' poetry (and my own) that I learned the process had a formal name—"ekphrastic poetry" (or, alternately, "ecphrastic")—from the Greek, meaning poetry that takes its inspiration from visual art. In its earliest, most restricted sense, *ekphrasis* referred to the verbal description of a visual representation, often of an imagined object such as the shield of Achilles in the *Iliad*. With its principle of *ut pictura poesis* (poetry as a speaking picture and painting as mute poetry), Horace's *Ars Poetica* expressed the ekphrastic ideal of giving voice to painting. From Ben Jonson to William Blake to the Romantics, many poets, most famously Keats with his urn and Shelley with his fallen statue, have allowed art to tease them "out of thought." Rainer Maria Rilke, the Surrealists, W. B. Yeats, Marianne Moore, W. H. Auden, and William Carlos Williams continued the tradition in the twentieth century. Nowadays, as semioticians and other literary theorists try to resolve the temporal/spatial dualities of text/image, one promising sign is a literary journal, appropriately titled *Ekphrasis*, which publishes the work of the many contemporary poets who continue to find inspiration in visual art.

It seems that works of art, in and of themselves, have the power to create creativity. According to poet Edward Hirsch, looking at a work of art is like looking into the act of creation. "Works of art," he says, "initiate and provoke other works of art; the process is a source of art itself."[1] From the outset, engagement with visual art requires something different from engagement with the day-to-day world. Art gives us imagery—images that are representational rather than "real." Art requires leaps of perceiving and experiencing. Like viewers of René Magritte's *Ceci n'est pas une pipe*, we are suddenly confronted with something that is, yet is not, what it seems. This "otherness," or detachment from the rest of the world—which the philosopher Suzanne Langer defines as characteristic of every genuine work of art—may be one reason why art can provide such a wonderful stimulus to writing. As Langer aptly puts it: "Sometimes, in the presence of great art, attention to the actual environment is hard to sustain."[2] Painting, she explains, creates a sense of "virtual space," or semblance; we experience it the way we experience a dream, abstracted from ordinary reality, yet vivid and real, alive in its own terms. Henri Matisse's view that "a drawing must . . . bring to life the space which surrounds it"[3] is echoed by many artists. This virtual space is a living space, capable of drawing the viewer into a meditative or dream state where eye, heart, and mind journey together.

The long looking and close attention required to "enter into" artwork is strikingly illustrated by Rilke's *Letters on Cézanne*. These letters by the poet, written to his wife Clara and composed in Paris in 1907 when he was paying daily visits to a salon exhibiting Paul Cézanne's work, reveal his conviction that art demands *participation* by the viewer, not just intellectual understanding. That the process deeply penetrated Rilke's psyche can be seen in some of the phrases he used to describe colors in Cézanne's paintings. For Rilke, Cézanne "so incorruptibly reduced a reality to its color content that that reality resumed a new existence in a beyond of color."[4] Instead of language that labels, Rilke gives us language that responds: a "deeply quilted blue," a "listening blue," a "self-contained blue," and more—all coming from a realm of words far removed from such tags as *indigo* or *cerulean*. In the paintings of Cézanne, Rilke found a way toward the language of "pure objective telling" that he sought in his poetry; as he said of the fruits Cézanne painted, they "cease to be edible altogether, that's how thing-like and real they become."[5]

Ekphrastic poetry involves the writer-viewer in a variety of stances toward the art: one may describe, address, or reflect upon the subject of the work. But perhaps the most useful of these stances, especially with painting, is "entering"—which, as poet and critic John Hollander explains, encourages us to make the spirit and space of the work of art our own. Czeslaw Milosz's poem "Realism," which begins, "We are not so badly off if we can admire Dutch painting," takes the reader on a journey reminiscent of Keats's negative capability. Midway into the Milosz poem, the speaker states, "Therefore I enter those landscapes," before joining the human figures in the scene, "becom[ing] one of them who vanished long ago." This process of entering and becoming is so fundamental to engaging in a work of art that it almost seems too basic to point out, save to note that the intense, absorbed state of mind that one has when looking at art is similar to the intense focus of writing. As we step inside the artwork and let its space become our space, we more easily get into that state that poet Jane Hirshfield calls "flow"—"the moment willed effort falls away and we fall utterly into the object of our attention."[6]

Terry Blackhawk

An astonishing variety of strategies for ekphrastic poetry can be found in the work of contemporary poets. These can go beyond the examination of a single work; many poets find the life or oeuvre of a painter just as intriguing as the paintings themselves. Mark Strand and Charles Simic have each devoted an entire volume of poetry to a single artist—Edward Hopper and Joseph Cornell, respectively. Lisel Mueller, in her poem "Monet Refuses the Operation," evokes well-known images from Monet's paintings as well as the artist's philosophy of flux and flow. Monet firmly informs his eye doctor that he has no intention of "correcting" his vision and abandoning "haloes / around the streetlights in Paris" in order to embrace "fixed / notions of top and bottom" or "return to a universe / of subjects that don't know each other." After all, he says, it had taken "all my life / to arrive at the vision of gas lamps as angels." In *Text and Contexts*, Geoffrey and Judith Summerfield explain how writing from a persona or an assumed role can help the writer make new discoveries and connections. "The framework of the role . . . [its]vicariousness . . . is perhaps its greatest virtue. No personal confession is involved. But the very detachment promotes, paradoxically, a greater intensity and concentration of 'existential presence,' of personal truth."[7] Monet's persona becomes a mask through which Mueller expresses a kind of artistic or philosophical manifesto.

Many other poets use carefully selected details from an artist's life in their poems. Stanley Kunitz's "The Crystal Cage," for example, addresses the artist Joseph Cornell directly: "Three days you fasted / to bring you angels." After a catalogue of symbols and images from Cornell's work, Kunitz has the artist slowly ascend a bell tower of imagery until the last lines ("What if, below, / your twisted brother is calling?") pull Cornell back to the reality of the handicapped brother he cared for. Alicia Ostriker's four-part poem "Caravaggio: The Painting of Force and Violence," draws the viewer-reader into a meditation on violence in the work of "an ignobly modern man / a quick man with a sword." In *The Art of Loss*, Myrna Stone weaves narrative details of the lives of Botticelli, van Gogh, and Degas into poems about these artists' work. Botticelli's grief over Savonarola's execution, van Gogh's last days as a guest of Dr. Gachet, and Degas's mourning for Rouart form the background of poems that also guide the reader's eye through the canvases in question. Poet Patricia Hooper, in "Monet's Garden," uses quotes from the artist's diary to reveal the almost clinical interest he took in the change of colors in his dying wife's complexion.

The encounter with art can also provide poets with an imaginative substratum through which difficult personal subjects can surface. In a recent conversation, Linda Nemec Foster discussed how Gerrit Beneker's *Provincetown in Winter, 1918*, a subdued painting of boats and sky, enabled her to write, finally, about the deaths of her mother's two sisters, which came before her mother was born. The painting's date helped her make the connection between the time of her mother's conception ("Halfway into the continent, in a place of factories /not boats, my mother is being conceived / by her immigrant parents") and the evocative, almost vanishing boats "leaning into each other / as if in unmarked graves. The sky, / gray and calm, waiting to be born."[8] Bob Hicok's poem "Rivera's *Golden Gate Mural*," in which a father and daughter view Rivera's artwork together, reveals much about the mural and its two viewers. What the child likes—what interests her, what she asks or doesn't ask about—helps the reader both to see details in the mural and to learn about the fragility in the father/daughter relationship. The girl wants to know, finally, about "the tree of Life and Love," and if her father loved her mother, to which the speaker lies and answers, "Yes."

The fact that the actual images described in ekphrastic poetry are seldom present to the reader can create a very lively triangle among the artwork and poet, poet and reader, and the reader and the art described in the poem. And while the contemporary poet may fulfill the traditional ekphrastic goal of making the reader "see," the poem frequently goes beyond this, embracing the writer's associations or concerns and even reflecting on its own "being" as a poem. One extraordinary example of this is John Ashbery's "Self-Portrait in a Convex Mirror," a sixteen-page meditation on the painting by Parmigianino of the same name (see figure 1), in which the poet examines and seems to take delight in multiple facets of art-poet-reader-text connections. The poem alternately addresses the artist (by his first name, Francesco) and the reader; includes visual details of the painting as well as critical commentary and facts about the painting's history and Parmigianino's life; and lets us know when the poet first saw it and where the painting now hangs. But primarily it takes the reader on a luxurious excursion through memory, reflections on the soul expressed in art, and the writer's meditations upon himself and the poem he is writing. The elusive nature of the whole endeavor keeps cropping up as Ashbery invites all the contradictory impulses, thoughts, and associations evoked by the painting to surface and contend with one another. Near the end, the poem itself becomes suspect:

Terry Blackhawk

> ...the way of telling
> ...somehow intrude[s], twisting the end result
> Into a caricature of itself. This always
> Happens, as in the game where
> A whispered phrase passed around the room
> Ends up as something completely different.[9]

Elizabeth Bishop's "Poem," by contrast, is an example of a poet trying to capture precisely what she sees—in this case, in a work of art that is not a masterpiece. Bishop is not alone in finding inspiration in amateur painting or common artifacts. "Outsider" art and folk installations have sparked poems by Mark Doty ("Dickeyville Grotto") and Sandra McPherson ("Outsider: Minnie Evans" or "Reposoir: Four Legends for Mose Tolliver's *Flowering Tree*")—to name just a few contemporary poets who understand that the so-called "quality" of the art does not determine the writing. As Marcel Duchamp says, "Art is not about itself but the attention we bring to it." Through attentiveness to the artwork's exact size, color, detail, and purpose, Bishop teaches us that nothing is unworthy of attention, not even a modest painting that "never earned any money." About halfway through the first page of the poem, she "enters" the scene, declaring "The air is fresh and cold," before arriving at the sudden realization, "Heavens, I recognize the place, I know it!" This recognition returns her to the "literal small backwater" where both she and the unknown artist lived, their memories "cramped / dim, on a piece of Bristol board, / dim, but how live, how touching in detail."

Many encounters with works of art engender similar shocks of recognition. Stephen Dunn initiates his poem "Slant," a wry take on Mark Tansey's painting of a cow in a room looking at the unveiling of painting of a cow in a field, with a description of a peaceful, fairly ordinary day. But the disjuncture prompted by this hyper-real painting jolts the speaker, who suddenly feels as if he's been "invited / into the actual, someplace / between the real and the real." Perhaps the most famous poem that conveys this shock of recognition is Rilke's "Archaic Torso of Apollo," a meditation that ends with an injunction: "You must change your life." A more recent example of artistic-poetic shock value is Jim Daniels's collection of poems based on paintings by Francis Bacon. Daniels's vernacular ekphrasis seems less inclined to capture visual detail than to get at the emotion or existential truth of the paintings. With lines such as "we got an amusement ride called / the electric chair—how about you?" or "I'm part buffalo, part / human virus. I wear a red tie / to hide the fat pill of my sick heart," Daniels creates and enters personae that are extreme, often vile and hard to watch—intuitive and fascinating poetic doppelgängers of Bacon's tortured figures.

This survey of ekphrastic writing by contemporary poets barely scratches the surface of a genre as varied as the writers who employ it. Nevertheless, I hope it points to the rich interactions and crossovers that occur when word-folk try to express their encounters with the work of image-folk. The following examples will show that engaging with visual art can be just as lively and productive for student writers. In the words of writer and teacher Anne Berthoff, "visualizing, making meaning by means of mental images, is the paradigm of all acts of mind. Students who learn to look and look again are discovering their powers."[10]

✧   ✧   ✧   ✧   ✧   ✧   ✧   ✧   ✧

Because art offers such compelling reality and mystery, the Hippocratic motto of "Do no harm" is probably appropriate to keep in mind when trying ekphrastic poetry with students. While it's tempting to get carried away with one's own excitement and discoveries, as a teacher I try to intrude as little as possible. I want to present art not as an occasion for an art history lecture, but first and foremost as an aesthetic experience. Generally, student writers do find "a way in" to a work of art, but when they need help I may suggest that they simply describe, reflect upon, or directly address the work. Primarily, however, I rely on "entering." "Go into it," I say. "Use your senses." The instruction is usually enough. In this example from one of my classes that participated in the annual Detroit Institute of Arts writing project, ninth grader Lesley enters Martin Heade's *Hummingbirds and Orchids* through the sense of sound.

7

Terry Blackhawk

Natural Sound

Hmmmm mmm mmm mmm mmm mmm mmm

mmm   mmm   mmm   mmm   mmm   mmm

The Surround Sound of Nature

DRIP   DRIP   DRIP   DRIP   DRIP   DRIP   DRIP

DROP   DROP   DROP   DROP   DROP   DROP

Let It Penetrate You

AS   KS   RI   AS   KS

K   H   E   K   H   E   K   H   E   K

S   RI   AS   KS   RI   A

Fill Your Body, Every Last Drop

Hear the environmental orchestra tuning up

The crickets hitting A-major

The fish swimming synchronized

The orchids at full figure

Sun light breaks

And the Symphony Begins.

This approach of calling on the senses works equally well, and often helps students overcome their initial resistance to abstract art, which tends to prompt nervous responses such as "You call that *art*?" or "I could do *that*!" Here is one student's response to Helen Frankenthaler's painting *The Bay*.

What I See!

Standing at four thousand feet
on the top of this mountain
I fear nothing
     but
  the feeling of impact
    on the gold-colored
    sand.
The ocean's waters
  bit by bit
     huddle
to form the person
  I most fear.
As the spirit begins to
    speak
I turn up the volume
  on my consciousness
    to inhale
LQC (large quantity of common
  sense). I listen with an open
    ear as my giant shadow
     stretches
      across the lonely
  deserted beach, surrounded
  by a heartwarming smile
which by itself
creates this beautiful
positive poem about my
innocent shirt that Mom
    washed,
warding off life's soapy cycles.
And about my loving
    personality

                    that she stretched, and pressed
                    and hung out
                            to
                                dry!

                    —Tyrone Davis

In her essay "Poetic Responses to Art," Marilyn Bates points out that an intense, personal identification with a work of art can provide students with "catharsis and insight into heartfelt concerns."[11] Tyrone's "discovery" of his mother in his poem "What I See!" bears this out. The next example reveals a different type of discovery.

Assuming the voice of the collective in Reginald Marsh's *Savoy Ballroom*—a crowded, colorful painting of a 1930s Harlem dance hall—enabled eleventh grader Shysuaune to make what Detroit Institute of Arts juror Nkenge Zola called "an excursion into the political, social (cultural) issues of the era."

Blues Remedy

    we dance
        red
            to the
            blues
    we're boom-bastic
        yellows
            and delicious
                    browns
    we entwine
        ourselves
                in the dark riches of
    Marvin Gaye's voice

    aggressions leave
    with the incoming rhythms

of soul,
　　black soul
　　　we smell the inner city
in a ring of cigar smoke
　　hear it in a bell
　　of cognac
the gray sign
　　of a time
　　when worried black clouds
got lost in Motown
　and depression
　became platinum
pleasures passed
　in the embrace of a slow dance.

　　　　　—Shysuaune Taylor

Perhaps the most interesting and important thing that encounters with the otherness a work of art can promote in the viewer is empathy with its subject-matter or its maker. Catrina's poem shows that students can develop an affinity for individual artists much like Rilke's for Cézanne or Williams's for Breughel:

Vincent Van Gogh: Self-Portrait

Can you see the uncertainty I feel
Or are you fooled like countless others?
Through my eyes, my afflicted heart begs
For release, but no one comes to call
Or quench my fires of frustration.
So I paint.

Can you not see that the sky is
Burdened with birds of ill omen,
Darkened with fluttering anger,
A hell-bent fury, the storming winds.
They loom larger, fly faster

On their damning flight to rage,
And still I paint.

As I look out into the streets
Even the town trollops and strumpets
No longer approach me
But with sudden quickness
Their feet step diligently out of reach.
Yet still only can I paint.

Surely someone has the key to let me
Out of my dungeon of torment.
Trouble won't last always
But for the constantly haunted, morally
Wounded, and rapidly aging
Always sounds longer than all ways,
So yet, and still, I paint.

   —Catrina King

Terry Blackhawk

In an essay on having students write ekphrastic poetry to help them learn about the Holocaust, Nancy Gorrell suggested that the experience of "entering" encourages an openmindedness that students will likely carry over into other aspects of their lives. That this process can help students imagine their way into other cultures, at least to a degree, is evident in the following example. After viewing the rich, wooden "Bowl in the Form of a Beaver"—a Northwest Woodlands Native American artifact—Ellery wrote this empathic poem:

Beaver-Shaped Bowl

My round back surfaces
cut from the burl
that held my soul.
I paddle and shape myself
to their calloused hands.
I roll over
and give myself gladly.

They take what sustains
them in this life,
kneading it in my smooth belly.
My feet woven
to this homely shape
hit hard to the ground.
Eyes stare at me
with quiet agreement
and hands pull forth
the food that I bring
for their existence.

—Ellery Cason

Notes

1. *Transforming Vision: Writers on Art*. Selected and introduced by Edward Hirsch. (The Art Institute of Chicago/Little, Brown, 1994), p. 10.
2. Suzanne Langer, *Feeling and Form* (New York: Charles Scribner's Sons, 1953), p. 81.
3. Ibid, p. 84.
4. Rainer Maria Rilke, *Letters on Cézanne* (New York: Fromm International Publishing, 1985), p. 65.
5. Ibid, p. 33.
6. Jane Hirshfield, *Nine Gates: Entering the Mind of Poetry* (New York: HarperCollins, 1997), p. 4.
7. Geoffrey Summerfield and Judith Summerfield, *Texts and Contexts* (New York: Random House, 1986), p. 210.
8. Linda Nemec Foster, *The Contour of Absence*, unpublished manuscript.
9. John Ashbery, "Self-Portrait in a Convex Mirror," in *Self-Portrait in a Convex Mirror* (New York; Penguin Books, 1972), p. 80.
10. Anne Berthoff, *The Making of Meaning* (Montclair, N.J.: Boynton Cook, 1980), p. 65.
11. Marilyn Bates, "Poetic Responses to Art: Summoning the Adolescent Voice," *Journal of Poetry Therapy* 6, No. 3 (1993), p. 149.

Adams, Pat, ed. *With a Poet's Eye: A Tate Gallery Anthology.* London: Tate Gallery Publications, 1986.

Ashbery, John. "Self-Portrait in a Convex Mirror," in *Self-Portrait in a Convex Mirror.* New York: Penguin Books, 1972.

Bates, Marilyn. "Poetic Responses to Art: Summoning the Adolescent Voice." *Journal of Poetry Therapy* 6, No. 3 (1993).

Berthoff, Anne. *The Making of Meaning.* Montclair, N.J.: Boynton Cook, 1980.

Bishop, Elizabeth. "Poem," in *The Complete Poems, 1927–1979.* New York: Farrar, Straus & Giroux, 1984.

Buchwald, Emilie, ed. *The Poet Dreaming in the Artist's House.* Minneapolis: Milkweed Editions, 1984.

Daniels, Jim. *Blue Jesus.* Pittsburgh: Carnegie Mellon University Press, 2000.

Dunn, Stephen. "Slant," in *Loosestrife.* New York: W. W. Norton, 1996.

Foster, Linda Nemec. "The Contour of Absence," in *The Contour of Absence*, unpublished manuscript.

Fried, Philip, ed. *Acquainted with the Night: Photographs by Lynn Saville; Poetry selected by Philip Fried.* New York: Rizzoli, 1997.

Gorrell, Nancy. "Teaching Empathy through Ecphrastic Poetry: Entering a Curriculum of Peace." *English Journal* 89, No. 5 (May 2000).

Heffernan, James. *The Museum of Words: The Poetics of Ekphrasis from Homer to Ashbery.* Chicago: University of Chicago Press, 1994.

Herbert, Zbigniew. *Still Life with a Bridle.* New York: The Ecco Press, 1991.

Hicok, Bob. "Rivera's *Golden Gate Murals*." In *The Legend of Light.* Madison: The University of Wisconsin Press, 1995.

Hirshfield, Jane. *Nine Gates: Entering the Mind of Poetry.* New York: Harper Collins, 1997.

Hollander, John. *The Gazer's Spirit: Poems Speaking to Silent Works of Art.* Chicago: The University of Chicago Press, 1995.

Hooper, Patricia. "Monet's Garden." In *At the Corner of the Eye.* East Lansing, Mi.: Michigan State University Press, 1997.

Kandinsky, Wassily. *Concerning the Spiritual in Art.* New York: Dover, 1977.

Kunitz, Stanley. "The Crystal Cage." In *The Poems of Stanley Kunitz, 1928–1978.* Boston: Little, Brown, 1979.

Terry Blackhawk

Langer, Susanne. *Feeling and Form*. New York: Charles Scribner's and Sons, 1953.

Milosz, Czelaw, "Realism." Translated by Robert Hass. *The New Yorker*, 11 April 1994, 70.

Mueller, Lisel. "Monet Refuses the Operation." In *Second Language*. Baton Rouge, La.: Louisiana State University Press, 1986.

Ostriker, Alicia. "Caravaggio: The Painting of Force and Violence." In *American Poetry Review* 29, No. 5 (September/October 2000).

Rilke, Rainer Maria. "Archaic Torso of Apollo," in *The Selected Poetry of Rainer Maria Rilke*. Translated by Stephen Mitchell. New York: Vintage Books, 1989.

Rilke, Rainer Maria. *Letters on Cézanne*. Translated by James Agee. New York: Fromm International Publishing Corporation, 1985.

Scott, Grant. *The Sculpted Word: Keats, Ekphrasis and the Visual Arts*. Hanover, N.H.: University Press of New England, 1994.

Simic, Charles. *Dimestore Alchemy*. Hopewell, N.J.: The Ecco Press, 1992.

Stone, Myrna. *The Art of Loss*. East Lansing, Mi.: Michigan State University Press, 2001.

Strand, Mark. *Hopper*. Hopewell, N.J.: The Ecco Press, 1994.

Summerfield, Geoffrey, and Judith Summerfield. *Texts and Contexts*. New York: Random House, 1986.

Tillinghast, Richard, ed. *Visit to the Gallery*. Ann Arbor: University of Michigan Press, 1997.

Transforming Vision: Writers on Art. Selected and introduced by Edward Hirsch. Boston: The Art Institute of Chicago/Little, Brown, 1994.

Zola, Nkenge. "Juror's Statement." In *Blues Remedy: Student Writings about Art*. Detroit: The Detroit Institute of Arts, 1996.

Unfamiliar Ground
Inspiring Students with Abstraction

by Gary Hawkins

*t*HEY SAY "EVERYTHING IS BIGGER" in Texas, and there is no shortage of awesome landscape to contemplate in the state. For the poet in Houston, however, some of the most stunning and inspiring vistas emerge as drawings, sculptures, and paintings within the city's museums. For entire afternoons, I have been bewildered by the constructed boxes of Duchamp and Cornell in Dominique de Menil's collection. I have passed unknown time before the calming and terrifying canvases that surround me in the Rothko Chapel. And, repeatedly, I have stepped inside the Cy Twombly galleries to attempt to fathom *Untitled [Say Goodbye Catullus to the Shores of Asia Minor]*, Twombly's enormous and epic work that fills a long room with explosions of color, silences, and the heavy scent of oils (see figure 2). It would make sense then that, as a poet with Houston's Writers in the Schools, I have sought to kindle creative writing among elementary school children using what awakens me, this local well of abstract twentieth-century art. To inspire students with non-representational art is to watch them face the limits in their own visions and surpass them, and teaching with such art has made me face many of the same challenges.

These challenges come down to a set of understandable resistances. I say "understandable" because the discomfort that students suffer in their efforts to come to terms with abstraction are what most viewers suffer at the hands of it. It is a purposefully unsettling form of art that intends to defamiliarize every viewer. Each time I walk into a gallery lined with canvases on which there are no human figures, no animals, no distinct objects from nature, I am immediately in unfamiliar territory, and no final appreciation of the work will dissolve that fact. I am forced to confront my own deep-seated faith in representation.

Teaching with abstract art in a museum setting also upsets a few long-held pedagogical faiths. There is no regimen of desks all facing toward the front, no strict schedule for any lesson. Instead of the rigid outlines of textbook chapters, there are the intricate nests of galleries. I find the museum rejects anything too straightforward. My students are allowed to sit or stand or lie down and are encouraged to take different angles on the work. I have my plan for what I want to show them, but I also stay attuned to the mood of the tour and to their reactions to what they see. This often means I spend a great deal of time in one spot or make a spontaneous stop in front of a particular Jean-Michel Basquiat I have forgotten. But if it fits in with the fantastic journeys I have been suggesting to them, I'll ask them to fill with words the blank space on the left side of the canvas, which seems to be where the painting's skeleton man is heading. Although I primarily look for ways to press my students beyond silence or rejection, I don't set goals for what they should produce in these galleries. Instead, I orchestrate repeated collisions between the students and their expectations of art, the kinds of encounters that will change their ways of seeing even after they leave the place.

To accomplish this, I have to get my students to resist their own resistance, including that of a young student who proclaims that *Midland #11*, one of Robert Ryman's landmark, all-white paintings, is something that "a first grader could do." I'm not trying to get my students to understand the irony and understatement of Ryman, but I do want to get them to sit still long enough to look into the details of the piece. So while flexibility is the order of the day, rules and etiquette still have their place in this kind of teaching, and I always discuss with my students how I expect them to behave before we start out. Primarily, I show them that while art need not be worshipped, it still has much to teach us. Once these guidelines of respect are in place and the students see how seriously I take them, I can relax them a bit. I encourage the students to feel comfortable as they settle in around a piece of art. I am fortunate in that the Menil Collection opens early to allow my classes to tour the galleries before the general public arrives. I am also blessed by a museum staff that follows Dominique de Menil's belief that a gallery should be a comfortable and not a staid place. I am able, therefore, to protect the art, supervise the children, and insist on their close attention to the paintings, without resorting to military discipline.

Sometimes the discipline of attentiveness requires a bit of enforcement, especially since, over the course of a morning, I replicate for them my own long experience of coming to terms with the abstract. Our path through the museum is designed to move incrementally from the more easily recognizable to the wildly abstract. A typical tour begins with a Warhol soup can (where I might ask the students to think about who would eat from a tin that big) and then proceeds to one of George Segal's full-sized plaster figures, in the presence of which I ask them to consider what a *Seated Woman* might think about all day inside her cast. These steps past the more familiar territories of the pantry and the human figure are crucial in a course toward the abstract.

When we encounter something that is unusual, we map the new upon the set of givens that make our worlds, and thus make the new more familiar. Abstraction interferes with the knowing that seeks to identify. It highlights the dynamic between our desire to ground a work of art by naming what it represents and our hidden willingness toward more imaginative, associative comprehension. This is the dynamic moment of the lyric, the hinge of metaphor. For this work to inspire I must allow my students the chance to locate known forms and simultaneously look for ways to break from the known into lyric territory. After they circle the Segal sculpture, I start with the literals: What is this? (A woman.) What is she doing? (Sitting.) What's her expression? (Downturned.) Then, since I feel the best way to access strong, imaginative association is through empathy, I tell my students that instead of an anonymous woman inside there, they should imagine themselves wrapped in that plaster. I give them first the open-ended prompt: "Tell me what you are thinking." I keep them writing by dropping new prompts, asking new questions at intervals: "How did this happen?" "What were you doing just before that?" "Where were you headed?" "What are you trying to say?" "Who do you want to hear you?" "Who are you missing?" I want the writing to include the expected responses of "Let me out!" But I also want it to surpass the practicalities of escape. By imagining themselves inside the sculpture, they become immediately and concretely involved with it, and through their conjecture they move beyond the literal moment.

While we can't imagine ourselves into an abstract painting in quite the same way as we can into a sculpture, there is much about abstract painting that encourages involvement. In the figureless field, shapes and textures resonate before us, brushstrokes move with a kinetic energy. All this is a convenient and tactile way to engage the students with a piece of art, by drawing their attention to the material of it and to the drips and pours of how that material is employed. What this also means is that the students need to spend some time in front of the work, allowing its subtleties and gestures to form in their imagination. Place a group of young students in front of *Requiem Blue*, Yves Klein's rough azure of speckled canvas and attached rock-like structures, and it won't take long before most of them see a lunar landscape through the painting's monochrome. They will quickly enter the work of substitution, like a game of picking pictures out of the clouds. To keep such substitution from becoming its own kind of reductive interpretation, I make the students depart from the moon and call out other terrain. Soon, I'm hearing of strange blue-sponge lawns and indigo surfaces of microscopic creatures. Often classes will set a challenge among themselves, each student trying to outmatch the others with his or her discoveries.

Each room in the museum can be a new discovery, and a constant movement between galleries helps keep students from settling into any pattern of perception. When I think they need a more dramatic shift, we move outside and cross the street to the separate building that houses the work of Cy Twombly. Just inside its front doors is a slightly darkened gallery lined with what appear to be three huge blackboards covered with rows of spiraled lines like warm-up penmanship exercises. At first sight, the students declare that this is all so much "scribble-scrabble." But when I ask them to move closer and look at the surface, they admit that the "chalkboard" is indeed a canvas and that the "chalk" itself is an illusion of the paint. Once they grasp that this is not mimesis and that their attempts at reference lead them to a dead end, they begin to make some progress along the road to understanding abstraction.

If abstract forms like Twombly's are a perfect training ground for furthering the work of visual metaphor, this training can can be a rough course in troping, both for the teacher and the student. Sometimes when I go around the circle asking what those rows of spirals look like, I hear repeatedly: like lines, like spirals, like curls, like paint. All claims that abstract art is hermetic find evidence in these authentic replies. Sometimes I have to give my group of students an idea of how far afield from the literal they might venture. "These spirals look like all the rings of hair cut today from the heads of a hundred princesses," I might say, "Or like wrinkles, like terrible rain." Inevitably, one student will raise his hand and set the bar by saying something such as: "They look like fields of wheat blowing in the afternoon wind."

There are always some students, though, for whom the leap to metaphor is not nearly so easy. I prompt them by asking if these shapes *remind* them of anything else, or what they could be *made into*. I know that this method seems to go against all I have previously said about avoiding the tyranny of representation in an abstract work. Yet while to ask of a painting, "What is it?" encourages a singular response, to inquire into what a painting is "like" elicits the more expansive responses of metaphor and simile that do not try to close down a work in a single explanation. So if those "lines" remind a boy of "circles," I keep pushing him until he makes them into a "row of circles." I ask him if those circles might be part of something bigger or if they are moving anywhere. But I am not always successful. All my prodding sometimes only takes a young writer up to the brink of figurative language and shows him the rewards on the other side. Ultimately, the leap is one that he must make himself.

More and more, I am headed away from the visual analogue in favor of a different kind of portrayal. Instead of asking my students to depict the literal or suggested objects in a painting, I try to get them to evoke the feelings within. I further this process by asking my students the simple yet provocative question: "What do you think the artist was feeling when he painted all these spirals?" The responses range wonderfully from "frustration" to "excitement." For each of the emotions the students name, I ask them to point to a specific part of the painting that led them to arrive at that answer. Still, I don't want them to lose sight of the larger work or to forget that the effect of the whole is as important as any given part. I maintain this holistic view by having the students stand in silence for a minute in the center of the gallery, their only permitted movement that of their heads as they scan all the walls. At the end of the minute, I ask them what it feels like to be surrounded by these paintings, and they take a moment to write their responses. Again, the reactions vary, from "It feels like everyone is yelling at me" to "I feel like I'm a baby again." As we exit the gallery, I encourage them by pointing out the ways in which they have transformed what appeared to be "scribble-scrabble" into a much more complex entity. Now they are prepared for even grander abstraction.

No method into abstraction can hope to encompass every instance of it in art. I do not always "get" this work myself, but I recognize that confoundedness and awe share a sector in this world with inspiration. My purpose in taking my students to see Twombly's perplexing *Catullus* is personal as well as pedagogical. This piece stretches for over fifty feet, filling one entire length of the gallery and reaching to its high ceiling where the day's shifting light slants through the louvered roof. There is nothing else in the room. I have the students assemble in the doorway, ready their writing materials, and then I lead them into the gallery in a line. As we walk parallel to the painting, I pause at intervals along its length to situate each student in a spot where he or she will remain for the duration of our visit. I turn him or her toward the painting and sketch out the swath of it from top to bottom that I designate "yours." In this way I form a row of children covering the entire length of *Catullus*. I tell them that I love this work but that I'm not always sure I've seen or know all of it. It is, I emphasize, enormous, and I ask for their help in exploring it. We will, I explain, try to get a sense of this painting by first observing and writing alone, and then assembling our responses into a larger poem. I remind them that they are responsible for their sections, down to the tiniest dot of paint.

Now I pull out Walt Whitman's *Leaves of Grass*, a section of *Salut Au Monde!* that I have edited to highlight the poem's grandeur and metaphor. Alone with the children in the gallery. I take full advantage of the acoustics that are as large as both Whitman and Twombly. The children look at the painting as I walk slowly behind them, reciting Whitman:

What do you see Walt Whitman?
Who are they you salute, and that one after another salute you?

I see a great round wonder rolling through space,
I see diminute farms, hamlets, ruins, graveyards, jails, factories, palaces,
    hovels, huts of barbarians, tents of nomads upon the surface,

I see the shaded part on one side where the sleepers are sleeping, and the
            sunlit part on the other side,
I see the curious rapid change of the light and shade,
I see distant lands, as real and near to the inhabitants of them as my land
            is to me.

Gary Hawkins

I see plenteous waters,
I see mountain peaks, I see the sierras of Andes where they range,
…
I see the tracks of the railroads of the earth,
I see them in Great Britain, I see them in Europe,
I see them in Asia and in Africa.

I see the electric telegraphs of the earth,
I see the filaments of the news of wars, deaths, losses, gains, passions, of
            my race.

I see the long river-stripes of the earth,
I see the Amazon and the Paraguay,
I see the four great rivers of China, the Amour, the Yellow River, the Yiang-
            tse, and the Pearl,
I see where the Seine flows, and where the Danube, the Loire, the Rhone,
            and the Guadalquiver flow,
I see the windings of the Volga, the Dnieper, the Oder,
I see the Tuscan going down the Arno, and the Venetian along the Po,
I see the Greek seaman sailing out of Egina bay.
…
I see the places of sagas,
I see pine-trees and fir-trees torn by northern blasts,
I see granite bowlders and cliffs, I see green meadows and lakes,
…
I see vapors exhaling from unexplored countries,
…
I see male and female everywhere,
…
And I salute all the inhabitants of the earth.

Immediately, without any pause for talk or questions, I set them to writing, saying, "Look at your section of the painting and tell me what it is you see."

Parts of *Catullus* are filled with huge splashes of color while others are subtle gradients of washes and grays, but throughout the painting there is energy of movement and there are shapes suggesting images both fantastic and mundane. Everywhere there are words and phrases scrawled onto the surface, or indecipherable beneath layers of paint. I have the students write in silence. For those who are still struggling to get beyond statements like "I see paint," I kneel down and ask them, again, what they could turn that shape of paint into. Or I point to a section up near the ceiling and ask them to be the first to detail the sight of it.

The true finale is the assembly of their individual views into a larger, collaborative poem. I ask them to re-read what they have written and choose the two lines that they like the most and mark each of them. Then I set the stage directions. They will stand up and remain facing the painting. I will walk behind them and one by one tap them on the shoulder. This is the signal to read their favorite line loud enough to fill the whole room. When I reach the end of the row, we will repeat the process until each student has read both of his or her lines. I walk to the far right-hand side of the painting, where those explosions of color are, and hold the gallery silent for a moment before I tap the shoulder of the first student, and we begin.

I wish I were not always in the midst of conducting this performance so that I might get a better sense of how it comes off. But from my perspective as well as what I can divine from the faces of the guards, the effect of these group poems that build down the face of the painting and rise to fill the room is stunning. I rarely direct any more writing after this event. It seems the perfect culmination of their visit. I have never transcribed one of these choral works, but I do hold onto the individual poems they write in front of *Catullus*. Time and again these young poets find sublime elements and remarkable moments deep within Twombly's abstractions.

I See

I see colors and colors like on a paint palette.
I see words about the emotion.
The colors look as if they were dancing with one another.
It looks as if some are slowing down and some are speeding up.

It looks like some are happy and some are sad.
Some are filled with a great heart, others not.
I see a beautiful painting that can describe every good thing or bad thing.

—Jaclyn Rosenthal, fourth grade

Gary Hawkins

Big Painting

I see writing written on the walls and big and small words. I see a cloud bursting with white which no one can describe. I see ice cream, smushed, reminds me of the flavor sweetcream. I see a bundle of stars, all squished like they are hiding a secret, which they don't want to tell anyone. I see a cluster of colors like fireworks flying into the dark gray sky. I see shiny white air trembling. I see rain.

—Sydney Sadick, fifth grade

A Mile Long

I see a story
Blobs of smoke
The daytime coming
The rain from the
clouds The firecrackers
and the madness
of people The
one fist out on
the paint from a flyer
I see the
tears of a baby
but behind
Ally off his—every
thing I see
behind the rain
The smoke the
baby's tears the

story the mad people
I see a smile
a nice big smile

—Andrew Scheinthal, fourth grade

Gray rain falling down on the boats of the explorers in it
fighting for their life! Words and prayers they are saying.
Some of them are saying,
"There is land close by,"
or, "Look over there, there is light and dark
everywhere." Some people praying to not die
and the fight to stop. Journals, people are
writing in sloppy writing because it's cold
and boats are shooting, putting holes in other boats.
The boat is rocking very hard. Suddenly
I . . .

—Hannah Goetz, fourth grade

When such final, confident offerings come to me at the end of a morning at the museum, I am forced to realize that the hesitation of my first, conservative attempts at using art to inspire poetry were the result of my own uncertainty. In the face of my desire that my students produce something, some exquisite object of poetry as the product of each encounter I offered them, I concocted a limitation. Feeling the representational to be a safe path to orchestrated creativity and abstraction to be the road to—well, who knows—I made a divide between them. Such is too often the fate of pedagogy: the theory precludes the experiment or the plan eclipses the immediate situation. Yet, in fact, my resistance and trepidation were crucial to my creation of a strong path into this experimental realm.

If anything, my students have confirmed for me that abstraction is often the most suggestive type of art. Surely I knew this—otherwise why would I have stood there so long in front of Twombly's work with a wealth of thoughts and emotions pouring over me? The difficult part is taking that confused overflow of inspiration and then starting forward into the work that is necessary to turn it into art. Working with young writers reminds me that maturity is not the best opening to art, but that creation yields best to awe, that most youthful position.

Gary Hawkins

ACKNOWLEDGMENTS: I am indebted to several colleagues for conversations about the use of visual art in teaching poetry. For sharing their methods in approaching specific works of art, some of which I have adapted here, I owe many thanks to David Bernardy and Delores Bustamante.

The Train in the Chimney
Teaching Writing by Discovering Art

by Barbara Flug Colin

*d*URING MY ELEVEN YEARS as a writer-in-residence at the Henry
Viscardi School, a state-funded school for physically challenged
students, I've learned that "childhood's freshness," Henri
Matisse's term for what he sought in art, cannot be taught. But it can be
invoked by great art.

When my students see Joan Miró's early conventional tree become a
tree with an eye and an ear, or Matisse's early dim dining room become
outrageous red, they *feel* the meaning of the words "original" and "imagination."

I've learned that art brings out something intrinsically human, what
Miró—like Jung—called a "collective unconscious." For instance, Nate, a
third grader, listening to my tape of loons on a Maine lake, heard "an interested train in the chimney."* He had not seen René Magritte's surreal
painting of that image (see figure 3).

I've learned that in the process of looking at paintings, the facts of
what we see *can* yield to poetry. It is a circular process: saying what we see,
then seeing what we say. Ninth grader Tess turns a postcard of Matisse's
Dance sideways and sees the misshapen oval of the dancers as "a bottle."

---

* The names of my students have been changed to protect their privacy. In the final section,
however, the name Dominika was retained with my student's permission.

Then Jon sees "a guitar." Julio free associates: "Or a lightbulb or a chicken leg or a bowling pin." Looking at *Dance*, Celine writes:

The Spirits

Barbara Flug
Colin

A tango of the mind
surprises them. They
have nothing to hide.
They are mysterious
like ghosts from another
life. They're out for a night
on the town. The pirates are
waiting and stalking them
like live prey.

Celine's originality does not give her high marks on standardized tests. She is in a class for students whose physical disabilities affect their scholastic capacities. Celine's discovery of her writing talent gives her coveted status among her peers. It also gives her self-confidence—the self-confidence to head for the computer when I arrive, to ignore my class exercises, and to write what is coming *through* her.

I've discovered the value of discovery. Matisse said his process was one of "form filtered to its essential." I have created a class exercise called "Matisse Mysteries" to point out this filtering process. To solve a "Matisse Mystery," students must find Matisse hidden in his paintings, or find past paintings hidden in later ones. Looking at *Dance*, we can see that it is "filtered" from *Harmony in Red*, in which a black-roofed pink house in the window anticipates the black-haired pink bodies in *Dance* the following year. We can see that *Harmony in Red* is filtered from *Breton Serving Girl* and *The Dinner Table*. We can see what is alike in all three: a servant tends a table. And what is different: among other things, only the final version shows a scene through the window. We can see that six circling naked dancers deep in the background of *La joie de vivre* become five in the foreground of *Dance*.

We discover this same process occurring in two drafts of William Carlos Williams's poem "The Locust Tree in Flower." I pose these questions: "In the second version, how many words did Williams leave out?

How many people did Matisse leave out?" The answers act as a starting point for a class poem that fifth grade students dictate to me.

Leaving Out

William Carlos Williams left out 21 words
in the final version of "The Locust Tree in Flower."
Matisse left out 11 people from *La joie de vivre*
to paint *Dance*.
He also left out trees, goats, the horizon, figures.
He changed the sky color.
He left out yellow that they're standing in.
And pink, orange, and red.
He left out whiter bodies.
The dark blue becomes light blue in *Dance*.

Discovering this process in Matisse and Williams helps us in our own processes. For two years, fifth grader Lyle wrote mostly humorous, verbose poems. After these editorial discoveries, he wrote the following unexpected incantation while looking at a postcard of Matisse's *The Yellow Hat*:

"The Waiting Is Killing Me!!!!!"

She is a housewife.
She is waiting
for her husband.
She begins to walk.
She can't find him.
She kneels down.
She begins to cry.

We have learned to respect our originality: that we see the same thing differently. In Matisse's *Chinese Fish*, for instance, James sees "the *x*'s are laughing at the blue sky /. . . Red lips are big, are laughing at a joke they heard." Looking at the same painting, Ann, a seventh grader, writes:

Combination

I see pink and purple
clouds. They are standing in
a line.

Have you ever seen a white
leaf? I can! See it in my
imagination.
A green box with a white
frog and yellow grass can be
strange, but when you think
about it, it can be beautiful.
I've never seen an orange
smile with yellowish orange
leaves around it. It can be
odd and realistic at the same
time.

Barbara Flug
Colin

We discover deeper things, become more curious, look harder, and say more, bringing into consciousness a language for something else that has much to do with ourselves. Celine identifies with the woman and the fish in Matisse's *Woman Before an Aquarium*:

The Mystery of a Goldfish

As she stares at the bowl wondering what are they
thinking. Wanting to be like them but why? What makes
them so different? Why didn't god make us the same?
Don't you sometimes wonder? About life? And why we
sometimes get so sad at the world.

We have learned that being in the museum "is like finding a treasure":

The Train in the
Chimney

Being in the museum is like finding a treasure.

In the museum Madame Matisse is hiding behind a mask.

The Conversation was bigger.

You could see how he painted over the skirt,

it came out near her feet but he painted over it.

In the museum *Dance* was huge with beautiful colors:

lighter peach than in the postcard;

more vivid orange than in the book.

In the museum you could see the woman who was sitting

in *The Painter's Family* was crying.

She is his wife.

In the museum, *The Moroccans* was unique with green

fruits and then a glass in the middle.

That was strange.

Why didn't he paint more than one nude man?

—Ninth and tenth grade class

"I like poetry because when you write a poem it's like a whole different world," says Mary. "I don't have to be afraid to speak." Mary is shy in class, but at the Matisse retrospective she summons me to *The Young Sailor* and then to the *Portrait of Pierre Matisse* to show me how alike they are. Then to the *Portrait of Mme. Matisse* to see how "her lips are smiling but her eyes are sad."

Cheri, who is pushing Mary's wheelchair, drags me over to *French Window at Collioure* to tell me she loves this one the best. Then Cheri takes me to *The Yellow Curtain* (1915) and says, "It looks like his cutouts." Of course, she's right, though she hasn't been taught this, hasn't even calculated that the cutouts come much later, in the late 1940s. But she is familiar with the cutouts, can sense the similarity in her spontaneous apprehension of something very complex.

Similarly, Victor, who did not know that Matisse hoped to "translate the totality of things with a sign," says that the window rail in *Conversation* looks "like a word, *NOX* or *NON*." In *Women and Monkeys* and *The Thousand and One Nights*, James sees "Chinese and Hebrew letters."

There is an uncanny resemblance between fifth grader Dominika's words and those of Matisse:

Dominika: Charcoal . . . it's almost nicer if you can use your imagination for the colors.

Barbara Flug
Colin

Matisse: A colorist makes his presence known even in a charcoal drawing.

Dominika (looking at a painting of Nice): It's really a great picture. You know he's worked out all the details before and all he does is . . . lines.

Matisse: Sift . . . details . . . selecting . . . the line that expresses the most and gives life.

Matisse: Colors win you over more and more. A certain blue enters your soul. A certain red has an effect on your blood pressure. A certain color tones you up. It's a concentration of timbres. . . .

Dominika: The colors look so awesome on one another. The colors fit together like they were meant to be that way. I've never seen colors so bright. It's like, wow, that's a great orange. Now, let's stare at the purple. It's amazing. I'm going to sleep here tonight. I'll wake up in the morning and I'll see the whole exhibit again. And I'm going to spend thirty minutes at each painting. Or rather thirty minutes at each color. Gee, that was a great pink.

Art Is for Everybody

by bell hooks

*i*N HIGH SCHOOL I PAINTED PICTURES that won prizes. My art teacher, a white man whom we called Mr. Harold, always promoted and encouraged my work. I can still remember him praising me in front of my parents. To them art was play. It was not something real—not a way to make a living. To them I was not a talented artist because I could not draw the kind of pictures that I would now call documentary portraits. The images I painted never looked like our familiar world and therefore I could not be an artist. And even though Mr. Harold told me I was an artist, I really could not believe him. I had been taught to believe that no white person in this newly desegregated high school knew anything about what black people's real lives were all about. After all, they did not even want to teach us. How, then, could we trust what they taught? It did not matter that Mr. Harold was different. It did not matter to grown folks that in his art classes he treated black students like we had a right to be there, deserved his attention and his affirmation. It did not matter to them, but it began to matter to *us*: We ran to his classes. We escaped there. We entered the world of color, the free world of art. And in that world we were, momentarily, whatever we wanted to be. That was my initiation. I longed to be an artist, but whenever I hinted that I might be an artist, grown folks looked at me with contempt. They told me I had to be out of my mind thinking that black folks could be artists—why, you could not eat art. Nothing folks said changed my longing to enter the world of art and be free.

Life taught me that being an artist was dangerous. The one grown black person I met who made art lived in a Chicago basement. A distant relative of my father's, cousin Schuyler was talked about as someone who had wasted his life dreaming about art. He was lonely, sad, and broke. At least that was how folks saw him. I do not know how he saw himself, only that he loved art. He loved to talk about it. And there in the dark shadows of his basement world he initiated me into critical thinking about art and culture. Cousin Schuyler talked to me about art in a grown-up way. He said he knew I had "the feeling" for art. And he chose me to be his witness: to be the one who would always remember the images. He painted pictures of naked black women, with full breasts, red lips, and big hips. Long before Paul Gauguin's images of big-boned naked brown women found a place in my visual universe, I had been taught to hold such images close, to look at art and think about it, to keep art on my mind.

Now when I think about the politics of seeing—how we perceive the visual, how we write and talk about it—I understand that the perspective from which we approach art is overdetermined by location. I tell my sister G., who is married to a man who works in an auto factory in Flint, Michigan, and has three children, that I am thinking about art. I want to know whether she thinks about art, and, more importantly, if she thinks most black folks are thinking about art. She tells me that art is just too far away from our lives, that "art is something—in order to enjoy and know it, it takes work." And I say, "But art is on my mind. It has always been on my mind." She says, "Girl, you are different, you always were into this stuff. It's like you just learned it somehow. And if you are not taught how to know art, it's something you learn on your own."

We finish our late-night conversation and it's hours later when, staring into the dark, art on my mind, I remember Mr. Harold. I close my eyes and see him looking over my work, smell him, see the flakes of dandruff resting on his black shirt. In the dark, I conjure an image of him: always in black, always smiling, willing to touch our black hands while the other white folks hate and fear contact with our bodies. In the dark of memory, I also remember cousin Schuyler, the hours of listening and talking about art in his basement, the paintings of naked brown women. And I think Sister G. is wrong. I did not just learn to think about art on my own—there were always teachers who saw me looking, searching the visual for answers, and who guided my search. The mystery is only why I wanted to look while others around me closed their eyes—that I cannot yet explain.

When I think of the place of the visual in black life, I think most black folks are more influenced by television and movie images than by visual arts like painting, sculpture, and so on. My sister G. told me: "We can identify with movies and we don't feel we know how to identify with art." Black folks may not identify with art due to an absence of representation. Many of us do not know that black folks create diverse art, and we may not see them doing it, especially if we live in working-class or underclass households. Or art (both the product and the process of creation) may be so devalued—not just in underclass communities, but in diverse black contexts, and, to some extent, in our society as a whole—that we may deem art irrelevant even if it is abundantly in our midst. That possibility aside, the point is that most black folks do not believe that the presence of art in our lives is essential to our collective well-being. Indeed, with respect to black political life, in black liberation struggles—whether early protests against white supremacy and racism during slavery and Reconstruction, during the civil rights movement, or during the more recent black power movements—the production of art and the creation of a politics of the visual that would not only affirm artists but also see the development of an aesthetics of viewing as central to claiming subjectivity have been consistently devalued. Taking our cues from mainstream white culture, black folks have tended to see art as completely unimportant in the struggle for survival. Art as propaganda was and is acceptable, but not art that was concerned with any old subject, content, or form. And black folks who thought there could be some art for art's sake for black people, well, they were seen as being out of the loop, apolitical. Hence, black leaders have rarely included in their visions of black liberation the necessity to affirm in a sustained manner creative expression and freedom in the visual arts. Much of our political focus on the visual has been related to the issue of good and bad images. Indeed, many folks think the problem of black identification with art is simply the problem of under-representation: not enough images, not enough visible black artists, not enough prestigious galleries showing their work.

Representation is a crucial location of struggle for any exploited and oppressed people asserting subjectivity and decolonization of the mind. Without a doubt, if all black children were daily growing up in environments where they learned the importance of art and saw artists that were black, our collective black experience of art would be transformed. However, we know that, in the segregated world of recent African-American history, for years black folks created and displayed their art in segregated black communities, and this effort was not enough to make an intervention that revolutionized our collective experience of art. Remembering this fact helps us to understand that the question of identifying with art goes beyond the issue of representation.

We must look, therefore, at other factors that render art meaningless in the everyday lives of most black folks. Identification with art is a process, one that involves a number of different factors. Two central factors that help us to understand black folks' collective response to art in the United States are, first, recognition of the familiar—that is, we see in art something that resembles what we know—and, second, that we look with the received understanding that art is necessarily a terrain of defamiliarization: it may take what we see/know and make us look at it in a new way.

In the past, particularly in segregated school settings, the attitude toward art was that it had a primary value only when it documented the world as is. Hence the heavy-handed emphasis on portraiture in black life that continues to the present day, especially evident if we look at the type of art that trickles down to the masses of black folks. Rooted in the African-American historical relation to the visual is a resistance to the idea of art as a space of defamiliarization. Coming to art in search only of exact renderings of reality, many black folks have left art dissatisfied. However, as a process, defamiliarization takes us away from the real only to bring us back to it in a new way. It enables the viewer to experience what the critic Michael Benedikt calls in his manifesto *For an Architecture of Reality* "direct aesthetic experiences of the real." For more black folks to identify with art, we must shift conventional ways of thinking about the function of art. There must be a revolution in the way we see, the way we look.

Such a revolution would necessarily begin with diverse programs of critical education that would stimulate collective awareness that the creation and public sharing of art is essential to any practice of freedom. If black folks are collectively to affirm our subjectivity in resistance, as we struggle against forces of domination and move toward the invention of the decolonized self, we must set our imaginations free. Acknowledging that we have been and are colonized both in our minds and in our imaginations, we begin to understand the need for promoting and celebrating creative expression.

The painter Charles White, commenting on his philosophy of art, acknowledged: "The substance of man is such that he has to satisfy the needs of life with all his senses. His very being cries out for these senses to appropriate the true riches of life: the beauty of human relationships and dignity, of nature and art, realized in striding towards a bright tomorrow.... Without culture, without creative art, inspiring to these senses, mankind stumbles in a chasm of despair and pessimism." While employing sexist language, White was voicing his artistic understanding that aesthetics nurture the spirit and provide ways of rethinking and healing psychic wounds inflicted by assault from the forces of imperialist, racist, and sexist domination.

As black artists have broken free from imperialist white-supremacist notions of the way art should look and function in society, they have approached representation as a location for contestation. In looking back at the lives of Lois Mailou Jones and Romare Bearden, it is significant to note that they both began their painting careers working with standard European notions of content and form. Their attempt to assimilate the prevailing artistic norms of their day was part of the struggle to gain acceptance and recognition. Yet it was when they began to grapple within their work with notions of what is worthy of representation—when they no longer focused exclusively on European traditions and drew upon the cultural legacy of the African-American diasporic experience—that they fully discovered their artistic identity.

Lois Mailou Jones has said that it was an encounter with the critic Alain Locke that motivated her to do work that directly reflected black experience. Locke insisted that black artists had to do more with the black experience and, especially, with their heritage. Although Romare Bearden was critical of Locke and felt that it was a mistake for black folks to think that all black art had to be protest art, Bearden was obsessed with his ancestral legacy, with the personal politics of African-American identity and relationships. This subject matter was the groundwork that fueled all his art. He drew on memories of black life—the images, the culture.

For many black folks, seeing Romare Bearden's work redeems images from our lives that many of us have previously responded to only with feelings of shame and embarrassment. When Bearden painted images reflecting aspects of black life that emerged from underclass experience, some black viewers were disturbed. After his work appeared in a 1940s exhibition titled "Contemporary Negro Art," Bearden wrote a letter to a friend complaining about the lack of a sophisticated critical approach to art created by black folks. "To many of my own people, I learn, my work was very disgusting and morbid—and portrayed a type of Negro that they were trying to get away from." These black audiences were wanting art to be solely a vehicle for displaying the race at its best. It is this notion of the function of art, coupled with the idea that all black art must be protest art, that has served to stifle and repress black artistic expression. Both notions of the function of art rely on the idea that there should be no non-representational black art. Bearden's work challenged the idea that abstraction had no place in the world of black art. He did not accept that there was any tension between the use of black content and the exploration of diverse forms. In 1959 Bearden wrote, "I am, naturally, very interested in form and structure—in a personal way of expression which can perhaps be called new. I have nothing, of course, against representational images, but the demands, the direction of the sign factors in my painting now completely obliterate any representational image."

Although Bearden was a celebrated artist when he died in 1988, his work has reached many more black folks since his death. Those black audiences who have learned to recognize the value of black artistic expression revere Bearden for his having dared to make use of every image of black life available to his creative imagination. As so much traditional black folk experience is lost and forgotten, as we lose sight of the rich experience of working-class black people in our transnational corporate society, many of us are looking to art to recover and claim a relationship to an African-American past in images.

The writer Ntozake Shange offers a similar testimony in *Ridin' the Moon in Texas.* In a "note to the reader" at the beginning of the book, she shares the place of art in her life. Talking first about growing up with a father who painted, who had a darkroom, she continues: "As I grew I surrounded myself with images, abstractions that drew warmth from me or wrapped me in loveliness. . . . Paintings and poems are moments, capturing or seducing us, when we are so vulnerable. These images are metaphors. This is my life, how I see and, therefore, am able to speak. Praise the spirits and the stars that there are others among us who allow us visions that we may converse with one another."

Revealing to the reader her privileged background in this note, Ntozake evokes a domestic black world in which art had a powerful presence, one that empowered her to expand her consciousness and create. While writing this piece, I have spoken with many black folks from materially privileged backgrounds who learned in their home life to think about art and sometimes to appreciate it. Other black folks I have talked with who have access to money mention seeing black art on the walls while watching

The Cosby Show and developing an interest. They speak about wanting to own black art as an investment, but they do not speak of an encounter with the visual that transforms. Though they may appreciate black art as a commodity, they may be as unable to identify with art aesthetically as are those who have no relation at all to art.

I began this essay sharing bits and pieces of a conversation that did not emerge from a bourgeois standpoint. My sister G. considered the role of art in black life by looking critically at the experiences of black working-class, underclass, and lower-middle-class folks in the world she has known most intimately. Looking at black life from that angle, from those class locations that reflect the positionality of most black folks, she made relevant observations. We both agreed that art does not have much of a place in black life, especially the work of black artists.

Years ago most black people grew up in houses where art, if it was present at all, took the form of cheap reproductions of work created by white artists featuring white images; some of it was so-called great art. Often these images incorporated religious iconography and symbols. I first saw cheap reproductions of art by Michelangelo and Leonardo da Vinci in Southern black religious households. We identified with these images. They appealed to us because they conveyed aspects of religious experience that were familiar. The fact of whiteness was subsumed by the spiritual expression in the work.

Contemporary critiques of black engagement with white images that see this engagement solely as an expression of internalized racism have led many folks to remove such images from their walls. Rarely, however, have they been replaced by the work of black artists. Without a radical counterhegemonic politics of the visual that works to validate black folks' ability to appreciate art by white folks or any other group without reproducing racist colonization, black folks are further deprived of access to art, and our experience of the visual in art is deeply diminished. In contemporary times, television and cinema may be fast destroying any faint desire that black folks might have, particularly those of us who are not materially privileged, to identify with art, to nurture and sustain our engagement with it as creators and consumers.

Our capacity to value art is severely corrupted and perverted by a politics of the visual that suggests we must limit our responses to the narrow confines of a debate over good versus bad images. How can we truly see, experience, and appreciate all that may be present in any work of art if our only concern is whether it shows us a positive or negative image? In the valuable essay "Negative/Positive," which introduces Michele Wallace's collection *Invisibility Blues*, Wallace cautions us to remember that the binary opposition of negative versus positive images too often sets the limits of African-American cultural criticism. I would add that it often sets the limits of African-American creative practice, particularly in the visual arts. Wallace emphasizes that this opposition ties "Afro-American cultural production to racist ideology in a way that makes the failure to alter it inevitable." Clearly, it is only as we move away from the tendency to define ourselves in reaction to white racism that we are able to move toward that practice of freedom which requires us first to decolonize our minds. We can liberate ourselves and others only by forging in resistance identities that transcend narrowly defined limits.

Art constitutes one of the rare locations where acts of transcendence can take place and have a wide-ranging transformative impact. Indeed, mainstream white art circles are acted upon in radical ways by the work of black artists. It is part of the contemporary tragedy of racism and white supremacy that white folks often have greater access to the work of black artists and to the critical apparatus that allows for understanding and appreciation of the work. Current commodification of blackness may mean that the white folks who walk through the exhibits of work by such artists as Bettye and Alison Saar are able to be more in touch with this work than most black folks. These circumstances will change only as African Americans and our allies renew the progressive black liberation struggle—re-envisioning black revolution in such a way that we create collective awareness of the radical place that art occupies within the freedom struggle and of the way in which experiencing art can enhance our understanding of what it means to live as free subjects in an unfree world.

Bibliography

Benedikt, Michael. *For an Architecture of Reality*. New York: Lumen Press, 1988.

Shange, Ntozake. *Ridin' the Moon in Texas: Word Paintings*. New York: St. Martin's Press, 1988.

Wallace, Michele. *Invisibility Blues: From Pop to Theory*. New York: Verso Books, 1990.

Our Story Quilt
Memories in Words and Fabric

by Susan Karwoska

This piece of fabric reminds me of a story: Once upon a time in Pakistan my mother was sewing with her sewing machine. I was watching her. I was three years old. When my mother was going to throw out this piece of fabric I started to cry because I wanted it, so my mother gave it to me. Then I was laughing and I was really happy. When I grew up to be about seven, I would put it in my closet to make sure that it was safe because when I was seven I came to New York and I saw all the things in New York so I kept it in my closet. I've had it for nine years, but now I am giving it to Ms. K. and she is going to make a quilt out of it.

—Maria Tanvir

*i*MAGINE AN ELEMENTARY SCHOOL in Queens, New York, one of the most ethnically diverse counties in the country. Entering the school's foyer you see a new tile mosaic and a banner that proclaims: *We Reach for Our Dreams at P.S. 16*, in English and in Spanish. If you climb the stairs to the fourth-floor classrooms, you can catch a glimpse of Shea Stadium, home of the Mets and of America's favorite pastime. Out of another window, you can see the Unisphere, a twelve-story high, stainless steel model of the earth that stands as a relic of the 1964 World's Fair and of its motto, *Peace through Understanding*. Such oversize promises as these have drawn people to this borough for years, from every corner of the globe, including many of the families whose children attend the school.

Susan Karwoska

On the first day of my ten-week position as writer-in-residence at P.S. 16, I went up the front steps behind a young girl with dark skin and long, shining black hair. Her mother, dressed in a sari, accompanied her. On the girl's back was a pink plastic backpack, emblazoned with a picture of a blond, blue-eyed Barbie staring with doll-like incomprehension at the diverse sea of faces swarming up the steps behind her. It was an odd juxtaposition, one that struck me as a potent image of the difficulties faced by the children of this community. The families of the students I was to teach hailed from Peru, Pakistan, India, the Dominican Republic, China, Puerto Rico, Colombia, Ecuador, Mexico, Honduras, and many other countries. Some spoke English at home, but many did not. The class list read like a patchwork quilt of names. What were their stories? I wondered. What had they carried with them from their pasts, and what had they discarded? How did they see themselves fitting into this classroom, their community, and the larger world?

The class I designed for this group of kids explored these questions through a semester-long project in which we made two quilts together, one composed of fabric and one composed of words. Why quilts? First and foremost, I believed I could use the creative process of quilting to illuminate the creative process of writing. For many of my students, the prospect of creating a finished piece of writing could seem overwhelming. I wanted to find a way to break it down for them, to make it seem possible, even likely. And quilting, like writing, is the art of putting things together, of making connections. It is an act of conjuring, of turning insignificant scraps into something eloquent.

I have been writing for as long as I can remember, but came to quilting only recently. Learning this new art brought me into fresh contact with the nature of the artistic process: Where do you begin? How do you translate your vision into the work? When is it appropriate to tear things apart, start over, push on through? How do you finish? When you are working with fabric, the connections and choices you make are concrete and visible: here is where this piece of fabric ends and this one begins. See how they go together, or how they clash. See how this one brings out the pattern in the piece next to it. I thought that if the writing and quilting were done side by side, my students might come to understand something about the way creativity works that would help them grow as writers.

There was also another reason why quilting with this particular group of students seemed appropriate. Many of the students in my classroom were struggling to define themselves within the diversity of their community. In the making of a quilt, an old and widespread art, history and culture are present at each step of the process, in the choice of fabric, technique, pattern, color, and design. But while steeped in tradition, a quilt can also embrace invention. This has made it a distinctively American art form, one that has integrated the traditions brought here from all over the world, and, from necessity and by intention, reshaped these influences into something unique to this place, this time. This, I believed, was not unlike the task my students faced: choosing what to hold onto from the past while making a place for themselves in a new culture.

Finally, I wanted my students to see what, to me, is the beauty of a quilt: each piece, no matter its provenance, becomes an indispensable part of a new whole, while still retaining its individual integrity. For whatever it was worth to these fourth graders, I wanted to make that metaphor available to them: that all of them are important members of their community, and that it is possible for them to claim their own place within its diversity and still remain true to themselves.

Getting Started

This piece of fabric is special to me. My grandfather gave it to me, but now my grandfather has died. He gave it to me because it was from his sister. He gave it to me two days before he died. He was born in 1872, in India.

—*Gaganpreet Kaur*

In Peru I used to ride a donkey and one time I fell and ripped this piece of cloth so that's why I brought it in. It makes me remember Peru, and riding a donkey. I had a cow for milk. In Peru I would herd the cow to the gate so the cow could give us fresh milk to drink in the morning. In the morning I would also go to the garden to get apples, oranges, pears, and strawberries. I would put them in a bag so we could eat them when we were coming back to the house.

—Victor Sierra

Susan Karwoska

The piece of fabric I brought in is memorable to me because it is a piece of my father's shirt, and he wore it all the time. It smelled good when my mother washed it. When I was little my father bought a guitar for me. He taught me how to play it. He knew a lot more than I thought he did.

—Muhammad Maroof

On my first day at P.S. 16, I described the project to my students and let them know that they would each be contributing a piece to the quilt and to our final anthology (our word-quilt). Our focus in both activities was to be on memories—collecting them, exploring them, stitching them into our quilt and writing them down. Each week, I told them, I would do a little work on the quilt and bring it in to show them how it was coming along. I hoped that the quilt itself—made of all our scraps—would provide inspiration for the students' writing on memories, and that watching the quilt come together would help them to understand how a finished product—a quilt or a piece of writing—that seems all-of-a-piece is actually made up of many smaller elements.

Besides keeping track of the quilt's progress, our class time each week was to be spent reading and writing. During the course of my residency, we looked at the works of various authors who had written about their own childhood memories: *House on Mango Street* by Sandra Cisneros, *Family Pictures* and *In My Family* by Carmen Lomas Garza, *Childtimes* by Eloise Greenfield, *I Remember* by Joe Brainard, *The Rag Coat* by Lauren Mills, and *Appalachia* and *When I Was Young in the Mountains* by Cynthia Rylant. After we read each piece, we would talk about it: where the idea for the story might have come from, what we liked about it, how the author managed to keep our interest through voice and style. I told them, for instance, that Rylant said she was highly influenced by James Agee's short piece, "Knoxville, Summer 1915," and had the voice of that piece in mind when she wrote *Appalachia*. Reading, we agreed, was one way to get ideas for writing. In *The Rag Coat*, a girl wears a coat made of all the cast-off scraps from her schoolmates' clothes, which, when they are recognized, give voice to each child's memories. This led us to a discussion of how simple objects, such as our own scraps of fabric, may be used to evoke half-forgotten memories. We talked about how memories that are buried deep within us may be brought to the surface with surprising force by things that stimulate our sense of taste, touch, smell, hearing, or sight.

The students' first assignment was to bring in a piece of fabric from home. I knew that this would not be an easy assignment for many of these kids, so I sent each student home with a sheet of paper detailing the necessary size (about 5" x 5") and making suggestions for where they might find it. I also emphasized that the fabric didn't have to be anything fancy, just a piece cut out of an old shirt, a baby blanket, a piece of cloth from the country their family came from, something that had some meaning for them. The response was better than I and the teachers had expected. Almost three-quarters of the kids managed to bring something in before the next week's class. For those who didn't, I brought in a selection of fabrics, cut into squares, from which they could choose. We were ready to begin.

Awakening our Memories

The fabric I picked is gray and when you touch it you feel silk. One day I saw my mother use it as a scarf. It looked beautiful. It shined through the sun. When she wore it my mom looked like a model. I was five when I saw her wear it. I guess she doesn't like it anymore. It stayed in my mom's closet for a long time, and now I have it! I like it. Some of my classmates say it is soft, and I think so too. Now it is on a beautiful quilt, shining.

—*Asia Garcia*

I remember when I was eight years old. I was at my Grandmother's house and went to buy a candy for my cousin Christian. I bought a candy called a "cry-baby." When I went into the store it smelled like cake. I was wearing gray pants and a shirt. It was in September 1998, in the autumn, on a sunny day. My cousin was following me, but I did not know. Then, when I was at the store, he was crossing the street when I heard a crash. I knew when I heard the crash that my cousin had been hit. He was hit by a van. The van was the color of a peach. I started crying because he was only two years old. We took him to the hospital and the doctors operated on him but he died. Now I am nine, but I still have not forgotten him.

—*Lissette Ferreira*

This fabric reminds me of the night sky with shining stars. It reminds me of a party my family had outside our house. We ate and then we threw fireworks in the air. It was spectacular how the colors shone in the sky. They looked like they were going to touch the sky.

Susan Karwoska

—*Oscar Vilchez*

What is memory made of? Where does it reside? In the mind, of course, in bursts of neural energy, but this explains little. It doesn't explain why memories take the shape they do—the oddest details highlighted, the important ones subdued or forgotten. Nor does it tell us why memories lie coiled in objects, smells, sensations, and a thousand other unlikely places. *When I went into the store it smelled like cake. The van was the color of a peach. It shined through the sun.*

The truth is, our memories are skittish and shot-through. We see something and think that we will remember it all our lives, but a year goes by and that memory is dim and full of holes, while another memory, a mere scrap of perception, is recalled in perfect, aching detail: the smell of a certain room in your grandmother's house, or something someone once said in passing. I wanted to show my students how memory is tricky this way, how it hides in the odd details, but, with luck, it can also be found in them.

The art of memory, developed in ancient Greece and practiced by scholars and orators throughout Europe for centuries after, was based on the discovery that the mind recalls images more easily than words or abstract ideas. Practitioners of this art would train themselves to recall specific thought sequences by connecting them with specific images in their minds. Images that held powerful emotions were found to be particularly powerful mnemonic devices.

Carl Jung talks of forgetting as a normal and necessary process, but asserts that these forgotten ideas and images are not lost, but sit "just beyond the threshold of recall, where they can arise spontaneously at any time." Often, he says, what is needed to recall these memories to the conscious mind is some kind of stimulus to the senses, or a story that acts as a trigger.

Without this trigger, my students found that many of their memories were inaccessible to them. When I first asked my students to write about their memories, many felt they had to write down the "important" ones—which meant, in most cases, memories of holidays or birthdays. But too often these memories were recalled in generalities that erased all traces of the individual child. The mental snapshot of the event was missing.

Listening to the reminiscences of others was one way to jog the students' own memories. In one of our first classes together, I read them excerpts from *I Remember* and from *House on Mango Street*, in particular the piece called "Hairs," in which Cisneros describes the characteristic head of hair of each member of her family. I wanted to show them how the most interesting memories are not always the big events, but the small, day-to-day occurrences, and that the way to make these memories come alive is with images. I re-read both pieces aloud, stripping them of most of their images, and then we talked about how boring they were that way, how the interest of each piece lay not so much in the particular events or situations, but in the power of the images that were used to convey them. The kids enjoyed hearing the two pieces, and more importantly, began to better understand their reasons for liking them.

Our other pathway to the particulars of memory was through the pieces of fabric the students had brought in. "The language of the poem is the language of particulars," says the poet Mary Oliver. These pieces of fabric, with their various colors, bright or faded, with their unique textures and smells, helped the students recall these particulars. After our discussion, I handed them back their fabric squares, labeled with their name on a piece of masking tape, and asked them to look at them again, to feel them, smell them, to think about their origin, and then to brainstorm a web of associations, writing down as much as they could in the remaining time. I think the immediate sensual appeal of these fabric squares assisted the students in recalling images and memories that had resisted conscious thought.

Connecting the Pieces

I chose this piece of a violet sweater because when I was young I used to get close to my mom and get cozy. My mom used to wear this sweater. I used to get close to her and get warm whenever I got cold. I liked that sweater when I was young. My mom liked her violet sweater too.

—*Jonathan Aguilar*

This is about a time in my family when my mom had a baby girl. Everybody was excited. They looked like they had never seen a baby! I was crazy. The baby was on the bed, and I was saying that she was a cute baby. Mom was next to my sister Nadine. Dad was going bananas for having such a beautiful daughter. My little cousin was there too, fooling around our house. It was the greatest time ever in history!

—*Diana Fernandez*

I like this fabric because it is from China and it is beautiful. Some people in China used to make big beautiful fabric like this, and people gave the big beautiful fabric to the king. The king would give money to the people and use the fabric to make something to put up in his king's house.

—*Wei Huang*

Susan Karwoska

I planned to put the students' fabric pieces together in what is called a "progressive strip quilt." I chose this type of quilt because it was easy to make, could incorporate many different fabrics and colors into a coherent whole, and because I'd always liked the way the finished product resembled the spines of books sitting on a shelf. The first step was to sew the individual pieces together to make four long strips, two for each class. When this was done, I brought them back to class and hung them on the blackboard before the students came in to start their day. The students were excited to see their pieces as part of something new, and came up to the blackboard in small groups to look at the strips.

Over the next few weeks, they witnessed the quilt taking shape bit by bit. The four strips were sewn together with a strip of plain black cloth between them, and I added a border of this same cloth around the whole piece. Each week I would hang the work-in-progress from the blackboard and explain what I'd done to it since last week's class. The kids would come up and look at it, locate their pieces and their friends' pieces, and to their great chagrin, without meaning to, pull the thing down. It survived just fine.

While the quilt was coming into focus, the students continued to write down all kinds of memories. I tried to let the writing and quilt-making processes overlap in an organic way, not forcing the comparison, but drawing attention to it when it seemed appropriate. One day I brought in Carmen Lomas Garza's books—collections of illustrated vignettes drawn from the author's Mexican-American childhood, written in English and in Spanish. After reading the English version of one narrative to the class, it occurred to me to ask if anyone wanted to read the Spanish version. Hands shot up all over the room. I called on a boy in the back, and he read it nearly flawlessly. When he finished, the students broke into spontaneous applause. It was the same with every piece of Garza's we read that day. A current of electricity seemed to flow through the room when the Spanish version was being read. For many, the spark came from hearing these cozy familiar words—watermelon (*sandía*), birthday (*cumpleaños*), barbecue (*barbacoa*)—in an unfamiliar context, the world of home and family and the world of school overlapping in an unexpected way. This, I told them, was how I saw our quilt and our collection of writings: scraps from the past brought into the present to claim a new place in the here and now.

Putting It All Together

This piece of fabric reminds me of the stars and about the time when I didn't even know what they were. I was three years old when I first saw stars. I thought they were salt in the sky. But one day I looked through a telescope and my grandfather told me that those lights were stars. I thought it was funny but I believed him. I looked in it and said the stars were so big! Then I wanted my own telescope, and I thought that the stars would look different through it, so I bought my own. When I saw the stars through my telescope I saw they were not different at all. They were the same. So now I know stars are not salt in the sky, and they are not different. Now I know what stars are.

—*Anthony Villegas*

Do you know about the really terrible thing that happened to me in the second grade? Well, I will tell you. It was lunchtime when I went to play with my friend. When I sat on the chair I fell! I got a bump on my eye. My friend took me to the lunch teacher and she sent me to the bathroom. The teacher didn't know that I had a bump on my eye because I had covered it. When I came back she was surprised that I had a bump. The bump was getting bigger and

my eye would only open a little bit. Finally I had to go home. My sister was
calling me "One-eye" because I was just able to open my eye a little bit. But
soon it was better and I went back to school again.

—Rabia Shaikh

This is a piece of fabric from a bib that used to keep me from getting dirty
when I ate. I took it everywhere I went. I also liked to smell it. I even slept
with it. I like it because it is soft and fun. I chose this piece because I thought
I was too big for it now, but I still like it a little bit. It reminds me of my father
who died. It reminds me of my father because I had this when I was little and
he was still alive.

—Peter Valencia

Finally the quilt was nearing completion, and the students were
ready to pull together their written pieces. I had finished the top of the
quilt, and I was working on putting it together with the batting and the
back, tying it, and sewing the binding. Two weeks before our last class, I
brought the quilt in and hung it on the board as usual, explaining how I
was going about finishing it. "This is what I want you to do with your writing now," I told them. "I want you to take all the memories you have gathered during our time together, and all the lessons you have learned about
making your own story come alive, and use them to tell me the story of
your own piece of fabric, now a part of this quilt."

Before the students got to work, I told them the story behind the
piece of fabric that I myself had contributed to the quilt, and their classroom teacher and my intern did the same. Then I asked the students to take
the brainstorming web they had developed when they first brought their
fabric in, and select the ideas that they wanted to expand upon. While they
wrote, their teacher, the intern, and I walked around the room, reading what
they'd written, asking and answering questions, and sometimes prodding
them to keep working. In the next class, they were asked to work on their
pieces some more and to select one additional piece of writing that they
had produced during the residency for inclusion in the final anthology.

At our last meeting, I gave each student a copy of his or her page in
the anthology and invited those who were interested to read their pieces
to the class. I also brought in two plain pieces of fabric for the students to

sign. These I later sewed to the back of the quilt, next to a square inscribed with the name "Our Story Quilt." Two weeks later we had our final event: a reading and an unveiling of the finished quilt in the school auditorium, to which the students' families, the school principal, other school staff, and the editor of the local paper were all invited. The quilt looked wonderful, an amazingly diverse collection of fabrics brought together into a colorful whole (see figure 4). I placed it on an easel on the stage where everyone could see it, and on easels to the left and right of it I displayed large sheets of poster-board with each student's story about his or her piece next to a small scrap of that student's fabric. These boards functioned as a legend of sorts, allowing the audience to identify and read the story behind any given piece of the quilt. All of the students read their pieces, and then received their own copy of the anthology, which featured the work of all the students and a color-copied photo of the quilt on the cover. After the event, the quilt and the boards accompanying it were given to the school and displayed on the auditorium wall.

My piece of fabric is from my mother's dress. She wore it when she was having me, when I was in her stomach. When my mother gave it to me it felt soft and comfortable. It was in 1990 that she wore it. I remember my mother told me she used to rub her stomach and it felt really soft. She was right. It is soft and comfortable and it still feels that way. That softness has lasted from 1990 until the year 2000!

—*Mary Perdomo*

The first time that I ever spoke: I began speaking when I was two years old. Even though I was able to speak, I didn't understand what I was saying. Everyone's first words are usually Ma Ma and Pa Pa. When I first began speaking it was very low and soft. My mother said I spoke this way for the first couple of weeks. It's very strange.

—*Chunrong Jiang* (translated from Chinese)

I remember a time when my cousin got asthma. I was five years old and my cousin was eight years old. This was the third time this happened to her. It all started when my aunt told my mom to take care of my cousin because she had to go to New York for a year. We lived in Colombia at that time. My cousin's name was Yessenia, just like mine. When my cousin's birthday came she was very happy. Then I saw her acting very weird. Suddenly, my cousin couldn't breathe. I took her to where my mom was. My mom called the doctor. When the doctor came he said that my cousin had asthma. My mom was nervous. Then, in a minute, my cousin stopped breathing. The doctor said that she had died. I remember that she was wearing her favorite dress. The next day my mom and I went to the cemetery. When we came back my mom called my aunt and told her the news. I heard them. They were crying a lot. I felt very lonely.

—*Yessenia Garcia*

I remember a time when I lived in the Dominican Republic and I was eating fruit. There were grapes, apples, oranges, bananas, pineapples, and that's all I remember. I was four years old. The fruit smelled good, and my brother and I were eating a lot. My uncle's wife and my other aunt were there. They peeled the pineapple, and we ate it. There were mangos too. We were eating in my house. That's where I was born, in the Dominican Republic. My parents lived in New York, and my aunt and my uncle's wife took a picture of us eating the fruit and sent it to New York so my parents could see that my brother and I were okay.

—*Anthony Espinal*

The piece I chose reminds me of my grandfather and father. My grandfather died five months ago. It reminds me of the hat he wore all the time. It looks like the hat in the picture on the fabric. My grandfather was eighty years old. He was funny and was always telling jokes. He was big and strong, but he died because he had cancer. When I last saw him he gave me a twenty-dollar bill.

—*Milton Puma*

I have a picture of all my students posing with the quilt shortly after the reading. They are a smiling, colorfully dressed group, this big bunch of nine- and ten-year-olds. Having worked with them for those ten weeks, I can look at this kid or that one and remember the stories they wrote down, sad or funny or sweet or angry. It gave me great satisfaction to have helped them articulate these memories, yet even more fulfilling was being a witness to the magic that occurred when these memories were collected together. The pieces of the quilt and the writings in our collection began, in ways small and large, to speak to each other. In so doing, they also spoke to their particular place and time in a way that the individual pieces alone could not. Author Roland Freeman calls this magic "a communion of the spirits." In his book of the same name—on African-American quilters and their stories—Freeman says this communion "refers to the power of quilts to create a virtual web of connections—individual, generational, professional, physical, spiritual, cultural, and historical." Suddenly, what the students and I had created was something greater than the sum of its parts. The voices and fabric contributions of all the students put together gave each individual voice and piece of fabric a context. The experiences they wrote about were no longer just isolated stories, but the stories of individuals who were a part of a fascinatingly diverse community. Themes and patterns emerged in both the quilt and the anthology of writings that could not have been seen without looking at all of the contributions put together as a whole.

When I started this project, I had a clearly defined idea of how I wanted one creative process—quilting—to illuminate another—writing. I believe that this worked well, and was engaging and thought-provoking for my students. What surprised me was that the ways in which one creative process spoke to another were more vast and complex than I had imagined. This may be the most important lesson of this project: that once you begin the creative process, interesting and unexpected things start to happen. Being open to this can produce wonderful work. Whatever the scope of your plans, the important thing, of course, is to begin; and these kids learned that that can be done with just a single image, just one small scrap of fabric.

Bibliography

Brainard, Joe. *I Remember.* New York, Granary Books, 2000.

Cisneros, Sandra. *House on Mango Street.* New York: Vintage/Random House, 1984.

Freeman, Roland L. *Communion of the Spirits: African American Quilters, Preservers, and Their Stories.* Nashville, Tenn.: Rutledge Hill Press, 1996.

Garza, Carmen Lomas. *In My Family*. San Francisco: Children's Book Press, 1996.

———. *Family Pictures*. San Francisco: Children's Book Press, 1990.

Greenfield, Eloise, and Lessie Jones Little. *Childtimes*. Drawings by Jerry Pinkney. New York: Harper Trophy/HarperCollins, 1979.

Mills, Lauren. *The Rag Coat*. New York: Little, Brown, 1991

Rylant, Cynthia. *Appalachia*. Illustrated by Barry Moser. New York: Voyager Books/Harcourt Brace, 1982.

———. *When I Was Young in the Mountains*. Illustrated by Diane Goode. New York: Puffin Unicorn/Dutton Children's Books/ Penguin, 1982.

Taback, Simms. *Joseph Had a Little Overcoat*. New York: Viking Penguin, 1999.

Susan Karwoska

Igniting the Inward Prodigy

by Will Alexander

SINCE THE WATERMARK OF THE CARTESIAN, meaningful thought has been construed as moving "in a clearly defined direction" toward a clearly incontestable outcome. Such structuring of the mind puts supreme concentration upon selective thinking, which proceeds sequentially, moving step by each justifying step. We see this, and the resulting codification, in most aspects of our day-to-day living, especially in education, in standardized student testing. All goals are recognizable, all progressions accounted for. It is like addition by abacus: each thought is a "digit in its appropriate column."

The mind most treasured in this world is the one that brilliantly complies with the strenuous complication of the unadorned result. Of course, this is the left hemisphere of the brain working at its optimum. In such a climate, the discontinuous is viewed with perpetual suspicion, and those minds lacking the same measurable fluency are marked as having an ignominious intelligence.

At the beginning of my educational sojourn, I was marked by this lessening. I know firsthand that this marking causes pain to the self and that this pain inhibits the power beginning to accrue in one's being. By age seven, I already felt as if I had failed to secure stability in this life. I had not developed the tools to join the established reading collective; to interpret written characters, and to gain sense from their arrangement. So I was banished to the lowest rung of that collective. To compensate, I engaged in imaginative forays. I turned great fig trees into winged vertical blueness, I imagined ancient sienna cities that I would arrange from stones that I'd find, and I modeled cinnabar ponies from mud. These inner flights helped me reconnoiter the shadows of fear. I could say that in this, my first poetic experience, I was intuitively understanding the rudiments of Edward de Bono's "lateral" world, much in advance of his findings. This is not to say that a seven-year-old had evolved any trenchant understanding of the anti-linear as technique. But I knew my indwelling grasp by touch, solitude, and the inner dialectic, which formed my basic principle of balance. Thanks to the diligence of one concerned instructor, a Mr. Beacon as I recall, the characters began to coalesce to such a degree that the print became comprehensible enough that I was able to work at an "acceptable minimum." Reading is a practical necessity: it allows one to gain a working into this world and also the capacity to counter its tenacious reasoning. It was a skill that ultimately allowed me to illuminate my inner complexity by engaging me in subjects as disparate as botany and poetics.

I am not presenting myself as a singular case. There are many others like me. As a writing instructor, I am always looking to restructure the classroom. "Advice," "restrictions," and "explanations" no longer subsist as guiding forces. What I seek to create is a hive of tactile opportunity, what I call "verbal painting." For instance, I take the noun *bird* and then ask the students what a bird does. Immediately hands go in the air. From there we get into colors, types of birds, patterns of flight, the difference between sea birds and land birds, types of food consumed, night birds, day birds, birds that fly, birds that walk over land. We delve into geography, diet, animal behavior, and astronomy. Rather than a sterile topography of facts, this creates a scent, an inner motivation to encounter worlds that students never knew existed. The students become immediately involved.

The only way knowledge becomes an inspiring element in one's life is through a lifelong motivation that outstrips diplomas and titles. As catalyst/instructor, my objective is to allow the students' interior presence to emerge without the facts being a restricting force. This is how curiosity exudes so that student and instructor can meet an existential mean, and all the facts from the instructor fall on fertile aural scapes, allowing unforeseen growth to transpire.

I have found this type of approach fruitful to a vast array of communities—from challenged fifteen-year-olds in south central Los Angeles to poets and writers five times their age in the comfortable setting of Hofstra University on Long Island. Whether the student is fifteen or seventy-five, of whatever ethnicity, the issue is to find out what motivates him or her so that an inward sparking takes place and dialogue is established. This dialogue needs to be more than simply between student and instructor in the classroom. It needs to be an ongoing connection for the student, so that an unmonitored arousal takes place in his or her being.

It is vital that the catalyst/instructor be most concerned with the individuals he or she is communing with. Not only at the college or university teaching levels is this essential, but also at those interesting levels where the fifteen- or eighteen-year-old has not evolved beyond the basic rudiments of reading. This is where the "Eastern"—or more particularly, African—model comes into play for me. According to traditional African values, "the person preexists and by incarnating himself . . . seeks to open himself, to grow, to insert himself always more effectively" into the larger society. The person is central in this context—not the institution, as in the West.

With these ideas in mind, I bring prints or paintings to class as a stimulus to writing. The students are excited not only by subject matter and color, but also by the artists' biographies. Miró is a perfect example. What I stress when discussing him is the purity of his creative character, a character infused with anxiety, transmutation, and discipline. While speaking to the students about how to achieve balance in a poem, I use *The Farmer's Wife*, one of Miró's early paintings. Why this painting rather than a later painting from his oeuvre? Because I instinctively learned from this painting the art of verbal equillibrium. How the weight, the coloration, and the alchemical linkage of each word creates an unerring magic. I tell the students what Miró said concerning *The Farmer's Wife*—that he had made the "cat too large," throwing "the picture out of balance." He went on to say that this was "the reason for the double circles and the two angular lines in the foreground" of the painting. From this visual example I introduce the idea of interior sonority. How, in the magic of a poem, tables, stars, and rivers can blend as immaculate homonyms.

During a recent class at the Naropa Institute, I made up a random list of words ranging from *ice* to *fire*, from *Ecuador* to *pyramid*, from *hummingbird* to *gold*. I then asked each student to connect these particles elec-

Will Alexander

trically. The results were singular, and each piece carried its own particular coloration. What I was stressing was not some pre-determined motion, but a response that charged each composition—electricity being the difference between quotidian and poetic levels of language. Creation needs to continuously germinate in the mind of the reader, listener, and viewer. This is what Antonin Artaud once termed the "electrical revolution," the transmuting of electricity by means of spontaneous resonance.

Working over the past three years with Theatre of Hearts/Youth First, a non-profit Los Angeles-based arts organization, I have encountered students who have been abandoned and forgotten by the conventional institutions of learning. These are young people who have been detained by law, who are transitioning into the challenges of schooling after recent incarceration. For them, the great Afro-Cuban painter Wifredo Lam is an inspiring example. Lam made groundbreaking works engendered by his African heritage. I show them how he lit the volcano of Orishas in painting his symphonic trance called *The Jungle* (see figure 5). Lam commenced work on *The Jungle* in 1942, and from its beginning it was a magnetic sum of his imaginative powers. I use the painting as an example of artistic courage, the courage to express who you really are.

In Lam's own words, *The Jungle* "was intended to communicate a psychic state." After all, Cuba is not a land of jungles. This painting is therefore a prime example of trusting one's interior cosmology. I tell students to think of the shapes and colors as words, as if the picture were a splendiferous verbal anatomy. Seeing the audacity of Lam's painting gives a kind of license to these nouveau verbal practitioners. It lets them know that one does not use conventional means to express artistic power. I tell them that to create and sustain power, one must study one's medium with an inward patience in order to raise one's writing to a level of perpetual quality. This turns their concentration toward the interior state, in this sense transmuting the negatives of their former street activity into the seminal activity of language. Working from this state of mind, they produce stunning writing. Being exposed to great artists, whose backgrounds at times echo their own, inspires them to meet life's challenges with another form of lightning in their eye.

We are educating people, not numbers. The most important thing is to understand that each individual is capable of providing unique insights into the subject at hand. I always try to employ de Bono's concept of "suspended judgment," which allows the possibility for increasing new, seemingly curious, approaches. Not that all approaches will prove significant in the end, but in their sum they generate motion, which in turn generates further motion. What takes place in such a conclave are unforeseen outlooks which help to draw out hidden powers from the subject at hand. It's like moving around a seemingly stationary chandelier, seeing at one angle blue-green, at another orange-red, at yet another lilac or ocher. The combinations proliferate. The effect of these combinations may not occur until three weeks after working with a group in this mode of free exchange, but even so, a tacit understanding begins to make itself felt. As David Bohm has so artfully stated, "If we are communicating at the tacit level, then maybe thought is changing." It is the duty of the catalyst/instructor to stir up the life force in all students, the seventy-year-old as well as the fifteen-year-old, so that inner circulation is activated. Even if it is for a fleeting moment that they see a wider possibility, it is the first opening to a freedom that soars beyond the harried routine of debility.

Bibliography

Bohm, David. *On Dialogue.* New York: Routledge, 1997.

Chipp, Hershel B. *Theories of Modern Art.* Berkeley and Los Angeles: University of California Press, 1968.

de Bono, Edward. *Lateral Thinking.* New York: Harper Colophon, 1973.

Erny, Pierre. *Childhood and Cosmos.* New York: New Perspectives, 1973.

Investigating the Process of Portraiture

by Ezra Shales

Dallisha's Written Portrait of Ashley

I think she is a nice person. Then she is sometimes bad. Ashley has a white t-shirt blouse and gold kinda pants, and her hairstyle in braids. She was friendly the first time I met her. She's kind and generous. I think she was cool in the picture. She has a scratch on her face. I was not wearing a white t-shirt blouse and gold kinda pants, and I did not have that kind of different braids in my hair. She and I have big ears. I have big lips, and she doesn't.

Ashley's Response to Written and Photographic Portraits by Dallisha

I think my picture looks ugly because my eyes are closed. Not really ugly but . . . not right, like . . . terrible. It just doesn't look right. I don't like it. See, if my eyes were open I would look better and pretty and . . . well better than I look in the picture. If my eyes were open I would also look mature. Not too old, older than nine years old, younger than eleven. Dallisha is right: I am friendly, kind, generous, and I don't have big lips. I am nice, sort of. I have big ears. Dallisha is like me. Her ears are sort of big, not big like Martin's ears.

You know, the Martin on TV—you know, Shanana, that Martin. Thank you Dallisha for all the nice things you said about me. If one day I have to write about you, I will write something good about you, unless your personality changes.

PORTRAITURE IS A WAY FOR STUDENTS to gain perspective on their own lives and on those of their classmates. Portraits can be written or drawn in the presence of the subject, or they can be derived from a visual artifact, such as a photograph or a painting. As the teacher of an after-school photography course, I have discovered that exposing students to more than one way of making portraits helps to emphasize the process over any finished product. By teaching verbal and visual portraiture, I help my students discover for themselves that each medium has its own strengths and limitations. They also realize that a picture is interpreted differently than a written description and that by combining a picture with writing they leave less room for misinterpretation. Learning to respect the value of each medium is a significant part of the lesson. The following exercises emerged from a recent after-school class in which I taught twelve third graders. The exercises were designed to sustain and build students' concentration spans and to increase their observation skills, their self-confidence, and their self-awareness.

Exercise 1: Portraits in Memory

I began the first class by discussing what cameras do, how they are used, and what images they make. I was particularly interested in introducing the idea of time and memory. To do so, I showed them two photographs: a snapshot from my childhood and a photograph of a group of strangers that I had found. To instigate their curiosity, I asked them to concentrate on one of the photographs and respond to the following questions:

1. Where was the photograph taken?
2. What time of day was the photograph taken?
3. How long ago was the photograph made?
4. How do you feel when you look at the picture?
5. What was the person thinking who took the picture?

For each question the students had to produce a written response; I also asked them to draw a picture of the photograph from memory.

To personalize the exercise, I then suggested that the students remember a picture of their friends or family. We closed our eyes together, and I asked them to imagine where the photograph was in their house—on the refrigerator or on the wall, next to the television or beside the bed. Then I told them to take it one step further and visualize the people in the picture—whether they are standing up or lying down, whether they are inside or outside—and finally, to write all of these details down.

Ezra Shales

For homework, I asked them to bring in the photograph they had written about so that they could begin to compare their memory of the image with the actual object. Once each student had mounted the photograph beside the description on a piece of paper, they were paired off and asked to interview each other with the help of the following worksheet.

1. Does the photograph look different than you remembered?
2. Are there details in the photograph that you wish you had mentioned?
3. Does the photograph make you remember a specific time, place, or event?

After conducting their interviews, the students wrote down each other's responses and then presented them out loud to the class. Such oral reports were a fun way to get everyone acquainted and to foster a sense of community. And though some students wrote very little, they gave good presentations by gesturing and talking their way through, adding impromptu comments as they went along.

Exercise 2: Eyes for Cameras and Humans

In the next class I focused on the process of observation, and compared it to the act of taking a picture. A shutter lets in light, I told them, the same way as the human eyelid opens. I passed around a shutter so that they could hold it up and snap the trigger open and shut. The students had all seen a camera before, but some had never actually held one in their hands. I also passed around an oatmeal-box pinhole camera so that they could see how a manual shutter (in this case, a piece of tape) functions similarly. I encouraged them to think of cameras as tools for collecting memories, not simply as mechanisms for making pictures. "Catching light" gradually became the students' favorite metaphor for memory-making.

I also used this lesson to make the idea of point-of-view more concrete. Each student was asked to make a viewfinder by folding a piece of paper in half, cutting a square hole in it, and then drawing two parallel lines into the center of one side. We all sat in a circle and held up our viewfinders so that we were each looking through the paper frames at each other. I explained that everyone has his or her own view of the circle and that photography (as well as drawing) allows us to see each other's perspective. To demonstrate this, I asked the students to take the small squares of paper we had cut out of the viewfinder and make drawings of the three classmates who sat opposite them. When they were finished, each student passed around a rough drawing of three stick figures—each was labeled with a name—and the class began to understand that each student had a unique perspective. By perceiving how each view complemented the others, the group grew as a community.

After laying out the drawings in order, I compared the sequence to a roll of developed negatives. To make the point clearer, I passed a loaded camera around the circle and asked the students to take a photograph of those who stood opposite them. Using a camera gave the students a sense of joy and power—especially because the person who was holding the camera had everyone's attention. When the group looked at the results in the next session, they were able to compare the film with the stick-figure drawings and see the differences as well as the continuities. Here was proof that each person's perspective complemented the others' in both drawings and photography.

Exercise 3: Portraits of Places, Old and New

For the purposes of the third lesson, everyone received his or her own oatmeal-box pinhole camera pre-loaded with a sheet of photographic paper. Each box contained a piece of thin metal (or heavy-duty aluminum foil) with a tiny pinhole in it: this pinhole was made light-tight with a slab of heavy tape. The students sat at their desks and did a practice attempt at taking a picture by removing the tape without moving the box. After they made their exposures, the students took turns developing their prints in the makeshift darkroom I had created—a corner of the room containing a sink over which a piece of light-tight fabric and a tarp were hung. A red light bulb replaced the normal bulb over the sink and the trays all had lids to prevent light-leaks. The students liked being self-directed and enjoyed the magical quality of watching the black shapes emerge from a white sheet of paper.

To accompany this activity, I read them a brief paragraph from Steven Milhauser's *The Little Kingdoms: Three Novellas,* in which a man drifts through a childhood memory of watching his father develop a photograph. The reading sustained the students' focus and articulated the joy of developing a photograph.

> The paper was blank, but as he watched, tense with expectation, he became aware of a slight motion on the paper, as of something rising to the surface, and from the depths of whiteness the picture would begin to emerge—an edge here, a gray bit there, a ghostly arm reaching out of a shirt sleeve. More and more the darkness rose up out of the white.

I followed up the reading by asking the students to examine and write about three nineteenth-century albumen prints of monuments in France. The assignment was very broad: they could write a single description, they could write a comparison between two photographs, or they could make up a story. This activity was devised to make writing less of a chore, and it seems to have succeeded. Aliko produced expository writing that was rich and energized:

> I see statues that are beautiful. I thought that France was a village that just spoke a beautiful language. I learned that if you move when someone is taking a picture of you, you are not supposed to move. I learned that you can't move the camera if you're supposed to take a picture of someone.

Ashley summarized what she learned from comparing old and new photographs:

> What I learned is that when you move in a picture sometimes the person looks invisible. Something else I know is that a picture in color looks better in my opinion. Pictures from 100 years ago look very different from today. I

also learned that if you scratch the film it cannot be developed well.

The excitement of discovery was palpable, and the writing exercise made them reconsider what they wanted to photograph next.

After looking at the Parisian photographs, students were inspired to document their own surroundings, transferring the same style of careful observation onto their own worlds. Elementary School 73 is a beautiful old building, a half-mile from Yankee Stadium, with a neoclassical facade, large columns, old iron fixtures, and a beautiful portico. It is a great subject for photographs and a fluent transition from Paris. The students moved to the exterior of the school, and wrote briefly about what they wanted to photograph. "I think it will come out nice because I took the picture straight and still," wrote Massiel. Martin, describing the light fixture outside of the old school, wrote, "I want to take a picture about the light bell. It looks like it's been there centuries, and in black and white it will look like it's been there for generations."

Exercise 4: Portraits of Who We Are and How We Are Seen

For the final project, I asked each student to photograph one other student and to write a description of the person he or she had just photographed. The sitter then wrote his or her own response to both documents. I reminded the class that our project was similar to something they did every year: have their class picture taken. This would be a chance for them to create their own memory of how they looked and felt in third grade. I also reiterated my rule that the students not be mean to each other. In order to curtail feuding, I organized the sequence so that each student photographed a student who was photographing a third. The tough criticisms *were* provocative, but the students accepted what was written about them. And the writing was stronger for its lack of inhibitions and its earnest clarity.

The students devoted the next session to writing descriptions of the portraits they had produced. Many students chose to compare themselves to the subject of the portrait as a means of articulating personalities or physical attributes. The final class was spent mounting each student's 8" x 10" photograph to a board, along with the two typed descriptions. When the display in the school lobby was complete, several parents came by to see the work and were pleased with the results. It was an important source of pride for the students to have their work exhibited (see figure 6).

I.

Ashley's Written Portrait of Aliko

Ezra Shales

I think Aliko is a poor person because of his sneakers. They're dirty and raggedy. I think Aliko is too serious and needs to lighten up. Everyday Aliko comes to school with pieces of things in his hair. Aliko has a funny shaped head and funny big ears. His shirt is nice. I would wear it even if I had it, his pants too. Aliko is very, very smart like me. Me and Aliko are both smart and both know how to dress in style. When Aliko smiles he has dimples. Aliko has a mole, me too. In many ways we are the same—like me, I'm a girl, Aliko is a boy, I have longer hair than him, he has short hair. Me and Aliko use different bathrooms, he uses the boys' and I use the girls' restroom. Me and Aliko are a lot different and a little alike because everybody is different. Only about 60% of the world is different.

Aliko's Response to Ashley's Written and Photographic Portraits

I think I'm gorgeous. I look wonderful. My head is straight and not awkward. My ears are not big. Well, they are big, they help me listen a lot more. I also think that my shirt was nice like she said. I look more handsome than Jermaine in the five Jacksons. I think what she said about my sneakers is a lie. It's not true. Everything she said is not true. Except when she put I always have things in my hair. When she said that I have to lighten up, I don't have to. She should start getting a little more serious about her work than about things that I have or don't have. I do know how to dress in style. I like everything about myself.

II.

Aliko's Written Portrait of Jacinto

I think Jacinto is a little boy who doesn't behave and a person who calls me stupid. Otherwise, he looks good. That person is Jacinto. I think he's a little short person that doesn't behave sometimes. He's a friend that cares. He acts like a clown sometimes. His picture looks like he took it seriously but not as a big joke. He's wearing a blue shirt under. A yellow zipper with a pocket on the chest of the shirt. He also has a yellow outfit under the green hood. He's cool and nice like me. In many ways Jacinto and me have unusual names. Jacinto's short. I'm tall. His hands are little, mine are big. Omar is his best friend, I'm not. We both use the same bathroom. Jacinto doesn't have a haircut but his picture looks surprisingly great. We both have the same pencils.

Jacinto's Response to Aliko's Written and Photographic Portraits

I think I look good because I think Aliko took it very well, because he took focus and wrote good things about me. He wrote good things and he took the picture very nicely. I love it because I was a beautiful picture. I look handsome. I love myself. I don't like how I acted—it was so stupid and I hate my shirt I was wearing. I look different today. Today I've got blue pants and a blue shirt. Under it I am wearing a clean whiteshirt. I got my hair mess' up.

III.

Valerie's Written Portrait of Eric

I think Eric is silly because he takes pictures with his eyes really open and he always yells at people when they bother him. I think he looks dumb because he is always making faces in pictures. But sometimes he is really nice to people who don't bother him. Sometimes he gives people stuff, like when he gives me a pencil when I ask him to. He's always whining when he starts a fight. Sometimes he gets mad and has spit coming down his mouth.

Eric's Response to Valerie's Written and Photographic Portraits

Valerie is right: when I fight I win. I like Valerie, she's pretty. She has green eyes and I made two songs about Valerie! Your head is big! And green Valerie you smell like gasoline! Hey hey. And Valerie the red nose reindeer had a very humongous head, all of the other reindeer like to call her names, the end.

IV.

Ezra Shales

Martin's Written Portrait of Dallisha

I took a picture of Dallisha. Describing her, she has a blue sweater and light blue jeans and pigtails. In front of her, she has a gold and white necklace. She is sweet and friendly and her behavior is good. Dallisha is in third grade. She is smart, short. She goes to an after-school program. Talks a whole bunch. Looks young. Her white shoes are Fila shoes. She has black pules, white teeth. She does not make a lot of jokes, and Mr. Shales does.

Dallisha's Response to Martin's Written and Photographic Portraits

First of all, my necklace is not gold and white, it is silver. By the way I am smart and short. Anyway, I do look young, but I have a second chin, Martin. And old people have second chins, don't you notice that? I did have pigtails, but now my hair looks like another hairstyle. I am in third grade. I do talk a lot. I'm friendly. I wear Fila shoes and they are white. I go to an after-school program. My pants are blue. And my shirt was blue at the time. I'm fat and chubby, fo' god's sake. I mean, I took up the whole picture.

✧　✧　✧　✧　✧　✧　✧　✧　✧

Students exercised many different abilities over the course of this project. They evaluated their own memories and wrote in response to the memories; they contrasted types of photographs and composed their own photographs; they wrote about their intentions when taking a photograph and how they felt the resulting image functioned. The after-school program took many risks, the most dangerous of which was asking the students to write descriptions of one another. However, no censorship was needed; students worked with each other to edit themselves. Moreover, the students met my challenge to produce expressive and focused work. What they made surprised their teachers, who told me that the students' abilities expanded during the course. The course not only tested the limits of what can be done in an after-school program, but the work produced by these students demonstrated that juggling several media—writing, photography, and drawing—can be stimulating and productive, and that interdisciplinary work should not be the province of higher education alone.

The Image-Making Workshop
An Introduction to Creative Bookmaking

by Rosalind Pace & Marcia Simon

*i*MAGE-MAKING IS A WEEKLONG WORKSHOP in creative book-making based on a series of simple, carefully structured, parallel verbal and visual activities. Even though we understand why these activities work so well, we never cease to be surprised and amazed by what students achieve, regardless of age or skill. We developed Image-Making in 1976 and have taught it every year since then. The following essay describes how we teach Image-Making and why it works. We refer specifically to a week we spent at Poughkeepsie Day School, where we taught a group of fourteen: eleven first to twelfth graders, plus three teachers. Our goal is not only to stimulate creativity, but to make students realize that inside each of them is an endless source of rich personal imagery that can be articulated, developed, and shared.

Monday Morning: A Brief History of the Book Form

On Monday morning we begin with an introduction to the book form as a unique format. We talk about what existed before books—Assyrian clay tablets, Egyptian wall paintings, Hebrew scrolls. By becoming aware of what a book is *not*, students become more aware of what a book *is*. We tell students that inherent in the book form is a beginning, a middle, and an end. The act of turning pages creates possibilities for anticipation, memory, surprise, and resolution.

We then give out materials for the first visual project: one large sheet of white paper, two smaller sheets of black paper, and white glue. We tell students to fold the white paper in half three times, making books of sixteen pages (counting both sides of each page). Now they are ready to decide on the size and proportions of the book. This choice is the first of many intuitive decisions. Our only rule is that the book must be rectangular. This eliminates books shaped like butterflies or hearts—designs that impose too rigid a content and elicit preconceived ideas. Students then cut their books to size, being careful not to slice off the book's spine. In response to their inquiries about content, we give them the following instructions:

> The content of your book will be one black rectangle (or fewer) per page. The rectangle may be cut or torn or both. It may be any size or proportion and placed anywhere on the page. Begin with the first page (the front cover) and work consecutively through the book. Do one page at a time, one rectangle at a time. A blank page—a page without a rectangle—is not nothing, but signifies something when viewed in the context of the total book. The centerfold is a special place, and can be treated as one page or two.

Students often ask if they can break the rules. The answer is always yes, as long as the black shape can be recognized as a rectangle. We never give examples of what might be done because we don't want to influence the students' impulses. The possibilities within a limited framework are endless, and that is precisely the point.

We guide students through this activity by insisting that they do not have to know what their books are "about." "Just pay attention to what you want the rectangles to do on each page. This book is about rectangles." We also tell students to save *all* their scraps.

The parallel verbal activity, which occurs after we "read" the rectangle books, is to build poems from word-blocks drawn at random from a common pile of words. Each student contributes to the word pile by writing ten nouns and ten verbs on separate slips of white paper. We introduce this activity by talking about words as concrete things that not only mean themselves, but also have resonances and implications, just as the black

rectangles do. As with the previous discussion, we tell them what a poem
is, by emphasizing what it is not. A poem is not necessarily a preconceived
totality, we tell them, but a discovery—line by line by line. We read a few
poems with startling images: "Two athletes / are dancing in the cathedral
/ of the wind" (from James Wright's "Spring Images") or "gritty light- Rosalind Pace
& Marcia Simon
ning / of their touch" (from Mary Oliver's "Starfish"). We remind the students to use specific verbs (*stroll* instead of *walk*) and nouns (*trout* instead
of *fish*).

The common word-pile is then mixed up (with the words face-down)
and each student draws out ten words, no more than two of which can be
his or her own. The words become the raw material for building a poem.
Our instructions are:

> Use as many of these words as you can and as many other words as you
> need to. You may repeat words if you wish, and you may change the form of
> the word (for instance, *dream* can be changed to *dreamed* or *dreamers*).
> Write one line at a time, and don't plan ahead. Don't try to rhyme. Resist
> the temptation to put obvious words together (like *horse* and *gallop*). Allow
> for surprise.

We wait until our students are engrossed in the project to tell them
how much time they have. A time limit then does what our other rules
do—it encourages quick, intuitive decision-making.

Tuesday Morning: A Brief History of the Alphabet

On Tuesday morning, we begin with a brief history of the alphabet, paying
particular attention to how the letters "A" and "B" evolved from images of
concrete things—an ox's head, a house. We show alphabets in various lan-
guages to help students see letters as visual delights. The most beautiful
letters, we tell them, were designed by hand to please the eye. Each student then chooses a letter from a variety of alphabet styles (we use Frederic William Goudy's *The Alphabet and Elements of Lettering*). Without
telling the students what they will be doing with their letter, we ask them
to examine it closely, using a magnifying glass and a mirror, and to mea-

sure its parts carefully with a ruler. When they are familiar with their let-ter, students are asked to draw it in pencil on black paper, making it at least four times larger than the original. We assure students that scientific pre-cision is not required. They should pay attention to proportions, relation-ships of height to width, and to the spaces in or around the letter, but they should also trust their eyes. The students then cut out the letter and glue it onto heavy white paper, using as much or as little of the paper as they wish, since the relationship between the letter and the space it occupies is another important intuitive choice. We then tack the mounted letters to the wall for viewing (see figure 7).

For the parallel verbal activity, students make acrostic poems using the letters of their first and last names as the spine of the poem. They write with thin black markers on unlined, white paper. Our instructions guide students into their poems step by step:

> Write your name vertically down the left margin of the paper. Then, in a few seconds, write on a separate sheet of paper as many words as you can think of that begin with the first letter of your name. Now choose one of those words—any one. This is the first word of your poem. Write it on your first sheet of paper, using the first letter of your name as the beginning of the first word.

We tell students to be aware of all the white space to the right of each letter and to use as much of it as they choose. The lines of a poem, we remind them, do not all have to be the same length, and while the words of the lines can form sentences, not every line has to be a sentence. A single sentence can run the entire length of the poem. We also say, "Even though this is a poem held together by your name, it doesn't have to be about you. Just let the letters of your name—the letters of the spine—propel you through the poem." When the poems are finished, we read them aloud, slowly and clearly, much to the delight of even the shyest students. At the end of this session, we ask the students to bring in a bag of found objects for the following day—anything with a surface that can be inked and pressed to paper.

Students always bring in a wonderful variety of found objects: leaves, shells, flowers, feathers, paper clips, letters carved out of wood, thread spools, cut potatoes, lemon halves, lace, string, and fly swatters. At the beginning of the class these objects are placed on pieces of large white paper in a communal pile. Before introducing the day's visual activity, we present a brief history of printing. Particular emphasis is placed on the invention of moveable type, which, we explain, made commonplace and accessible what was previously considered magical and inaccessible (except to monks, priests, and scribes). We point out that the printed word, however, still carries with it a power beyond its literal meaning.

Rosalind Pace
& Marcia Simon

We then invite students to help themselves to the found objects and to an assortment of water-soluble printers' inks and papers (including black pastel paper, sumi or rice papers, and plain white paper). The purpose of the activity, we explain, is to explore the printing process—to experience the magic of the printed image emerging as an object in itself, which may or may not resemble the original object. In addition, we encourage our students to discover how repetition of an image can create rhythm and pattern. We ask them to do at least five sheets of prints, including at least one on black paper, and to simply have a good time printing. After they have finished, we clean up the rollers and inks, spread all the prints out on the floor, like a beautiful carpet, and marvel at them.

Then we tell the students to pick up their own prints and, using picture mats with different sized windows, find a section they like. As students look at the framed image they have chosen, we encourage them to let their minds go and to jot down their thoughts on a separate sheet of paper—what they see, what they are reminded of, what is happening in that space, what it might feel like to enter it. These jotted notes form the basis of the repetition poem, which is the verbal activity we proceed to introduce. We talk briefly about repetition as an organizing principle of poems and read a few examples: the repetition of sound (Emily Dickinson's "Soundless as dots–on a Disc of Snow"); the repetition of words (D. H. Lawrence's "Bavarian Gentians"); the repetition of phrases and syntax (Walt Whitman's *Leaves of Grass*); and the repetition of images (Wallace Stevens's "Thirteen Ways of Looking at a Blackbird"). Students then write poems, using their notes and as many kinds of repetition as they wish. The session ends with a group reading of their poems.

On Thursday and Friday, students compose and assemble their final books from the mass of material they have generated, including their scraps. We introduce the project by talking again about the book as a format for designing in time and space. Each page is both complete in itself and exists in relationship to what comes before and after. We look at several beautiful books, including Horace Rackham's *Sleeping Beauty*, Kenneth Patchen's hand-painted poem-books, and individual pages from *The Complete Graphic Works of William Blake*. Graphic images and words relate to each other not only in terms of content, we tell them, but also in the way that they look.

The students' first task is to discover the theme of their own books. They spend a lot of time looking at everything, re-reading their poems, fingering their scraps. Slowly, they begin to notice commonalities and echoes, the threads that run through their work. We tell them that what they have before them is raw material and that nothing they have done so far should be considered either finished or inviolate. Poems can be cut apart and reassembled, copied over. Their rectangle books, enlarged letters, and prints can be cut or torn to make whatever visual image they need. The point is that the final book is not a scrapbook. It is not a container for the previous days' activities. It is a new invention, made from the raw material already generated. More black paper can be cut, torn, or folded as needed, but no drawings or other materials can be added. We assure students that once they have discovered their theme, they will be amazed at how everything becomes relevant to it. We also say, "The title of your book already exists somewhere in your verbal material. All you have to do is find it."

Conclusion: Nurturing Creativity

Establishing the conviction within a student that he or she *is* creative is the critical first step in nurturing creativity, just as making students realize that they *can* master a given task is at the heart of all effective teaching. In the Image-Making Workshop, this belief emerges in two ways: when the student sees his or her own personal style or "signature" emerge in the verbal *and* the visual work, and when the student sees that the work has meaning and significance to others. The student's signature emerges when work is produced intuitively, that is, without a preconceived idea. There-fore, the first activities of the week are designed to circumvent the pre-conceived. In both the rectangle book and the word-block poem, students are forced to proceed from the materials themselves, the papers and the words, rather than from any conscious plan.

Rosalind Pace
& Marcia Simon

For intuition to operate effectively, students must begin with the act of choosing: choosing the size of each rectangle, choosing where to place it on the page, quickly writing down any ten nouns on ten slips of paper. If choices are made for the sake of choice, rather than for a specific "goal," the choice will be intuitive. And no intuitive choice can be a mistake, because it is automatically a reflection of the chooser. A student's artistic signature will manifest itself in a characteristic use of space, patterning, repeated images, and the quality of lines and edges. It can be seen in the way the words look on the page or in the relationship of the rectangles to the edges of the page. When verbal and visual activities are presented back to back, as parallel activities, and the same characteristics appear in both, students begin to recognize and respect their own patterns of expression.

The two of us teach *after* the fact, as opposed to the conventional practice that begins with the goal (or the rationale) followed by examples. In the Image-Making activities, the students work first, so intuition can operate freely, and later learn the why. We give simple instructions that allow students to work directly with the materials—e.g., use one black rec-tangle or fewer per page. Only after the work is done do we respond to it. Our responses are always based on finding the uniqueness in each work— not what we think it ought to be, but what is there. Students learn that everything counts, that every tear, wrinkle, and cut matters, whether they meant it or not. And it is because everything has significance that we insist the students keep all their scraps—their leftover cuttings, their first drafts, everything. By the end of the week, they learn that what they ignore can be as important as what they pay attention to.

The conviction that one *can* do creative work begins to be established on Monday morning when we read the rectangle books. First, everyone looks at the books in silence. This allows everyone to experience the books intuitively, or emotionally. Then we, as teachers, set the pattern for the lan-guage to be used to discuss the work, and very quickly the group begins to develop fluency in this way of looking and articulating. Rectangles fly and fall, explode from centerfolds, or slide off pages into space. We point out the sequential nature of each unfolding drama and how particular pages anticipate or recall other pages.

Everything we say about both the visual and the verbal work rein-forces the personal signature that is there. For example, the big letter "M" by Scott (Poughkeepsie Day School, tenth grade) was impressive in its grace, with its balance of thicks and thins, and its serifs waving gallantly. Placed in the center of a large white space, the actual center of the letter is slightly to the right, making the letter look as if it were moving across the page. The delicacy of the thins makes the letter seem fragile, more brave than assured. A little later, when we were looking at Scott's acrostic poem, several things were immediately apparent. In his poem, the tiny handwriting was strung out in long lines, and echoed the delicacy of his big letter "M." And the subject of his poem (moving through space, reach-ing, yearning), the soft echoes of sound, and the precise and sophisticated use of enjambment and internal rhyme, echoed the shape, movement, and intricate design of his letter. M for Motion. M for Melody. M for Moon. The first and last lines of the poem repeated the colors red and green in the same way that the bottom serif of the letter reiterated the top. Turned sideways, the shape of the poem itself echoed the shape of the letter. All of these correspondences served to make Scott aware of the coherent, rich personal imagery that informed his work every step of the way.

There are always two parts to the creative act: the artist's creation of the work, and another person's re-experiencing of the work. Until this communication takes place, the creative act is incomplete. This is why it is important to allow enough time for group viewing. What we look for in our students' work is evidence that a discovery has been made, that they have gone beyond the expected and the previously known. We facilitate this by insisting that they stick as closely as possible to both the materials and the task at hand. If the focus is narrowed, the vision expands.

During the group viewing and reading, we are able to demonstrate that each student's work is successful and has distinction and meaning, vitality and character; because the work arises from the individual's imagery and bears each person's artistic signature, it is unlike any other. Thus we accomplish our first goal as teachers, which is to provide activities that convince the students that they *can* do it, that they have within them the power to create.

Our second goal is to be sure that the work the students do is good—that the work itself is convincing as art. A convincing work of art is a work in which the form and content are one. The exercises we use and the way in which we discuss them are all geared toward this fusion. Therefore, how we talk about the students' work becomes an important part of our teaching. This articulation contains two elements: first, the intuitive response ("The 'A' looks like it's dancing"), which is a statement about the *content*. Students see that their work has an effect. Then we tell them why their work has that effect ("because of the way it is placed at an angle, freed from the horizontal and vertical edges of the paper, and because of the way this serif points delicately into the corner")—and this is a statement about *form*. This two-part articulation goes a long way toward dispelling the altogether too typical response to art and poetry, which says that it's whatever I want it to be and whatever I see in it and my guess is as good as yours. By teaching verbal and visual art together, we further encourage the fusion of form and content because we *read* the visual material as well as look at it, and we *see* the verbal material as well as read it. Students can no longer look only at the form and say: if it rhymes, it's poetry—no matter how trite the message. And they can no longer look at the content alone and say: it has mountains and a rainbow, therefore it must be art—regardless of how badly it is painted. Mere illustration can allow content to take over. Similarly, mere decoration can allow form to take over. Both can be nice to look at and fun to do, but they should not be confused with deeper creative activity, which results in self-revelation and which expresses the voice and vision of a unique individual.

Rosalind Pace & Marcia Simon

If a student understands the relationship between form and content, even intuitively, then that student can allow the materials to have their own life. Being able to do this comes from the belief in oneself: "I will play with these things. Something exciting is bound to happen." As teachers, of course, we never tell students that they are going to do exciting work, that it will be a lot of fun, and that they will learn important things about themselves. Nothing would be more intimidating. Instead, we focus their attention simply on the task at hand, and the possibilities they *must* consider in order to do it. The excitement comes afterwards, when we help them to see what they have done. When students begin, on their own, to see possibilities in the material that they had not seen before, they cross the line from being doers to becoming makers.

One of the most dramatic examples of this at Poughkeepsie Day School was when Joan, the librarian, dared to cut up her big letter. When she put her carefully copied, meticulously cut, fourteenth-century Lombardic "E" in the paper cutter, everyone gathered around to watch. Joan had become convinced that a page in her final book needed a certain shape, which cutting the letter would produce. She sliced it with understanding and enjoyment, sacrificing a beautiful form in order to create other forms that the content of her book demanded. With less fanfare, but with equal understanding, six-year-old Adrian incorporated the form of his letter "S" into his final book as a startling elephant's trunk that twisted off the page. What Joan and Adrian did, when they saw how their material could be transformed into new material, describes one level of the creative process. A further stage is reached when the maker is able to use that new material to discover even more new material. This stage sometimes incorporates the use of "accident" as a means of discovery.

The experience of Heather (Poughkeepsie Day School, sixth grade) demonstrates the second stage. She had finished her final book, except for the title. The book had coherence and theme, but up to this point she had sensed these only intuitively. "I know what my book is about," she kept saying, "but I can't find the words to say it." We insisted that she come up with a title, and kept asking her questions until she did. It was simply a matter of getting her to say out loud what had been floating around in her head as feeling. "It's about wishing," she said. She then looked at her cover with the big "B" in the middle. "What is the 'B' for?" we asked. "Beginning." "Then what is the title of your book?" "*Wishing and Beginning.*" But she was not satisfied. Then, the title came to her in a flash: "*In the Beginning, I Wish.*" She was thrilled. So were we.

Heather began to cut out the large letters of her title, and spent agonizing, intense minutes on the very small letters. The "I" in "Beginning" was half-black and half-white. Heather didn't plan this, but discovered it as an exciting possibility when the "I" landed on the edge of the black border as she glued down the black letters one by one. And it was the invention of this "I" made of positive and negative, black and white, one half the reverse of the other, that led Heather to the concept for the back cover. Here, the negative space of the "B" was used in the center, and became a new positive space, while the reverse of the title became the conclusion. "Beginning" was born out of the belly of the "B," like an invitation to turn the page into the future. At the end, there is no end, but rather a flourishing seed that has taken root and is growing. Heather was fully in control of her materials to the extent that she allowed herself to be led by them. She worked with utter intensity for about an hour and a half. She had become a maker.

Of all the group at Poughkeepsie Day School, Maggy, the fourth grade teacher, was the one most deeply affected by allowing her materials such a strong voice. Maggy's rectangle book had as its centerfold a black rectangle that unfolded by itself to become a three-dimensional black box. Some people reacted to this as a comic image; others found it frightening. Her word-block poem had as its central image a basket full of eggs. As the week progressed, Maggy's work continued to present contradictory, unrelated images, both visual and verbal. She wrote a terrifying poem, with images of rattling bones and a witch doctor, about the recent death of a friend. Maggy intended to make her final book a memorial. However, through our persistent efforts to have Maggy include *all* of her materials, not just the ones that obviously related to death, she was able to make an enormous leap into unknown territory. Once she saw that her black box was both basket *and* casket, and that her eggs were not only symbols of shame for her public display of grief (she used the phrase "egg on the face") but also stood for rebirth, she was able to relate the unrelated and, ultimately, to reconcile what was previously irreconcilable. Maggy said: "I was finally able to accept what had happened."

Rosalind Pace
& Marcia Simon

One of the advantages of working with the book form is that the dramatic and emotional content is inherent in the form itself. Just by turning a page, one is inescapably caught up in a particular structuring of time and space. And since our individual and collective lives are the stories we construct from the time and space we inhabit, the book form can become a metaphor for our lives.

When all of the books were finished, we took them to an empty room that had carpeted risers built into the floor, and we displayed them on large pieces of black or white paper. For about half an hour, the fourteen members of what we called the Poughkeepsie Scriptorium read each other's books. There was absolute silence. Often the most comfortable way to look at the books was to kneel before them on the bottom riser. It was an appropriate posture for the atmosphere in the room: the rapt attention, the amazement.

While everyone was still basking in the splendor of the books that had been created, the director of the school made this comment: "The book," he said, "is the least important part. The workshop could be done with science activities or in social studies. It is a workshop in creative thinking." And this is the whole point. The purpose of teaching creativity in the schools is not to train book designers or poets, or even to improve reading scores, but to develop people who can think creatively, who can find solutions to problems, trust their instincts, and go beyond the boundaries of the expected. The purpose is to develop people who can act as purposefully as Joan slicing her big letter; as energetically as Adrian inventing his bestiary; as intuitively as Scott letting his words reach out into the white space of the page; and as hopefully as Maggy daring to confront the darkest questions. In the structure of true education, creativity is the foundation, and not the ornament.

ACKNOWLEDGMENTS: The week at Poughkeepsie Day School was made possible by the generosity of Stella Chasteen. The Image-Making Workshop is taught at Castle Hill, Truro Center for the Arts on Cape Cod. For more information, contact:

Castle Hill, Truro Center for the Arts
P.O. Box 756
Truro, MA 02666
(508) 349-7511

or

Rosalind Pace and Marcia Simon
The Image-Making Workshop
P.O. Box 687
Truro, MA 02666
(508)-349-2487

Gestural Abstraction and the Art of Cy Twombly

by Holly Masturzo

Lines can move freely, as if they were following their own impulses. Every line is thus the actual experience with its unique story.

—*Cy Twombly*

*a*S A WRITER-IN-RESIDENCE who visits classrooms in concentrated stretches, I am well aware of the peculiar order of school culture—the procedures, schedules, and manners that are both necessary for the environment and create a tension within it. In school, students are rewarded for being still, both physically and, to a degree, intellectually. Sometimes it seems that dancing or running on fields out of doors is what we and the students most need to reinvigorate ourselves for creating. For a long time, I found myself longing for students' writing to come more from their bodies, from lived experiences. A major breakthrough came after a visit to a Houston museum, the Menil Collection, where I viewed the paintings of the American artist Cy Twombly.

It occurred to me that Twombly might exert a fruitful influence on my writing students because of the implicit connection in his work between the verbal and the visual. Poet Frank O'Hara describes his impression of the vitality of some of Twombly's early pencil-and-crayon canvases this way: "A bird seems to have passed through the impasto with cream-colored screams and bitter claw-marks."[1] What bird-force might tear through our writing? In a landmark essay titled "The Wisdom of Art," philosopher and critic Roland Barthes pursues the connection between gestural action and language, focusing specifically on Twombly's work. "[T]he gestures through which Twombly enunciates (should we say spells?) the matter in the trace" are scratching, smudging, smearing.[2] Twombly's paintings are streaked with letters, numbers, words and pictographs, and include references to literature and mythology. While the detached words and symbols are not directly "readable," they imply a narrative and suggest, along with Twombly's technique, writerly motions.

My students are especially taken with Twombly's large gray-ground works, often referred to as "blackboard drawings." White and gray lines appear at first to the students as magnified hand-scratching, but on further meditation just as easily suggest music, rain, or swaying fields of wheat. Many other sizable single-canvas pencil-and-crayon drawings are sparsely covered with letters, numbers, loose pictographs, and paint applied by hand. The materials are most often applied dry; the resulting scratching and smearing effect reveals not only the movement of the applying instrument but the force, angle, and speed of the application. The movement of the artist's hand over and against the canvas mimics the way the body moves through the world.

Many critics have termed the gestural quality of Twombly's work "childlike" or "primitive"—especially when compared with the measured, contemplative work of other abstract expressionist painters. Twombly's gestures, however, seem less to hark back to some repressed feeling or state than to move forward to realization. It is as though Twombly "had to give up brush for the pencil to suppress virtuosity and gain a childlike immediacy."[3] The markings manifest a palpable moment, a life-experience moving in a course that the canvas may only partially hold. It is this sense of trace, of art in its form and its process signaling its lived origins, that I hoped to kindle in my writing students through a strategic use of gestural abstraction as a pre-writing activity. This pre-writing activity proved so successful the first time that I have done it many more times in a variety of settings, from schools to community gatherings, and over a complete range of age levels, from kindergarten through twelfth grade—even with groups of teachers. Here is a description of the basic plan I follow for the pre-writing exercise.

We start with large, white drawing paper (at least 8 $\frac{1}{2}$" x 14" or 11" x 17"), positioned so that the long side runs horizontally, which allows for a sense of carrying gestures beyond the page. Each table or group of students has a selection of colored chalk, pastels, or crayons. (I prefer using pastels, which can be manipulated like traditional writing tools but are easier to scratch, smudge, and smear.) The students all position themselves around the paper, and I announce that we are going to scribble—not haphazardly, but with purpose. "Did you know there are different types of scribbles?" I ask. On a sheet of spare paper, I demonstrate with one color a slow, meandering scribble from end to end of the paper. With another crayon, I then scribble quickly in a tight zigzag. We talk about the differences in speed, pressure, and coverage. Eventually, the conversation turns to how what I was thinking or feeling inside may have made the scribbles different. "In that second one, it's like you were mad," a student will say. "Or you were relaxed at first," says another, "and then you got nervous."

I invite the students to select a color to begin with, assuring them that if their favorites are not available there will be plenty of opportunity to exchange materials. Then I ask them to connect with a feeling, thought, or memory. "Perhaps it is how you are feeling right now, in the moment, or perhaps it is a sensation or emotion, a memory or desire you wish to explore," I suggest. I have younger students make one extended scribble for ten seconds at most before I instruct them to move to another color and feeling. Four short intervals of this seem about right—the longer the students are allowed to gesture, the more congested the paper becomes with color and line, making later writing difficult. With older students, however, because they work so much more slowly and deliberately, I usually provide a window of time (ten minutes or so) with instructions to change scribbling techniques at least twice. If students seem to be having difficulty connecting a gesture with an internal sensation, I encourage them to think about different ways to move (jump, slide, roll) or suggest specific emotions (joyful, nervous, angry). Younger students may enjoy imagining they are something other than themselves—otters, water, airplanes; older students may scribble from a very specific memory or place, such as a fight with a parent or summers spent by a lake. The activity will work whether the scribbles are distinct sensations or are linked aspects of a single experience.

"Each line now is the actual experience with its own innate history," said Twombly.[4] For students as well, the potential to rediscover and refigure the experience of each line provides a dynamic—and highly personal—writing activity. While the most verbal parts of the activity (finding strong action words, shaping a work, revision) may be highlighted or downplayed depending upon the interests and needs of a given group, what remains central is the focus on the body and the non-verbal as the generating force of the material.

Recently, I presented this activity at a grief center, a non-school environment where children who have lost a sibling or a parent can interact. Grieving children carry much of their stories in their bodies. The grief that cannot be articulated often emerges during play: a shared utterance, a sudden punching, wild dancing, a cry. Finding spoken language is hard; finding written language through the layers of grief is often impossible. But as a writing teacher I hoped that gestural abstraction would provide a bridge between lived grief and the written word.

One young boy, Jeremy, always in his baseball uniform, regularly participated in the scheduled art activities with intense interest. For weeks he had verbally described to us scenes of the cemetery where his brother is buried. However, the writing activities intended to accompany or springboard out of the art projects never engaged him. During the session in which I assigned the gestural abstraction exercise, Jeremy wrote a word or a sentence for each of the lines he had "scribbled" to express his grief.

angry
confused
People lied.
The tree fell down on top of the stones.

—Jeremy, second grade

One of our great Southern storms had uprooted a large oak tree, sending it down over several headstones. Jeremy had walked past the tree and several shattered headstones on his way to his brother's grave. Concerned for the families whose plots were affected by the fallen tree, he wondered how the tree might be righted. Week after week he shared a version of this story. Unwilling to write any of it down, he continued to draw the tree as a thick, looming line over the headstones—one week in yellow, one week in green. The writing that followed his gestural marking was the only writing we witnessed from Jeremy all year. Writing need not be elaborate or detailed to be a powerful reflection of a person's knowledge. Often a line is the most—the best—a body can tell.

In elementary school classrooms, I frequently follow up on my gestural pre-writing exercise by asking students to consider verbs and words of motion in single worded lines. We build word banks from stories and poems we have read, or pull exciting verbs from the students' previous writings. I ask the young writers to place words along or around their lines, words that seem connected to how they felt when making their "gestures" and/or how they looked on the page. As students begin to see their lines as images or stories, they are ready to move from writing action verbs to writing phrases and sentences. Ashley's line demonstrates the movement inherent in this process:

> Moving, floating, swimming, in the air in the sky, eating the pretty
> pink honey.
> —*Ashley, third grade*

Just how this shift is achieved varies with each individual. Some students are comfortable only placing action words along their scribbles as a kind of addition to or labeling of their art. Many students begin straightaway with descriptive sentences, even stream-of-consciousness narratives. This intial writing is both verbal and visual, as students choose to write in colors and different handwriting. At this transitional phase of the activity—moving from gestural marks to written language—I do not press the students to shape their work, but ask them to focus on writing with immediacy. We pay attention to order, structure, and cohesion later, when students select lines or parts of lines to use as "starters" for an extended piece of writing.

Peter, a mathematically-minded fifth grader concerned with keeping his papers neat, chose to write only verbs, with wide spaces between them. When I suggested he take out a sheet of notebook paper to try to transform some of the verbs into phrases, he wrote a poem.

Cattle

I watch them trot around
wandering, wondering which way

has a safe place to rest
to stop uncontrollable motions of
the feet, stomping back and forth
the legs obeying the thoughts.

—Peter, fifth grade

Peter's family owns a ranch in Texas and he had observed the movements of cattle numerous times throughout his life. Recalling Frank O'Hara's bird sighting in Twombly's work, I suggested to another student in that particular class that she think about her lines as tracks left by an animal, person, or thing.

The act of putting away the colored pastels and picking up the pencil causes some students to become disassociated from their own markings. Their later writing need not *necessarily* reflect or reproduce the pre-writing experience of the gestures. I only ask that they remember the experience, particularly the pleasure and freedom of it. Following the pleasure of a movement across the page, some students (such as Peter) link the stories of their gestural lines together into one narrative. Others do revisit the emotions and memories, conscious and subconscious, that came to them during the pre-writing. Ashley's gestures had been slow and precise, yet continuous. When she began writing, she saw the marks as reminiscent of the marks left by her ice skates at skating practice—a time, perhaps, when she is relaxed and happy. She wrote evenly over each of her lines and then organized the sentences into a narrative poem.

Skating on Wet Ice

As I skate on the ice and twirl and turn,
I see little things in the snow.
I twist and turn, skating, skating, skating,
Past the trees and icicles.

I see snowflakes falling, falling, falling,
They fall here and there,
And in my hair and eyelashes
The dim sunlight shines on the ice.

I skate by the frozen trees,
And I see the sun on them, too.
I twirl again and again.
As I skate I find different things.

Suddenly, a person skates past me.
It's my friend and she slowly skates by me.
We skate together,
This time not twirling or turning.

We slowly skate on the shiny ice.
I turn here and she turns there.
It is time to go home.
We go and sleep.

As the sun is shining one last time,
It says goodnight to the world,
And to the moon,
Then falls asleep, too.

—Ashley, fourth grade

Holly Masturzo

Another fourth grader, also named Peter, enthusiastically wrote about the movements of snakes over his lines. Above one cluster of markings, in a corner, he wrote the word *hideout*. As he transferred his words to paper, he remembered the haikus we had written months earlier, integrating the spy-play he so loves getting away with on the way to the restroom or recess.

Secret Mission

I'm in the hallway.
Like a snake, I sneak past guards.
I run far away.
Home safe at my base.
I now have their secret files.
I am the top spy.

—Peter, fourth grade

Older students, though perhaps more suspicious at first, enjoy the experience of gestural marking just as much, but in different ways. More compositionally adept, many are more conscious (and self-conscious) during the marking process. The activity does not *require* a kind of unconscious spilling onto the page. Twombly's own work differentiates itself from the "automatic" writing of Surrealism to present a fusion of impulse and awareness. For instance, Hector, a quiet senior at an arts magnet high school, spent the majority of the first session with pastels in hand, scratching a few verbs in pencil before the end of the period. The next week, he returned to his drawing, finding verbs in his work that he used to create a prose poem about the weeks of winter rain we had endured:

Rainy Wednesday

Wednesday was a rainy day and everything was muddy. The rain washed away all the little kids' graffiti in non-permanent Crayola markers. The wind blew hard making the trees wave around crazy as if they were dancing. Candy wrappers, beer cups, and cigarette buds all blended and mixed with mud making freeform sculptures. The oil drips from cars in parking lots swirled up making cool marbled effects. Ankles twisted everywhere due to slippery floors puddled in rain water. The world turned soaked in water like a washing machine. Metals rusted and turned a red orange drippy tone. No longer shining in that nice glossy chrome. Lightning and thunder blasted like the greatest fireworks show. Nature was at its best with many things happening at once. But no one really came out on Wednesday because it was raining.

—Hector, twelfth grade

I particularly enjoyed Hector's "cigarette buds"—a litter that suddenly seemed salvageable. The phrase, like Hector's drawing and prose, was fully his own. Working first through the body had enabled him to access an easier if not more personal language.

Another high school student, Whitney, a dancer, stretched in many directions from her desk, revealing the limitations in its design and its failure to accommodate her body. After beginning with some central blue spirals, she eagerly filled in the surrounding spaces with heavy strokes of red (see figure 8). Then she wrote:

It's a new year

A new day

A new day needs new clothes

A silent,

    Still

    Listening

    Waiting

    Watching

Holly Masturzo

Powerful

Poisonous Red Snake

I shed my skin

Hibernating I have been sleeping

Dreaming of what's to come; what's happened

I awake now

Yawn, stretch, breathe

Inhale. I take in the world

Completely hollow, but so full

Exhale

The worries, thought, anticipation, anxiety

Gone.

I can just be me

(For a little while. In the morning.)

—Whitney, ninth grade

A further benefit of doing this exercise with older students is that it prompts them to experiment with form. I am careful therefore never to specify what the eventual writing product should be, in style, length, or genre.

Techniques

I. Shoalin

thrusting fists,
swinging feet,
bones as rigid as the mountains,

he accepts no pain
crushing the opposition,
piercing, jabbing, calculating,
the Shoalin technique
trains assassins.

II. Tai Chi

flowing as wind as water,
in effortless patterns,
whipping,
as the fish whips his tail,
gliding like the crane,
striking like the snake,
his motions coincide with nature
and the Tao.

—Jude, twelfth grade

Jude's work visually illustrates how this activity can provide an improvisational structure—a space to create forms. Jude has taken martial arts and as he worked with the pastels, black in one hand and gray in the other, he incorporated shadowing "techniques" he had learned in his martial arts practice.

Those in the disciplines of art and of literature, both practitioners and critics, have been much occupied in the last century with the degree and the manner by which the body determines our consciousness and vice versa—whether metaphor (and language) reflects or determines experience. Art, whether verbal or visual, should be an arena where body and consciousness, language and experience repeatedly and fruitfully interact. While it would be a mistake to understand gestural abstraction as a direct analogy for any aspect of experience, the lines created are knowingly askance metaphors, through which the writing process can be repeatedly refigured.

Of the work of Twombly, curator and art historian Kirk Varnedoe wrote, "[He] deals not only with opposite spheres of culture, but with upper and base body functions as coexistent and interdependent. . . . What his achievement may ultimately depend upon most heavily is the power he has drawn from within himself and from so many enabling traditions to isolate in a particularly raw and unsettled fashion that primal electricity of communication, in his apparently simplest acts of naming, marking, and painting."[5]

Holly Masturzo

Consciously connecting physical with cerebral process in the teaching of writing can be our dynamo. By helping students come to understand physicality as something subtle, complicated, wide-reaching, and layered—and not simply "primal"—we encourage them to trust their own impulses as stores of knowledge. This in turn helps them to understand that the process of writing, like the process of learning, moves between sensation and sense-making, between matter and mind.

Notes

1. Frank O'Hara, quoted in Kirk Varnedoe, "Inscriptions in Arcadia," in *Cy Twombly: A Retrospective* (New York: The Museum of Modern Art, 1994), p. 20.
2. Roland Barthes, "The Wisdom of Art," in *Cy Twombly: Paintings and Drawings, 1954–1977* (New York: The Whitney Museum of American Art), p. 10.
3. Varnedoe, op cit., p. 49.
4. Cy Twombly, quoted in Varnedoe, op cit., p. 27.
5. Ibid, p. 51.

Bibliography

Barthes, Roland. "The Wisdom of Art." In *Cy Twombly: Paintings and Drawings, 1954–1977*. Translated by Annette Lavers. New York: The Whitney Museum of American Art, 1979.

Cernuschi, Claude. *"Not an Illustration but the Equivalent": A Cognitive Approach to Abstract Expressionism.* Madison, N.J.: Farleigh Dickinson University Press, 1997.

Delehanty, Suzanne. "The Alchemy of Mind and Hand." In *Cy Twombly: Paintings, Drawings, and Constructions, 1951–1974*. Philadelphia: University of Pennsylvania Press, 1975.

Gibson, Ann. "Abstract Expressionism's Evasion of Language." Reprinted in *Abstract Expressionism: A Critical Record*. Edited by David Shapiro and Cecile Shapiro. Cambridge, Mass.: Cambridge University Press, 1990.

Herrera, Hayden. "Cy Twombly: A Homecoming." *Bazaar*, No. 3393 (August 1994), pp. 65–86.

Varnedoe, Kirk. "Inscriptions in Arcadia." In *Cy Twombly: A Retrospective*. New York: The Museum of Modern Art, 1994.

Text-Art Exercises
for Resistant Students

by Lee Upton

RITING EXERCISES THAT DRAW UPON VISUAL ART as a starting occasion have the potential to make students more sensitive to the visual arrangements of words and the imagistic capacities of language. Such exercises also have the ability to strengthen students' critical faculties. In some instances, imaginative writing that uses visual art as a prompt is actually carrying on criticism by other means. Yet, despite the strong potential of such exercises, students may resist them. My experience teaching college students suggests that this resistance emerges from a number of sources, among them:

1. *Parasitism*: Students sometimes suspect that to "work" with another art form in mind is the creative equivalent of larceny or that using visual art as an inducement is a kind of parasitism.

2. *Corruption*: Some students harbor the conviction that a work of art is corrupted when it is drawn upon for inspiration. This arises from the belief that respect for the visual artist demands that we refuse to "desecrate" his or her art by embarking on an imaginative exercise triggered by it.

3. *Diversion*: Some students are anxious about being overwhelmed by visual art. They believe that the acute pleasure of making their own written art on the page may be compromised, even sacrificed, by using visual art as a prompt. Rather than viewing a text-art exercise as a potentially fruitful encounter, these writers perceive it as a debilitating threat, a diversion from their own primary concerns.

4. *Comparison*: A corollary to the fear of diversion is the fear of being revealed as an awkward beginner—and being rendered mute—when confronted by a fully achieved work of visual art.

What interests me about all of these resistances is that they revolve around questions of power: the perception, for instance, that the student writer has the power to violate the art, or an equal and opposite anxiety regarding just how little power the student writer possesses in comparison to the mature artist. The artwork, as such, is not an incitement or a provocation, but a rebuke.

Such resistances sometimes occur for all the right reasons, and the questions that prompt anxieties about authority and appropriation are not likely to be entirely resolved, no matter how many successful examples we put before students. Nor does it seem sufficient to recall that the tables are often turned: visual artists have used written art to their advantage for a very long time. We might bear in mind the questions that Dannie and Joan Abse pose in *Voices in the Gallery*: "How many Bathshebas have posed in artists' studios? How many Ledas about to be disgraced? How many painters have drowned Ophelia?" Matters of appropriation and authority are ones that writers will meet in various forms throughout their careers, and surely such matters are not apt to be swept aside easily, nor should they be. Resistance, after all, represents an opportunity, not only for energetic discussion, but for writing that registers a productive tension. Rather than repeatedly defending the use of visual art in writing classes, we ought to consider asking students to write with resistance in mind.

What follow are exercises that take into account different aspects of student resistance. Most often, the exercises focus on writing poems, but they could be adapted for other genres as well. Although they employ static visual art images and ask students to manipulate images through their imaginations, they could be modified for use with moving images, such as those found in video, film, and computer graphics.

1. *Handwriting Exercise*: I admire Edward Lear's *View of Mt. Parnassus, 1849* for many reasons: among them, his airily sketched lines and, in the foreground, the words *marshy lake, faint blue snow, domestic bramble,* and *Tortoises!!!* in Lear's looping penmanship (see figure 9). His handwriting conveys his vigorous semantic and visual interest. Those students who believe that visual artists are alone in their attempts to create memorable visual imprints can learn a great deal from Lear's spontaneous meshing of the pictorial and the textual.

Lee Upton

     After looking at the drawing by Lear, I ask my students to concentrate on the art of their handwriting. After all, even though many of us use the computer to write, we must still sign our names. Although our signatures no longer register much of an impression for most of us, they do point to a period in our lives when working with even simple representations was arduous and complex. And signatures, it would seem, are not accidentally developed. I was recently reminded of this by an eleven-year-old acquaintance of mine who spent many hours experimenting with various handwriting styles—a tightly slanted rendering, a softly doughy alphabet, and a chunky triangular signature.

     For the purposes of this exercise, students are told to focus on and describe the visual qualities of their signature as a form of handmade self-presentation. Do they have multiple "hands"? Does their handwriting change according to the situation, mood, and the identity of the addressed? I also ask students to consider other signatures, including those that appear on works of art. What language does contemplation of the artist's signature arouse in them? By using handwriting as a prompt, that is, by using the visual that has grown "unseen" in its very familiarity, students are urged to look at visual presentations dynamically and in unaccustomed ways.

2. *Self-Defense Exercise*: In this exercise, I encourage students to render their resistance in a dialogue, a harangue, or any other form that accommodates the range of their hesitations. Conversely, students may opt to write a monologue in which the artwork defends *itself* from incursion. Conventional exercises can be easily adapted for this purpose: Write a poem that makes mobile what is immobile in the work of visual art. Allow a person or object in the artwork to leave it behind, or enable a brushstroke to change position. Ask the visual art to comment on its own experience, contending with or seducing the viewer.

3. *Interior with Extension Cord Exercise*: In an undated watercolor by Elizabeth Bishop, a lamp's extension cord captures our attention, traveling up a wall and across a ceiling. The cord partly frames a doorway that opens onto a garden. In my experience, student writers often include the verbal equivalent of the lamp and the garden—the obviously symbolic and the undeniably beautiful—but forget the extension cord. They fail to recognize that the ordinary, the practical, holds and extends its own line of energy. To assist them in this recognition, I instruct my students to write a poem that puts something functional and frequently ignored (or out-of-sight) directly in our field of vision. Doorstoppers? Vents?

4. *Equivalency Exercise*: In this exercise, students are asked to write the "equivalent" of an artwork. The challenge is to use few recognizable formal elements from the art, while at the same time attempting to create a text that in effect duplicates a pattern of energy exhibited in the original art. For instance, if the artist's image were a poem, what would its form be? Four quatrains, thick with consonants? An echo-chamber of repeated words? I invite my students to create a textual form that "rhymes with" the visual form. Or, conversely, to extrapolate the artwork's rules and seek to defy them. In any case, the final written product must acknowledge its debt to the artwork in the title.

5. *Multiple Points of View Exercise*: In Peter Carey's novel *Oscar and Lucinda*, the reader learns a good deal about the characters from their reactions to a church made of glass. For one character, the glass church is a sublime fulfillment of a dream. For another, the church represents utter folly. For this exercise, I encourage students to write a poem or a piece of fiction or drama in which various characters react to the same piece of art. What would each see? What elements would each ignore? What memories or projections into the future might emerge in each character's encounter with the art?

6. *Stages Exercise*: The Stages Exercise asks students to restore a particular image to an earlier developmental state. For instance, what did a given painting look like when it was wet? Or when the seventieth brushstroke was applied? What did a specific photograph look like in its first moments in the developing solution? What was the artist's model contemplating on the way to the studio? Describe the movements of the hands that arranged the pears glowing in the still life.

7. *Space-Shifting Exercise*: In "Two Views of a Cadaver Room," Sylvia Plath brings our attention to the small image of a country in the corner of a painting by Brueghel. In a similar manner, the Space-Shifting Exercise helps students bring attention to parts of a visual work that might otherwise be overlooked. Postcards work particularly well for such an exercise. I encourage students to imagine what is omitted or how details might be magnified—or shrunken further. I sometimes ask students to address what is missing from the artwork or to locate a point at which the art defies expectation.

8. *Sense-Shifting Exercise*: In some students' writing, the visual is already overly dominant. These students need to be encouraged to experiment with new perceptual practices. For instance, I sometimes ask them to make a counterintuitive attempt to discover non-visual sensory material *through* visual material. In some cases, students have added a "soundtrack" (voices, peripheral sounds) to accompany the visual art. Others have focused on the sensation of touch as it is triggered by contemplation of the artwork.

9. *Contextual Exercise*: As its name indicates, this exercise encourages students to research the artist and his or her time period. The exercise asks students to focus not only on the historical context for inspiration, but on the physical context of the artist or the art. What was outside the image as it was being created? What is outside the image now, in contrast? Students might even write about the frame of the visual work (if there is one) or the garden that surrounds a sculpture.

10. *Naïve Questions Exercise*: This exercise requires students to ask incessant questions about the work of art. They are to maintain the express aim of not sounding authoritative. I was recently reminded of the importance of inquisitiveness and naïveté when a four-year-old, upon seeing a reproduction of Hugo Simberg's *The Wounded Angel*, asked a series of wonderful questions. *Do angels have moles? Do angels take care of swans? Do swans bite angels?* When students are encouraged not to sound like experts and to allow themselves to "play dumb," they often write with greater inventiveness and enhanced insight. Somehow, I think Michelangelo's *David* will survive such scrutiny. At any rate, it has.

11. *Repeated Exposure Exercise*: This exercise requires students to write about the same piece of art on a daily basis for fifteen minutes over a period of seven days. It often surprises students to discover how their minds develop new strategies for re-encountering a visual image over time. Of course, the time period can be lengthened. Why not two or three weeks? Just when students believe they have exhausted every possibility, they may discover additional ways to respond. This exercise also helps them to create an ongoing (and often relatively charged) record of the ways in which their minds reflect on visual art, a record they may choose to mine for material in the future.

No single exercise can overcome student resistance—nor should we encourage students simply to dismiss their own misgivings. And, of course, no exercise can guarantee that the writing it prompts will be powerful. Yet in some cases strong writing emerges from students who are most reluctant to pursue text-art exercises, perhaps because their very discomfort signals a potential dynamism in their perspective. Resistance, balking, uncertainty—these are the writer's stock-in-trade. It is never too early for student writers to learn to take their own resistances seriously. After all, writing that uses visual art as a starting point may prod some students to raise the verbal stakes of their work and to examine the properties of their writing in unaccustomed ways. The visual work stands witness, in a sense, to the students' written works. It's a proximity that challenges students— and a summons to rise to a demanding occasion.

Bibliography

Abse, Dannie and Joan. *Voices in the Gallery*. London: Tate Gallery, 1986.
Carey, Peter. *Oscar and Lucinda*. New York: Vintage, 1997.
Plath, Sylvia. *The Collected Poems*. Edited by Ted Hughes. New York: Harper, 1981.

Drawing a Line
Making the Connection between Literature and Art

by Pamela Freeze Beal

*I*F YOU WERE TO STAND AT THE DOOR of my classroom and scan the walls, you would observe mobiles, posters, book jackets, and mosaics hung from, propped on, or cantilevered into every dimension of the room's space. Some of my students laughingly call my classroom a flea market; others call it a museum. Whatever label they attach to it, my classroom is something of a gallery, filled with art projects that connect to the works we study in my World Literature class.

These literature-based projects bring life to texts that initially seem alien to students so used to postmodern American culture. "Drawing the line"—making artistic links—from stories to art leads my students to a clearer understanding of world literature. It shows them how human thought and actions connect across historical epochs, helping them to make archetypal links between diverse cultures.

My school, Lee County High School in Sanford, North Carolina, has over 2,200 students of diverse ethnicities. My school's academic program offers both a College Prep and a Tech Prep curriculum. North Carolina mandates a world literature curriculum for sophomores, but allows a broad range of works from which teachers may select. Since students in our state study American literature in the eleventh grade and British literature in the twelfth, tenth grade teachers concentrate on works from "the world minus America and the British Isles."

Confronted by so much literature, my students naturally crave something in addition to words in print. In response, I offer them various ways to approach texts through individual and group art projects connected to individual written responses, including poetry, personal narrative, and analytical essays. The following is a sampling of the many literature-based art projects I do with them.

Hero the Man

Because many of the works we study are epics focused on one or more heroes, I introduce the curriculum each semester by defining the "hero journey," which we then trace in the texts we study. I use Joseph Campbell's terminology for the stages of the quest and the adventures the hero encounters. I explain terms such as *call to adventure, quest, threshold crossing, threshold guardian,* and *the return.* We talk about these terms in relationship to Odysseus and Hercules, as well as other heroes from stories they have read and movies they have seen.

The first work that we read is *The Epic of Gilgamesh.* After we have read and discussed it, I have the students write their own epics. To begin, a hero is required. This past semester, one class wanted to construct a hero and build him "bigger than life," to serve as the subject of their poems and to use as inspiration. One of our assistant principals, a large man in stature, agreed to serve as our model. He stood up against a 4' x 8' piece of plywood and allowed a student to trace his figure. Afterwards, students who were taking woodworking used a jigsaw to cut out the shape.

The next step was to give the hero-figure dimension by using a papier-mâché technique. Students balled up newspaper, wrapping masking tape around it to secure it to the plywood base and to smooth out the "flesh" form. They fashioned a nose and mouth, eyes and hands. Some painted his skin while others made his helmet, arm bands, shoulder pads, boots, and "skirt" from felt-backed tablecloth fabric. Thus, they constructed a larger-than-life hero. The class decided to name him "Hero," which suggested that he was generic rather than culturally specific. Once Hero was dressed and armed, he was ready for action and in need of an epic.

The class decided on a rhythm of iambic tetrameter (with some variations for interest). We brainstormed a basic story line as a class; then I divided the class into small groups to write the individual episodes. The result was quite ingenious.

Episode 1: A bard (named "Bard") narrates as Hero the Man hears the call to adventure and readies himself to go boldly into the unknown. *Episode 2:* He meets Wizard, the wizard who will be his helper throughout his quest. *Episode 3:* His first battle is a battle of wits with a troll who guards a bridge he must cross. *Episode 4:* He seeks to recover treasure in a ninja dragon's cave, but he must physically fight and defeat the dragon first. *Episode 5:* As Hero and Wizard make their way through a dark forest, they are attacked by enemies who seize their treasure and get away with it. The final battle—*Episode 6*—is the toughest: here Hero struggles alone with his innermost fears, facing questions about who he really is. He wages this lonely battle in the Night Sea while Wizard waits. *Episode 7:* When Hero emerges, stronger than ever, they continue the journey. Hero is lured into a trap by a Candy Goddess whose spell he overcomes; he steals her lollipop supply. *Episode 8:* Hero returns to his city, delivers his speech of success, and shares the lollipops with the citizens. Here is a short excerpt from *Hero the Man: An Epic*:

> Inspire me, Muse, to tell a tale;
>> give me words; please, do not fail.
>> The quest is dangerous, the journey far;
>> grant him a helper; give him a star
> to guide him through trials, to lead him—a man,
>> human, but fearless with an almighty plan.
>> His name is Hero, valiant and strong.
> Listen well while I sing his song.

Gilgamesh: A Pop-Up Book

Once students have read the entire epic, I divide the class into groups of three or four and assign each group a major episode of the text. The groups, in turn, subdivide each episode into specific actions by major characters. They each choose an action to recreate in pop-up style and write a sentence or two that captures the plot.

Each student receives a manila file folder. I then ask them to sketch designs for the action or event that they have chosen and to decide on two or three aspects of their sketch that, accentuated, would render the action or event three-dimensional. On the crease of the closed folder, they mark where the figures will pop up on the inside when the folder is opened. They then make two perpendicular cuts for each three-dimensional figure. One or two of these cuts should be approximately two inches across the crease for the three-dimensional figure, and one or two should be two-and-a-half to three inches for the figure(s) in the foreground. They then open the folder to create the scene inside. The "action-or-event aspects" of the scene (a tree, a character, an animal) are glued to the cut sections of the folder.

I give students a variety of ways and art forms to create the scene. They can choose collage, using pictures from magazines; they can draw or trace and color with crayon or markers; they can paint. Some choose to tear small pieces of paper and create the scene in a mosaic style; others combine two or more approaches, pasting pictures for parts of the scene and hand-drawing others. Any combination works so long as the action in the scene is apparent. Each student then types a summary statement of his or her scene and glues it somewhere on the pop-up picture—like the text in a child's pop-up book.

Here are two specific examples:

1) Anna illustrated the following excerpt from *Gilgamesh*: "There was a trapper who met wild Enkidu face to face, and the trapper was frozen with fear." The background of Anna's pop-up scene is made of pasted magazine pictures of a forest. The "bottom" flat page (when the book is opened) is made of pasted magazine pictures of grass and flowers and small animals like turtles. The three-dimensional pop-up pictures are also from magazines. The background pop-up is a deer drinking water; the right foreground figure, a man squatting down, his mouth open as if in surprise or fear; the center foreground figure, a man in a zebra-striped outfit who looks as if he is running toward the reader.

(2) Daniel illustrated: "When Gilgamesh had retrieved the flower of immortality, he sat it down to take a bath. A serpent snatched it away, sloughing off his old skin and returning to the well." With Daniel's pop-up, you open the page and see a painted scene of brown mountains, the sun, and a deep blue sky. The "bottom" flat page features a painted border

of grass, a brick well, and the figure of Gilgamesh. There are two three-dimensional effects: a large green serpent pops up in a standing position on his tail and faces a pop-up of a beautiful white flower.

When all pop-up scenes are finished, we glue the unadorned back of one folder to the unadorned front of another in chronological plot sequence. Once the glue dries, you can turn from one page to the next, reading the story and seeing the action take place in pop-up fashion! As a creative writing assignment, I ask students to use their knowledge of the story and their pop-up scene to answer the following questions:

Pamela Freeze Beal

1) If you were a character from the epic other than one pictured in your pop-up scene, who would you be?
2) Where would you position yourself, if you were in the scene?
3) What would you say or do or think as you observed the action?
4) Write a poem in which you take the point of view of the character you have selected and share his/her thoughts.

Anna, who illustrated the trapper frozen with fear at the sight of Enkidu, wrote the following poem:

From *Anu, Creation-Goddess, to the Trapper*

Run, Trapper, if you can move your feet!
Speak if you can thaw your tongue!
For Enkidu rules this forest—wild,
untamed; as swift as gazelles;
grass for his dinner, he eats with animals;
the waterhole is his goblet.
Strong like the clay he is made from,
innocent of man's ways
like water dropped from heaven,
he is mine, for I formed him;
I protect him and guide his feet.
Run now, Trapper, back to your home
before you, the hunter, become the hunted!

Daniel, whose pop-up scene illustrated the serpent who stole the plant of immortality from King Gilgamesh, wrote his poem from the point of view of Utnapishtim—"The Man in the Distance" who tells Gilgamesh about the plant and its power:

From *The Man in the Distance*

I weep for you, great Gilgamesh,
for you have lost the gift
you longed for,
the power you sought
over mountains and waters of death.
Pure water gave it up to you,
placed its white beauty in your hands;
in your grasp, you held what no man
has ever held before—eternity and all its glory,
lost now because you are a man,
weak, careless, tired;
your eyes beheld a vision
beyond your human capacity;
you blinked once and lost.
The proof lies in the serpent's sloughed skin—
a snake who outwitted your tiny brain
and stole your gift away.
Return to your city of great walls,
empty-handed now,
weary of travel;
rule well while you have life
for one day you shall die
and sit in a house of dust forever.

This writing assignment helps prove to the students and to me that they really know the text. It also adds the enjoyment of taking on another persona and writing from that viewpoint. This exercise requires that students set and maintain a mood and that they use specific details in order to capture the moment.

Another art project that my students have enjoyed is the retelling of the journey in mosaic pictures (see figure 10). As with the pop-up project, I divide the class into small groups, and each small group is given an episode to illustrate in mosaic. "Mosaic" here does not mean ceramic tiles; rather, it means small pieces of colored paper torn, not cut, from magazines. Torn edges and irregular pieces, rather than scissor-cut pieces, help create interesting effects.

Pamela Freeze Beal

On a 12" x 19" piece of construction paper, they glue thumbnail-sized pieces of paper torn from old magazines. No space is left uncovered. Once the mosaic pieces are in place and the picture is complete, we laminate the page with plastic laminating film, which adds to the brilliance of the mosaic effect. Once completed, all the pictures are combined into a book, with mosaics on the right-hand page and a summary statement or two on the left-hand page.

One small group illustrated the "Garden of the Gods" scene in *Gilgamesh* by tearing out pieces in several shades of blue paper to give variations of color to the river in the garden. They mixed several shades of green for the landscape and scattered colorful flowers on the banks of the river. The effect is quite stunning.

Another created a mosaic "Cedar Forest" where Gilgamesh and Enkidu travel for timber. They pieced together shades of browns for tree trunks, greens and browns for the ground, greens for the foliage, and blues and lavenders for the sky. As with the mixing of paints, the colors are varied and vivid.

My personal favorite was a mosaic illustrating the epic's final scene in which Gilgamesh's body, a roughly torn piece of light brown, lay on a dark funeral pyre with triangular shaped pieces of orange, red, and yellow. Interspersed and reaching upward were pieces in the shapes of human hands and arms, signifying the people beseeching the gods, who are represented with a swirl of reds, blacks, yellows, oranges, blues, and lavenders.

The writing assignment I use to accompany this art project is similar to the one for the Gilgamesh pop-up book. Students are asked to "become" a character in their scene and write from that persona. Most choose to write poems. Here is an excerpt from a collaborative poem written by a group of four students who designed the mosaic of the Cedar Forest:

Humbaba roars and shakes his mangy locks—
Fire in his eyes, hatred in his nostrils:
"Who dares tread on my hallowed forest ground?"
The earth quakes with fear while its master growls.
"I am the guardian here; no man leaves alive,
for I will crush his bones and smother his breath
until he is nothing but dust."
A chorus of Cedar Trees moans,
bent by the winds that answer a prayer
from heroes who dare to face Humbaba,
defying his power in the Forest.
"Tall and strong we stand together
here on a mountain protected
by gods and the guardian of our land;
but the winds bring change
with the smell of stone axe blades
and human scent of men
who know no fear.
Mercy to them who face the giant
that rules these acres
where cedars grow dense
to cover the door of his lair.
Mercy to us who will fall by the axe
and make timber for walls of Uruk."

—Chas, Lauren, Hillary, and James

Further Projects

Each semester I dream up a new type of art project for my classes as the
culminating activity after weeks of reading and research. About eight
weeks before the end of the semester, each student chooses a novel or book
of plays from a list I provide. These range from Tolstoy, Dostoevsky, and
Molière to modern works by Italo Calvino, Albert Camus, and Eugène
Ionesco. The range of choices also includes works by African and Asian

writers, and when students share their reports and projects, the class again has the opportunity for a "survey" of archetypal connections.

Each student chooses a different work, reads it, and writes the traditional research paper explaining how the author uses symbols, imagery, characterization, and conflict to illuminate a theme. Afterwards, the real fun begins—the artistic interpretation, creative writing response, and oral presentation.

Pamela Freeze Beal

Literary Themes in Silhouette

One option I give students is the "Literary Theme in Silhouette." I ask them to choose a critical dramatic scene, and I give them these guidelines:

> 1) The figures in your scene should be kept simple, like objects in a child's coloring book. These figures will be cut out of black construction paper.
> 2) The black figures will be imposed upon a background, not necessarily of white (although that is a choice), but of a color that is symbolic to a theme in the book.
> 3) The silhouetted picture on the colored page needs a narrow black frame around it to polish its look.
> 4) At the bottom of the page, leave room for a one- or two-sentence explanation of the silhouetted scene. Include the title and the author.

Before they begin, we as a class explore further techniques. We look at silhouettes in books, observing how details of a face or body or texture, such as strands of hair, can be conveyed by cutting out spaces in the black image so that background color shows through. We also look through magazines, graphic arts books, and coloring books for more ideas. The actual process is simple: just cut an image out of a coloring book or magazine or make a photocopy of an image in a literature or history book—then superimpose the cut-out on a sheet of black paper and cut around it. Voilà! A silhouette!

I follow up this art project with a creative writing assignment—a poem about a character in the silhouette or one whose life is affected by a character in the silhouette.

The poem below is about Fantine in Victor Hugo's *Les Misérables*. Emily's silhouette was a beautifully artistic rendering of Fantine: a tear streaming down her cheek, her hair so long that it connects with and becomes her daughter Cosette's skirt. Cosette has a happy expression on her face and waves her arms up into the air, outstretched as if receiving new joy in life. Emily's summary of the scene reads as follows: "In the historical novel *Les Misérables* by Victor Hugo, the character Fantine sacrifices everything for her daughter Cosette. The selling of Fantine's hair symbolizes what we sacrifice for those we love."

Fantine

Down an alley strewn with crumpled paper
and dirty bottles reeking with sour gin;
over a threshold of thin, gray shadows;
into a room where thieves steal souls
of desperate men and homeless women;
Fantine—cold, poor, homeless Fantine;
her face, a crevice of worry and fear;
her body, a skeletal ghost grown old
from labor too hard for a fragile girl;
but her hair—her hair, a mass of luscious wealth;
soft like silk in a man's rugged hand;
luscious and rich like jewels of the sea;
her hair—a lifeline for sweet Cosette
who toils long hours of dreadful days—
so young a slave; no time for play
while watchdogs leer and glare with hate.
An invisible bond between mother and child
tears at the heart and cuts the hair;
sacrificial death, a saving grace—
the light of love in a mother's face.

Three-Dimensional Book Jackets

Another art construction project I use effectively to energize students' interest after the tedious process of research is the three-dimensional book jacket. Once again, the guidelines are simple and results are typically original, colorful, and interesting. Using a cardboard box that has an attached lid, students paint the front cover of the jacket (the lid of the box) with colors that are appropriate and/or symbolic of a major aspect of their book, adding a title, the author's name, and an image. In the box itself, they re-create a scene that is important to the story line. Sarah, for example, created a visually striking scene of Meursault, the protagonist in Albert Camus's *The Stranger*, walking on the beach under the hot sun. She cut wavy strips of yellow and orange foam board for the background, off-white foam for the sand, and "hot" colors for Meursault's clothing. The colors as well as the figure of Meursault "jumped out" of the box at you.

Pamela Freeze Beal

On the back jacket (the bottom of the box), students write several brief reviews or blurbs. An accompanying writing assignment is for students to act as reviewers for a major magazine or newspaper and review the book as if it were new on the bestseller list. These reviews include brief plot synopses and assessments of the works as well as students' opinions about the authors' styles and techniques. Most students are fair, some are unmerciful, but all are honest about whether or not they like their books.

The Message in a Bottle Project

The "Message in a Bottle" project combines mosaic techniques with decoupage to project a visual message on a glass bottle which holds a written message from the author or a character. Each student brings a bottle made of thick glass with ample surface area on which to paste a design. Tearing off thumbnail-sized pieces of color from magazine pages, students glue the pieces on the bottles, weaving designs of color that are symbolic in their arrangement—circular, vertical, striped, stacked, twisted, or swirled. Some students superimpose on the mosaic foundation a face or some other figure representative of a character or event in the book. In the design, they also include individual letters torn from magazines to compose these words: "A Message from (Author or Character's Name)." Once all the paper pieces are glued in place, a layer of water-based sealer is added. Then we spray the bottles with clear acrylic to add a sheen and to fortify the strength of the glass.

Inside the bottle is a message from the person whose name is on the outside of the bottle. The message is addressed, in some instances, to "Whoever finds this bottle" and, in others, to a specific character. The message can be any of the following: a plea for help, a confession, a love letter, a warning, congratulations, an invitation, words of advice, a discovery, a secret, or an accusation—whatever is appropriate. The messages are written in black felt-tipped pen on brown parcel paper, rolled up, and deposited in the bottles. After she had read Elie Wiesel's *Twilight*, Tiandra wrote this message from the perspective of Wiesel.

Drawing a Line

To the person that finds this bottle:

I truly condemn those who think that they are better than others—those who put down others because of their race, religion, or nationality. I am a survivor of the Holocaust, which changed my life dramatically. The Holocaust happened because one group felt superior over another group of people. Many innocent people suffered and died because of this attitude that got completely out of control. I write to tell you that no one should die because of one human's intolerance of another based on prejudice. If you see this kind of intolerance taking place, please stand up and say something. Maybe if people would stop being silent, these acts against humanity would stop happening. The Holocaust grew into a terrible monster because of silence and indifference. I condemn anyone who allows indifference to lead to the harm of others. This message is a warning that, if you don't speak out against injustice, another entire population of people may be wiped out. You can make a difference. Join me in my campaign as a human rights activist.

A Final Word

Literature-based art projects are such a given in my classroom that recently a student walked in with a large bag full of empty coffee cans and announced, "I brought you something, Mrs. B. My grandmother was throwing away these cans and I was sure we could come up with some way to use them in this class!" She was right! A few days of brainstorming and we were off on a new project—drums! Each student decorated a can, using a papier-mâché technique to shape a drum and create a design, reflecting the mood and theme of a classic of world literature. Quotations from the book, the author's name, symbols, and other images were painted on the drum, and, of course, an appropriate fabric was stretched over the can like a skin head on a drum. After explaining individual design choices to the class, each student beat the "rhythm of the book" on the drum. We displayed all of the drums under the title "The Beat Goes On: Rhythms of World Writers." Then, of course, we wrote poems to match the beats of our drums.

Drawing the line from stories to art frees students to take creative risks, to make personal connections to the works we study, and to find excitement inside the English classroom. As he worked on his drum, Ronald, a "reluctant" student, grumbled: "I can't believe I actually *like* English this year!"

Pamela Freeze Beal

Bibliography

Camus, Albert. *The Stranger.* Translated by Matthew Ward. New York: Vintage Books, 1988.

The Epic of Gilgamesh. Translated by N. K. Sanders. New York: Penguin Putnam, 1972.

Hugo, Victor. *Les Misérables.* Translated by Charles E. Wilbour. New York: Ballantine Books, 1961.

Wiesel, Elie. *Twilight: A Novel.* Translated by Marion Wiesel. New York: Random House, 1995.

The World at the Tip of a Brush

Teaching Chinese Poetry, Painting, and Calligraphy to First Graders

by Beth Zasloff

i BECAME CAPTIVATED BY CHINESE BRUSH PAINTING when, as a ten-year-old, I visited the National Palace Museum in Taipei, Taiwan. I remember standing in front of a scroll taller than I was and gazing at the liquid sweep of a mountain landscape. Up in a crag, a tiny orange-robed monk meditated underneath the arc of a slender tree branch. With my eyes, I traced the winding mountain path up into a world of contemplation and serenity. To the side of the landscape were columns of Chinese characters. The bold dancing lines were things of beauty themselves. What did they say? The words seemed to be speaking to the picture, engaging the mountain and monk in conversation.

Thirteen years later, an exhibit called *Splendors of Imperial China: Treasures from the National Palace Museum, Taipei* came to the Metropolitan Museum of Art in New York City. At the time, I was a first grade associate teacher at Saint Ann's School in Brooklyn, preparing to teach a twelve-week curriculum focused on various artistic traditions from around the world. When I visited the exhibit, I was struck again by both the grandeur and intimacy of this vast array of classical Chinese works: the way a sweeping line of calligraphy expressed an artist's exuberant mood, or a single brushstroke invited you into a snowy landscape. I thought of my six-year-old students and our recent discussion of cave painting. They had been so eager to voice their opinions about why people began to make art and what these early lines and shapes might mean. They couldn't wait to begin painting their own impressions of charging buffalo and pregnant mares. But while they were eager to paint, many kids were still struggling with one of the major challenges of first grade: how to translate their visions into words on the page. As I looked at the remarkable combinations of pictures and words on the museum walls, I decided to devote several weeks of my art curriculum to a study of Chinese poetry and painting. I hoped that by bringing word and image together, these ancient scrolls would inspire the children to do the same.

Beth Zasloff

"Everything that exists in the world can be expressed at the tip of a brush," wrote third-century scholar Lu Chi in his "Essay on Literature." In the Chinese artistic tradition, poetry, painting, and calligraphy were known as "The Three Perfections," and each form relied on brush and ink. Each could create vivid impressions of both the outside world and the world within, and often shared the space of a single scroll, fan, or album leaf. An eleventh-century Chinese scholar called poetry "painting without form" and painting "poetry with form." A poem's vivid language was meant to create a mental picture, and a painting had to be expressive enough to inspire a poem.

Part of the artist's challenge, however, was to use no more lines than necessary to capture the essence of the image. An essay from the National Palace Museum website describes how, in the court of twelfth-century Emperor Hui-tsung, painters were challenged to illustrate the following line of poetry: "Scattered peaks conceal an ancient temple." While "most painters showed the tip of a pagoda, a roof, or even an entire building . . . the top candidate depicted only a banner peaking out from the mountains, suggesting a temple concealed within the vast landscape." The winner was the painter who economized his strokes, who was most attuned to the exact relationship between the lines of his painting and the line of poetry.

I began my class with a similar exercise that challenged the students to translate words into images and images into words. I divided the class into pairs and gave each student an art postcard, featuring a variety of both

European and Chinese paintings. As their first task, I asked the students to write a description of their postcard that was so specific that, after reading it, their partner would be able to draw the image. As a class, we made a list of the kinds of details they could mention, including colors, shapes, placement of objects, and areas of darkness and light. I told them to be sure that their partner couldn't see the postcard, and the secretive nature of the writing assignment became part of the fun. After they finished writing, the students put the postcards away and exchanged papers. Using index cards and crayons, they tried to draw what their partners had described. When everyone was finished, we regrouped and held the originals next to the drawings they had produced.

The following week, we were lucky to have Julie Quan, a parent of one of the students and an expert in Chinese brush painting, come into our classroom to give a demonstration. The kids gathered around the pushed-together desks and watched in hushed fascination as she held the bamboo brush vertically, dipped its white hairs into the black ink, and made swift strokes across the delicate rice paper. She explained that Chinese characters derive from pictures, and the students were delighted to see how the image of a running horse evolved into the character for horse. For children just learning to read and write, it was fascinating to think about the logic of a different writing system, and its closeness to drawing gave it immediate appeal.

The beauty of the instruments Julie used encouraged the students to see writing materials as things of value. Even the traditional vocabulary used to describe calligraphic tools emphasizes this idea: ink, inkstone, brushes, and paper or silk were known as the "Four Treasures." The children handled the objects with reverence (see figure 11). For kids whose writing instrument was most often the anxiously chewed pencil, the vision of a culture in which the tools of writing were revered seemed particularly fascinating. Historian Jonathan Spence describes the desk of a late Ming scholar in which "the elaborately carved brush holders of wood or stone, the luxurious paper, even the ink sticks and the stones on which they were rubbed and mixed with water to produce the best and blackest ink, all combined to make of every scholar's desk a ritual and an aesthetic world before he had even written a word" (Spence, 10).

Another object that Julie showed the students was a fan with a poem written vertically on its slats. For one student, this alternative format for a poem inspired a breakthrough in his writing. Angus was an intense, imaginative boy who possessed a distinct poetic vision but was slow in learning to read and found writing painful and laborious. His letters tended to wander over his pages, and he had difficulty spacing out his words. During free time on the day of Julie's visit, he asked me to fold a piece of paper into an accordion fan for him. Then, on the creased stripes, he wrote a poem called "Summer."

Beth Zasloff

```
S       T       T       A
U       H       H       N
M       E       E       D
M
E       G       R       D
R       R       A       E
        A       B       E
I       S       B       R
S       S       I
                T       S
H       I       S       H
O       S               E
T               A       D
        H       R
        I       E       T
        G               H
        H       H       E
                I       I
                G       R
                H
                        S
                        K
                        I
                        N
```

—*Angus Page*

What better way to express summer's heat than on a fan? Previously, Angus had been continually frustrated by his inability to get what was in his mind onto paper. "Do you ever have trouble drawing what you see in your imagination?" he asked an artist whose studio we visited on a field-trip. Seeing the fan's vertical format as an alternative orientation for writing may have offered him a point of connection between the images in his head and the tools of expression he was struggling to master. I resolved that next time I would have all the students write vertical poetry on a fan.

In the next class, I brought in examples of classical Chinese poetry. Like the brushstrokes Julie had demonstrated, the poems created vivid images in a few deft lines. If they closed their eyes, I asked the students, could they imagine the moments described by T'ang dynasty poet Li Po (701–762)?

Going to Visit Tai-T'ien Mountain's Master of the Way Without Finding Him

A dog barks among the sounds of water.
Dew stains peach blossoms. In forests,

I sight a few deer, then at the creek,
hear nothing of midday temple bells.

Wild bamboo parts blue haze. A stream
hangs in flight beneath emerald peaks.

No one knows where you've gone. Still,
for rest, I've found two or three pines.

Ching-T'ing Mountain, Sitting Alone

The birds have all vanished into deep
skies. The last cloud drifts away, aimless.

Inexhaustible, Ching-T'ing Mountain and I
gaze at each other, it alone remaining.

Sunlight on Incense-Burner kindles violet smoke.
Watching the distant falls hang there, river

headwaters plummeting three thousand feet in flight,
I see Star River falling through nine heavens.

Beth Zasloff

Thoughts in Night Quiet

Seeing moonlight here at my bed,
and thinking it's frost on the ground,

I look up, gaze at the mountain moon,
then back, dreaming of my old home.

In our discussion of the poems, I pointed out how the poet focuses on specific sensory details to create a vivid picture of a moment: the sound of a dog barking, the reflection of the stars in a waterfall, moonlight shining on a bed. Then I asked the students to think of a moment when they had paused to look at an animal, tree, or landscape. It didn't have to be from someplace far away, I told them. Maybe, like Li Po, they had once watched a cloud drift away. Maybe they also loved to gaze at the moon, seen hovering between tall buildings in the brightly lit city.

The children responded warmly, full of stories about deer, dogs, raindrops, and waterfalls. We discussed their ideas and made a list of the moments they remembered. Then I sent them to their desks to write their own poems. The results were reflective and personal.

I see a deer in the forest.
It is crying for its mommy.
It sees me and jumps away.

—*Nathaniel Buckholz*

The moon shone on them,
but they were scared of the car light.
They ran away.

—*Lauren Bridges*

Even the poems in which students described animals in exotic places felt intimate and immediate:

A monkey in the trees,
Swinging from branch to branch.
The sunset is gold, making a shadow on the greenish
gold grass.

—*Jordan Puryear*

I am a gorilla and my name is Michael.
I live in a jungle.
I have a wife and a baby.
I play with him in the morning.
Usually when we play we swing from tree to tree.
My baby collects all the green leaves he can find.

—*Joshua Barocas*

The next stage was the painting. The students received watercolor paper and pencils, and set about drawing pictures of the same moment that they had described in their poems. On vertically oriented sheets of paper, they carefully planned how to situate the pictures in relation to the words. I showed them more examples of Chinese paintings, pointing out how a poem can sit under a tree branch or dance across a mountaintop. When the students had decided where they would place their poems, they drew light pencil lines to mark the spot.

After they finished their pencil plans, they began their pictures in watercolor. The kids painted their animals and trees with short brush-strokes and bright colors, then mixed watercolor and water to create pale washes for their mountains and lakes. (My sister Eva, whose third grade class also made scrolls the following year, had her students use black ink and water, instead of watercolor, to create looser, monochromatic landscapes). When the finished paintings were dry, the first graders used skinny black pens to copy their poems onto the paper in their best handwriting.

Josh Barocas, who had written the poem about the gorilla, asked for black paint. Then, to the side of his painting of the jungle where Michael and his baby played, Josh painted the calligraphic character for "forest," which Julie had introduced. I quickly realized how much the Chinese character added to the scroll, and urged the other students to do the same. Even when the character didn't quite make sense (the character for horse leaping across a waterfall), the bold black lines contrasted beautifully with the pale watercolor paintings. The additions reminded me that in Chinese calligraphy, appreciating the expressiveness of the brushstrokes and the visual beauty of the characters themselves is as important as understanding their verbal meaning.

To assemble the scrolls, I glued the watercolor paper onto long pieces of brown paper. And, because many Chinese scrolls are framed by elaborately patterned fabric, I decided to have the students decorate the brown backing with colorful prints. On a rainy afternoon, students carved designs into slices of potatoes, spread their scrolls out on the floor, dipped their potatoes into plastic plates of tempera paint, and printed patterns on the paper backing. This process was quite messy, but fun. Finally, I glued wooden dowel rods to the ends of the brown paper and tied a silky red ribbon to the top of each scroll.

We displayed the scrolls in the hallway when the project was completed, and students often lingered there to admire each other's work. In many of the scrolls, the paintings and poems were combined in imaginative and harmonious ways. In Jordan's, for instance, dark pencil lines depict a smiling monkey, one hand on its hip, the other grasping a branch. A serene deer walks by, happy to have a mouse as a passenger on its back. A vine of green brushstrokes snaking around a corner of the page and through the lines of her poem completes the picture. In Yaffa Quan-Weinrich's scroll, a "baby swan, white as porcelain" nuzzles a girl whose swinging line of black hair echoes the brushstroke of the calligraphic character above it. Elisabeth Rosen's light blue washes fill the space of her scroll with the grandeur of the waterfall she'd recently seen in Brazil, and her words make the moment immediate: "I'm getting foam in my face. The trickle of the water is impressive."

The excitement about the scrolls transformed the classroom during the weeks we worked on them. At free time, kids made more scrolls and fans using white paper and markers. One student even penned another nature poem:

> When the leaves fall down in autumn,
> When the trees are almost bare,
> It makes me feel so calm,
> In a pleasurable sort of autumn way.
>
> —Eliza Martin

Yet another student sat in the "teacher's chair" and mouthed explications of Chinese paintings to an imaginary audience.

When we went to see the exhibit from the National Palace Museum at the Metropolitan Museum, our noisy, exuberant class moved with unusual calm, the students concentrating on the exquisite works of painting, calligraphy, and sculpture that surrounded them. I like to think that the contemplative natural spaces of Chinese brush painting drew them in, and that in their own writing and art, they were learning to create these spaces for themselves.

Bibliography

CURRICULUM GUIDES

China: 5,000 Years: Curriculum Guide for Educators. New York: Education Department, Solomon R. Guggenheim Foundation, 1998.

Splendors of Imperial China: Treasures from the National Palace Museum: A Resource for Educators. New York: Asian Art Department, Metropolitan Museum of Art, 1996.

BOOKS

Fong, Wen C., James C. Y. Watt, et al. Possessing the Past: Treasures from the National Palace Museum, New York/Taipei: Metropolitan Museum of Art/National Palace Museum, 1996.

———. *Beyond Representation: Chinese Painting and Calligraphy*. New York: Metropolitan Museum of Art, 1992.

Hearn, Maxwell K. *Splendors of Imperial China: Treasures from the National Palace Museum, Taipei*. New York/Taipei: Metropolitan Museum of Art/National Palace Museum, 1996.

Li Po. *The Selected Poems of Li Po*. Translated by David Hinton. New York: New Directions, 1996.

Spence, Jonathan. *The Search for Modern China*. New York: W.W. Norton, 1990.

WEBSITES

China Page: chinapage.com. Ming L. Pei, editor. This website contains a wide array of resources on Chinese history and culture.

The National Palace Museum: npm.gov.tw. This is the website of the National Palace Museum in Taipei. Information from an exhibition called *Representations of the Literary Mind: The Theme of Poetry and Literature in Chinese Art* is very helpful.

Beth Zasloff

The How and The Why

John Taggart's "Slow Song for Mark Rothko"

by Marjorie Welish

*a*LTHOUGH IN THE VIEW of certain abstract painters, poetry written *about* abstract painting is the most abstract register there is, I would argue that, in remaining extrinsic to the medium and so being *illustrative* of sense, poetry about painting often depletes the true content of the painting, reducing it to mere subject matter to be discussed. This descriptive tendency is, after all, a natural tendency of the literary approach to art.

There is another approach, however. A poem *through* abstract painting can be both expressive of the concrete register of painting and true to the medium of words, *if* some verbal analogue to the visual can establish itself on its own terms.

Thus, when as a teacher you ask students to write about a painting by Mark Rothko or another abstract painter—optimally, in its actual physical presence—the best directive is not "*Describe* abstract painting," but "*Construct* a verbal artifact commensurate with the visual one." As an example of this method, I will use a workshop I teach based on John Taggart's poem "Slow Song for Mark Rothko."

Taggart wrote his poem in analogy to a large canvas seen up close. I begin by pointing to the canvas. I point to it without describing it. Then I simply read the poem by Taggart, offering the students little if any background information. When preparing students to write in response to abstract art, it is important, as the teacher, to withhold information.

Marjorie Welish

(*Excerpt*)

To breathe and stretch one's arms again
to breathe through the mouth to breathe to
breathe through the mouth to utter in
the most quiet way not to whisper not to whisper
to breathe through the mouth in the most quiet way to
breathe to sing to breathe to sing to breathe
to sing the most quiet way.

To sing to light the most quiet light in darkness
radiantia radiantia
singing light in darkness.

To sing as the host sings in his house.

To breathe through the mouth to breathe through the
mouth to breathe to sing to
sing in the most quiet way to
sing *the seeds in the earth breathe forth*
not to whisper *the seeds* not to whisper *in the earth*
to sing *the seeds in the earth* the most quiet way to
sing *the seeds in the earth breathe forth.*

To sing to light the most quiet light in darkness
radiant light of *seeds in the earth*
singing light in the darkness.

To sing as the host sings in his house.

To breathe through the mouth to breathe to sing
in the most quiet way not to
whisper *the seeds in the earth breathe forth*
to sing totality of *the seeds* not to eat to
sing *the seeds* not to eat to
sing *the seeds in the earth* to
be at ease to sing totality totality
to sing to be at ease

To sing to light the most quiet light in darkness
be at ease with radiant *seeds*
with singing light in darkness.

To sing as the host sings in his house.

As we begin our discussion, I direct students not to the poem but to
the work by Rothko, asking them about the principles behind its composition. Perhaps they will say it is large. Or dark. Or repetitive. Or illegible.
Or abstract. I ask them how they know this and encourage them to be concrete in their responses. What sort of darkness is there and how is it made?
How does scale differ from size, and under what conditions does scale
change? I suggest that context might alter the meaning we attribute to
light, dark, size, scale, continuity, discontinuity. Having withheld information about Rothko's medium and his method of applying paint—laying oil or oil/egg emulsion over dry pigment—I describe it to them and
then ask what difference this knowledge of his aesthetics makes to their
experience of the work. Having withheld information about the architecture of the Rothko Chapel, I now tell my students about its dimensions,
and about the climate of Texas. I avail them of further knowledge of
Rothko's life and work. Next, we look at a number of Rothko's paintings
(see figure 12). I ask the students to note phenomena that repeat, and to
consider the similarities, then the differences, within such repetition.
Finally, I ask them to define *abstraction.*

Returning to the poem by John Taggart, I ask what aspects of
Rothko's paintings the poet has observed. How does Taggart express these
visible features in words? Indeed, what words has he chosen, and why? We
consider line breaks and variable line lengths in order to see how these
affect what is on the page. I ask how this poem's composition differs from

the compositions of poems they have come to expect as the norm. What is the significance of knowing what Taggart himself said, that his is a poetry of spaces?

Diverging from the issue of visual art in relation to the lyric, I ask how may it be said that musicality characterizes "Slow Song for Mark Rothko." We then compare issues of immanence and repetition in "Slow Song for Mark Rothko" with those in another Taggart poem, "Pen Vine and Scroll." We go on to consider how a poetic artifact is one that exercises the art of contemplation.

❖ ❖ ❖ ❖ ❖ ❖ ❖ ❖ ❖

The above schematic lesson may seem like one of those directives from medieval albums that say in effect: Make plan, build cathedral. But, keeping the lesson plan sketchy has its advantages. A general plan is readily adaptable to the relative and variable sophistication of the students, and importantly, adaptable to teaching non-illustratively. I want to teach students that the verbal artifact need not mimic the visual one; indeed, mimesis is best when it is selective, that is, limited to deriving one or two properties from the visual work. The resulting poem is thus freer to manifest the constitutive features of poetry as such. One must be careful not to naturalize the poetics of abstraction.

If you wish to teach abstract painting and poetry, some background reading will yield much in the way of theory and practice for the workshop. Taggart's own writing offers a guide to his Objectivist poetics, but other basic readings might include: the entry on "Objectivism" in a dictionary of poetics; one or more of Gertrude Stein's verbal portraits of artists; Stein's "Portraits and Repetition" and "Poetry and Grammar" in *Lectures in America*; poems by William Carlos Williams on paintings; and poems by George Oppen in *An Objectivist Anthology* (edited by Louis Zukofsky). From Taggart, I recommend "Deep Jewels (George Oppen)"; "Come Shadow Come and Pick this Shadow Up (Louis Zukofsky)"; the poems in his collection *Loop*; and especially "A Preface"—a piece addressing his poem "Slow Song for Mark Rothko," in *Songs of Degrees: Essays on Contemporary Poetry and Poetics*.

In "Preface," Taggart writes of the wandering process that at last brought his poem into being. The initiative of "Slow Song" actually came not from the painting by Rothko, but from two other sources: stained glass and Gregorian chant. Taggart's poetics recreate the direct imagistic properties of the two art forms; the palpable sensations are racheted up for chromatic difficulty whilst being modulated for contemplative states of attention. "Gregorian Chant: the dense and ultimately restful rhythms of which strike me as singularly close equivalents of stained glass," writes Taggart.

How these two art forms might be made palpably abstract is nowhere more realized than in Mark Rothko's paintings. Rothko (1903–1970) emphasized the importance of color over that of the brushstroke. Color, spread rather than drawn over an area, makes the two-dimensional surface of the canvas crucial to the essence of painting. Rothko's deliberate method of applying color contrasted radically with the methods of other Abstract Expressionists like Jackson Pollock, whose application of paint was more spontaneous and aggressive. Although this dialectical schema simplifies the historical situation as it existed in the New York School during the 1950s, there is some truth to it. In any case, that Rothko built his darkly luminescent abstractions through the application of several thin laminations of color in an admiring attempt to imitate a darkly vivid stained glass only strengthened Taggart' s resolve to conceive of the same—but through language.

"The answer is seeing. I repeat: not belief but the experience of seeing for ourselves what has already been seen by another," Taggart writes of poet Frank Samperi's work. Notice that Taggart places emphasis on seeing *for* himself rather than seeing *as* himself—as the confessional self would aggrandize the poet in the world. What Taggart has in mind is an impersonal objectivity. In "Preface," his essay on Rothko on the occasion of the artist's retrospective at the Guggenheim Museum in 1978, Taggart reports on Rothko's interest in the properties of stained glass. The key, writes Taggart, is seeing: seeing streaks in the stained glass as evidence of the impurities characteristic of the medium. Modern methods have yet to duplicate the elusive recipe of stained glass. Rothko's application of paint by hand would be inefficient if the point of painting were merely to cover a surface. If the point of painting is to ready a surface for seeing, however, then the hand-held implement of the brush applying paint in layers to create a

Illustrations

FIGURE 1 Parmigianino, *Self-Portrait in a Convex Mirror* (1523)

FIGURE 2 Cy Twombly,
Untitled [Say Goodbye Catullus
to the Shores of Asia Minor], detail (1994)

FIGURE 3 René Magritte,
Time Transfixed (1938)

FIGURE 4 Susan Karwoska's Students,
Our Story Quilt

FIGURE 5 Wifredo Lam, *The Jungle*（1943）

FIGURE 6 Ezra Shales's Students,
(clockwise from the top) *Portraits of Dallisha,
Dana, Joei, and Eric*

FIGURE 7 Rosalind Pace & Marcia Simon's Students, *The Image-Making Workshop*

FIGURE 8 Whitney Sparks,
Gestural Abstraction

FIGURE 9 Edward Lear,
View of Mt. Parnassus, 1849 (1849)

FIGURE 10 Pamela Freeze Beal's Students,
Gilgamesh: A Mosaic

FIGURE 11 Qi Bashi, *Scholar's Tools* (1947)

FIGURE 12 Mark Rothko,
Red, Brown, and Black (1958)

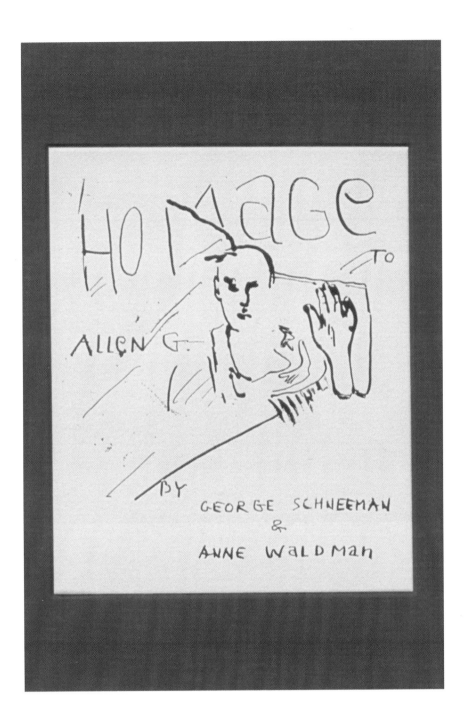

FIGURE 13 George Schneeman & Anne Waldman, *Homage to Allen G.* (1997)

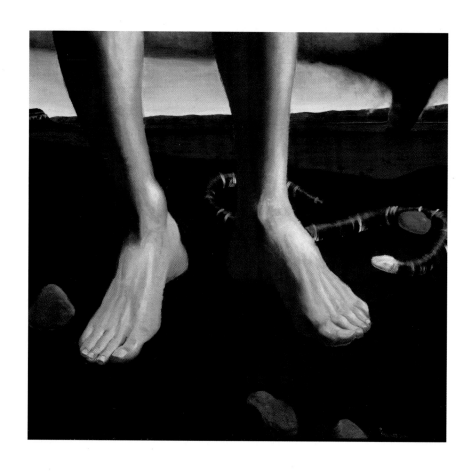

FIGURE 14 Erik Johnson,
An Allegory of Emotion(s) (2000)

I always wanted to start over

FIGURE 15 Amy Trachtenberg's Student,
I Always Wanted to Start Over

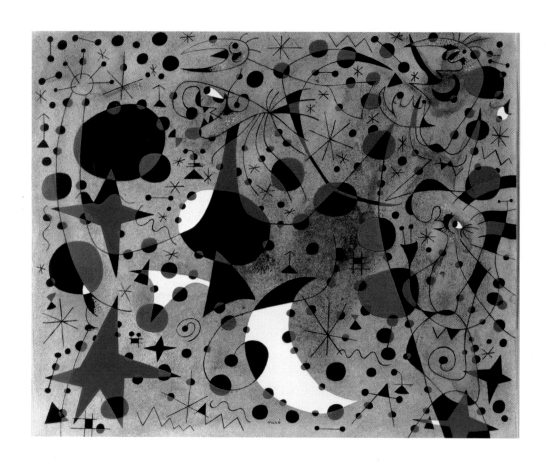

FIGURE 16 Joan Miró,
*The Nightingale's Song at Midnight
and the Morning Rain* (1940)

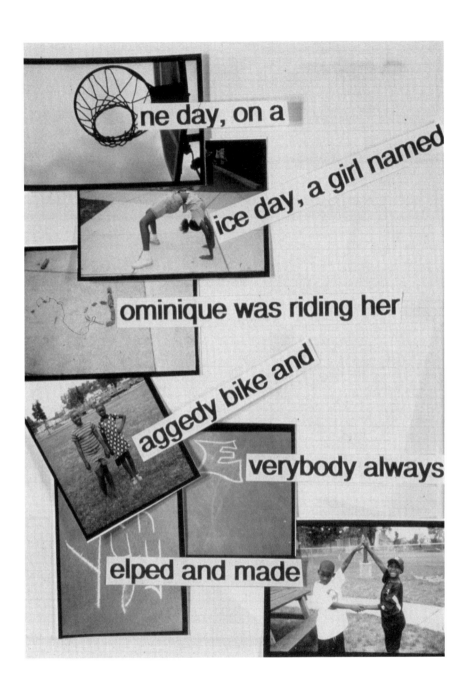

FIGURE 17 Ondreya Anderson,
One Day, On A Nice Day

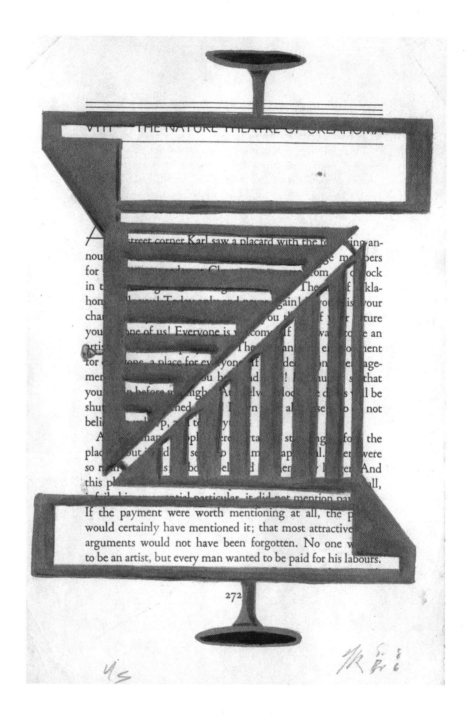

FIGURE 18 Nelson Savinon,
Study No. 30 for AMERIKA VI (1984–85)

Marjorie Welish

dense chromaticism is very much in order. The ethos in Taggart's "Slow Song," then, is integrity through directness, a directness sustained by way of repetition and the ardors of that written oral exercise.

The palpable experience Taggart strives for depends on the recitation and reiteration of a few words with controlled breathing; yet unlike other poems meant to be recited, "Slow Song" draws attention to breathing by using the verb itself (*breathe*). Naming what one is doing makes poetry a concrete pragmatic exercise of the spirit, not a vague idea. What Taggart has done is to embody in words Rothko's own belief that "it was never a question of being abstract or representational. It is really a matter of ending this silence and solitude, of breathing and stretching one's arms again." Words lyrical in their minimal expression of lyricism, repeated again and again with variants, become a sound poetry the aural qualities of which introduce a drone centering on the letter *E*. "To breathe," "to stretch," "to breathe . . . earth," or "to breathe . . . seeds"—all these give privilege to assonance, rhymes alternating with off-rhymes. Composing with closely-keyed linguistic sound, Taggart discloses that he is imitating the minimalism of musician Steve Reich as much as any poetic meter. Moreover, through the sounds' slight difference, "Slow Song for Mark Rothko" brings about a true aural translucence, with its sonorous depths established through palpable embodiment. To breathe, to stretch one's arms again: these words enact their own earthly immanence.

Composition through breath creates pattern as well, but unlike the long line of Projective Verse, which propels energy of intellect across the page, the breathing cycle that informs Taggart's contemplative lyric is as short as a syllable, word, or phrase. Pulling analogies from Rothko and Reich, Taggart finds ways to compose with blocks and lines of words. A device he mentions in "Preface"—that of isolating a line from a stanza—accomplishes two things at once: it reinforces the abrupt sound shift that has erupted, and anticipates the sonorities that are about to emerge as a block in the following stanza. This is analogous, in painting, to the line drawn beside a form to negotiate the transition between (abstract) figure and ground. In Rothko, that line may come about as a function of layering paint: chromatic difference demonstrably revealed along the color blocks' ethereally feathered edges. Taggart's "Slow Song for Mark Rothko" shows how language may be made to function the same way.

When we read (and hear) Taggart's opening lines:

To breathe and stretch one's arms again
to breathe through the mouth to breathe to

the displacement of phrases has established syntactical expectations for future hearing:

breathe through the mouth to utter in
the most quiet way not to whisper not to whisper
to breathe through the mouth in the most quiet way to
breathe to sing to breathe to sing to breathe
to sing the most quiet way.

To sing to light the most quiet light in darkness
radiantia radiantia
singing light in darkness.

To sing as the host sings in his house.

If a line within the stanza is likened to an utterance, it is meditative and fuses sense even as it differentiates syntax. This is quite distinct from employing the kind of repetition that Gertrude Stein used for emphatic assertion. Given the Objectivists' interest in the atomic units of language and their combination and recombination, it is no wonder that Taggart found Zukofsky's fugal interests for poetry as a means to creative verbal moiré more compatible than Stein's forcefulness. Taggart's "Julia's Wild," which plays upon close degrees of syntactical sense deriving from Shakespeare, shows this influence:

Come shadow, come, and take this shadow up,
Come shadow shadow, come and take this up,
Come, shadow, come, and take this shadow up,

These lines suggest how Taggart's lyric is constructed of syntactical sense. Taggart's verbal interference patterns for the poem tend not to mark one word as more interesting than another. The effect is not only subtle, but beyond sensibility: here is indeed an embedded rhetoric. When we read these lines:

To breathe and stretch one's arms again
to breathe through the mouth to breathe to
breathe through the mouth to utter in

we do not know in advance whether "to breathe through the mouth" functions as an infinitive or an imperative. There's performance poetry, and
then there's the performative aspect by which even the most self-conscious
literariness in poetry demands to be reconstituted with each encounter.
Taggart's poem draws attention to the ethics of the latter even as it clearly
aligns itself with the poetics of the former.

Marjorie Welish

✤ ✤ ✤ ✤ ✤ ✤ ✤ ✤ ✤

Assigning a creative exercise based on "Slow Song for Mark Rothko" need
not require a spiritual topic to induce a meditative lyric. Indeed, it is prefer-
able that the words be chosen first to let the content propagate through the
sound. Have students choose words first for their sound. Then they should
experiment by listening to the sounds of words, finding the new sonorities
the words make when repeated, as they compose their poems. Initially, with
a few simple words, then with words aggregated into phrases, and those
phrases varied for temporal emphasis, the reader becomes accustomed to
hearing a musicality based on breath rather than meter.

The displacement of words and the breaking of established
sequences is Taggart's method for varying the repetition of words. Music
in poetry can be accomplished through aural patterning rather than meter
or rhyme. With repetition, blocks of similar sounds precipitate, and
through repetition comes stasis. Hence the slowness in this slow song. Fascinating is how such slowness is invented.

Anfam, David, and Carol Mancusi-Ungaro. *Mark Rothko Chapel Commission*. Houston: The Menil Collection, 1996.

Ashton, Dore. *About Rothko*. Oxford: Oxford University Press, 1983.

Taggart, John. *Loop*. Los Angeles: Sun & Moon Press, 1991.

———. "Slow Song for Mark Rothko," In *Poems for the Millennium, Vol. 2*. Edited by Jerome Rothenberg and Pierre Joris. Berkeley and Los Angeles: University of California Press, 1995.

———. *Songs of Degrees*. Tuscaloosa: University of Alabama Press, 1994.

Going on Our Nerve
Collaborations between Poets and Visual Artists

by Anne Waldman

OLLABORATION IS A CALLING TO WORK with and for others, in the service of something that transcends individual artistic ego and, as such, has to do with love, survival, generosity, and a conversation in which the terms of language are multidimensional. I always work with people around me because it's a way to be in the world together and to make something that has intrinsic value. It is a statement of connection, of camaraderie, and it also goes beyond a particular relationship or duet and becomes what William Burroughs called "the third mind." Something new, or "other," emerges from the combination that would not have come about with a solo act.

As a poet, I have collaborated with other poets—particularly those associated with the so-called New York School, including Ted Berrigan, Bernadette Mayer, and Eileen Myles—and with many visual artists, among them Joe Brainard, Elizabeth Murray, Red Grooms, Susan Hall, George Schneeman, Richard Tuttle, and Yvonne Jacquette. Working together to produce poems and artworks has been necessary as a way of manifesting our aesthetics, which include a sense of community and collaboration. In the early days, these writings weren't being sponsored or produced. We were going on our nerve, getting inside each other's heads. We were work-ing to surprise ourselves, each other, sometimes to show off and get closer to one another, like birds in an elaborate mating ritual.

The genre of collaboration is a social activity: you know something of the artist, because he or she is a friend of yours or because you are familiar with his or her creative work. You may even have a shared sensi-bility, but even if this isn't the case you are willing to "wing it" without a prescribed agenda. You are not thinking about the concept, the finished product, or making money. So you *surprise* each other. During the 1960s and 1970s, collaborations were made possible by a particular bohemian lifestyle. You visited painters at work, and they dropped in on you. If there were a reading or performance coming up, and you needed a flyer, you'd stop in and ask someone to help you design it. If you were publishing small-press editions, as I was, you *needed* artists for covers and drawings. They enhanced the production, bringing fresh perspectives.

The painter George Schneeman moved next door to me on New York's St. Mark's Place in 1968. His studio, a small back room on the fourth floor, was filled with cutout images from old magazines as well as various crayons, paint, pens, and paper. George was also doing a lot of por-traits of poets at that time, and covers for small-press mimeograph edi-tions. We would get to work, have a tea break, and then his wife Katie would cook a delicious Italian dinner. Afterward, we would swoon and fuss over our brilliant productions.

Since our very first collaboration we have followed the same proce-dure. We begin with an open sheet—usually a quality Arches-type paper—on which George begins to dab a little color (paint, gouache, crayon, ink) or to draw an object, sometimes a cutout image. I usually have a few lines milling about in my head. If not, I go into a notebook or spontaneously riff off his shapes and pictures.

One of my favorite collaborations is one that I call *Amerigo Vespucci*. I think George introduced the tomato first, floating in the space like a planet or a star. Then, most likely, I wrote "vegetable love" and "egg love," followed by "I I I I I / it's a celestial little body." There's a postcard in the piece that looks hand-tinted, possibly from Italy, with children in an ordinary street setting, and underneath George inked "Spoleto: Festival of Two Worlds." I think we both agreed on embedding "A merry go around" inside the words "Amerigo Vespucci." In the way of readable images you see a car mirror, stars, a partial map of America, a zipper, and a tomato in the sky. Also the words "the afterlife," "goes on singing," "workers of the world unite." It's a very American work, you could say, about space, aspiration, discovery—and it's a field composition.

Collaborations reinforce ritual, the importance of making something together as an act of generosity or homage. For example, within hours of Allen Ginsberg's death, George and I had already begun collaborating on a memorial project. George had done a series of tracings of Allen's photographs, on which he had planned to have Allen write, scribble, and doodle. (In fact, we visited Allen at his loft so that George and he could discuss the project, and, although nobody knew—the cancer had not been diagnosed yet—Allen was dying at that point. He lay prostrate on the sofa, then got up bravely to cook us lunch.) The project took on a different tone after his death—the tracings of images were ghostly, haunted, you might say. It was consoling to have a place to put the sadness of his death—George's images also included the "literal" traces of Allen. I stayed up all night, sitting in front of George's tracings, writing a few lines at a time. The text is quite spare. Both the text and the tracings are black ink on white paper.

The finished project, called *Homage to Allen G.* (see figure 13), feels like more of a unified piece, in that the words seem extensions of the artist's own hand, his own line, which in a way continues the line of the photographer's (Allen's) eye. One page I particularly like is a drawing of poet-mendicant Gregory Corso holding a stick. The lines read "a bowl"—"a rod"—"a staff"—"Poetry's ACCOUTREMENTS"—"stabilize"—"the void." I was thinking perhaps of Mahatma Gandhi's possessions at the time of his death (a begging bowl, a staff, a pair of sandals), as well as of Allen's particular modesty. Steve Clay, the scholar of small presses and the mastermind behind Granary Books, published the edition.

Another artist I have worked with is Susan Rothenberg. As Susan lives in New Mexico, we created our collaboration through the mail. The project—finally entitled *Kin*—was also sponsored by Granary Books, which brought its own design and vision to the production. We began with my manifesto "Kali Yuga Poetics," which Susan decided she could not relate to. She wrote to me that she spent a lot of time going out and drawing "animals in the barnyard" (she lives on a ranch), and the tone of "Kali Yuga Poetics" was too ponderous. That was amusing to me actually, and being an admirer of her work and in particular the mythic quality of her horse paintings, I was comfortable letting her take the lead. The animals she drew were provocative as "subjects." I wrote a suite of eight poems I probably would not have written otherwise. I worked with responses to her drawings and thoughts about animal-realm dualities. I wanted to go along with her sense of a light touch, almost comedic at times. Her charcoal drawings in this project are quite lush. Whether it's two cats, crows, two horses, or a horse and a man in relation to one another, the images have a talky presence, and I picked up on that for the text. *Kin* is elegantly printed by Philip Gallo—each poem opens out into a triptych with the drawing placed at the center. Here's a little sample of the text, which includes the footnote "in winter they gather at night by thousands in communal rooks":

peck.

then head. along. home

pecking order
obviates
transmission
or cowpoke
kind of bliss
   flies thru here
to take scraps for supper
hungry
extemporize a 'caw'

I also worked on a project entitled *Her Story* with the painter Elizabeth Murray. (Elizabeth had been asked to do a project with Universal Limited Art Editions, so that was the "seed" for *Her Story*.) I made some notes in a little notebook after seeing some works-in-progress in Elizabeth's studio. She had also given me a couple of discarded scraps. The initial notes I took in her studio led to the text, and then we went back and forth a bit. I was responding to her drawings (she'd sent color xeroxes). At one point I revamped the text entirely, sent it to her, and she wrote back that she had been counting on the *earlier* version. In a way, I was pleased that she felt strongly about the words and liked them enough and didn't want me to keep messing about. I remember thinking the text was too simple compared to the complexity of the drawings. Her palate is grandiose. The drawings are coils, bursts of energy, fantastically witty, like cartoons gone awry yet made elegant in their transformation. She seems to be located in "things," but what are they?

Anne Waldman

I read the text of *Her Story* as a kind of serial poem. It has a narrative logic. It embeds being female, being pregnant, being in a kind of humorous, hormonal situation vis-à-vis the world, the "male." It's a contest, a struggle. Her drawings suggested a story, not necessarily hers or mine, but the story of a state of mind taking shape. In fact her work is generally very hieroglyphic, in that the imagery—which is suggestive, not literal—takes place in a zone of subtext, imaginatively wild. The finished product is very atmospheric—you could say it has a strong feminine quality—our signatures are in the watermark of the paper, which adds a kind of authorial depth to the whole creation.

✧   ✧   ✧   ✧   ✧   ✧   ✧   ✧   ✧

The ideas of collaboration that we work with come from a long lineage and tradition. "Shaped" poems or calligrams (from the Greek *kalli* and *gramma*, "beautiful writing") have roots in classical antiquity in the province of magical design. The dadaists and surrealists were long-time partners in collaborative extravaganzas and early "happenings" that featured costumes, visuals, and performative poetries and strategies. There is also a long tradition of various modernist artist/writer's book/broadside collaborations: Sonia Delaunay and Blaise Cendrars's *La Prose du Transsiberien et de la petite Jehanne de France*, or Picasso's numerous illustration/collaborations with the likes of Robert Desnos, Pierre Reverdy, Paul Eluard, René Char. As it moved to America, the tradition included lovely visual/poetry portfolios by Larry Rivers and Frank O'Hara ("Stones") and R. B. Kitaj and Robert Creeley ("A Day Book"), among others.

In his *ABC of Reading* the poet Ezra Pound, who was also an art critic, conjures *phanopoeia* or "the visual image thrown on to the reader's imagination" as one of the three necessary ingredients in the mix of poetry. *Logopoeia* (the dance of ideas) and *melopoeia* (the music, the charge of the sound) are the other two. Pound's notion is that the mix of these three elements charges language with meaning "to the utmost possible degree." This spark is ignited when the three elements all work together, when there is a kind of collaboration among images, sounds, and ideas.

Gertrude Stein provides a good example of this mix in action. She claims to have learned a lot by observing Pablo Picasso while he was painting. (She had over 80 sittings with him for a portrait he painted of her.) In a piece of writing entitled *Tender Buttons*, Stein tried to use words as an artist uses paint. Her writing is often described as "Cubist," which refers to the way an artist attempts to look *through* objects, to their other sides, concentrating on the angles and not relying on a fixed view. In Cubism, the eye is always in motion. Here are some short sections from *Tender Buttons*:

A Dog

A little monkey goes like a donkey that means to
Say that means to say that more sighs last goes.
Leave with it. A little monkey goes like a donkey.

A Blue Coat

A blue coat is guided guided away, guided and guided
away, that is the particular color that is used for that length
and not any width not even more than a shadow.

An Umbrella

Coloring high means that the strange reason is in front not
more in front behind. Not more in front in peace of the dot.

In the words of "A Blue Coat," one sees a blue coat in motion, fleeting by. The lines of "An Umbrella" seem an attempt to capture the mysterious way a person might look holding an umbrella. Could the "dot" modified by the word *peace* be the top of the umbrella, the center as one holds it out to close it? Whatever the interpretation, there is an intention in this particular piece of Stein's to look through ordinary objects and paint them using words—as a painter attempting to paint a cubist still life might.

The real key to a good collaboration is that the writing does not simply fall back on looking and describing and naming the things in the painting, but rather that it responds in a parallel fashion. That the writing becomes a kind of artwork, in and of itself. It's as though both the painter and the poet can speak through a contained field (the large canvas or sheet) that also comes alive in the way poetry does—off the page. Composition by field has been an important poetic stance for me and many of the writers and artists I've collaborated with.

Anne Waldman

✧   ✧   ✧   ✧   ✧   ✧   ✧   ✧   ✧

Of course, one of my biggest collaborations is with students, and I have found that introducing collaboration into the classroom allows them to think about their writing in a different way. The best thing about working with visual art in the classroom is that it is simple—it doesn't have to be overly complicated, with lots of materials and supplies.

I am always pushed by students as they question and argue aesthetics. I make them write on top of or in the margins of each other's writing, as well as bringing in visual images (photographs, postcards) to respond to. We collaborate on word portrait sketches of one another, which is evocative of the surrealist "exquisite corpse." The exquisite corpse is a collaborative technique that artists and writers still use to generate a poem or drawing—it can be done spontaneously, sitting around at party or in a cafe or working together through the mail. It works like this: divide the class into groups of four, and each group folds a piece of paper into four vertical sections, then unfolds it. In the top folded section, one person in each group draws the top of a body and refolds the paper so that the next person can't see what the first has drawn. The next person draws a body part in the second folded section—students should be encouraged to be wild in their interpretations of what a "body part" is. After all four people in each group have drawn a body part, the paper is unfolded, and an exquisite monster might appear. You might end up with a fish-headed creature with an hourglass waist, car beams for knees, and claws for feet. Each group can then share their exquisite corpse with the rest of the class.

This also works with sentences. Students write sentences in the folded parts, not knowing what the others have written. When the students read the combined sentences out loud, they revel in the strange juxtapositions of the new poem they have just created. One can also do cut-ups by "stealing" words and images from magazines and newspapers.

One of the very best writing experiences I know is simply taking students—of any age—to a museum at some point during the semester. As a start, I recommend leaving them completely free to wander through the space and see what catches their eye. Then they should linger for a few minutes in front of the art piece or sculpture that attracts them—but without looking at the descriptive placard or title. (No art history at this point—it might be inhibiting to the process.) This transforms the museum into an environment, a place distinctly removed from the outside world, where students may focus with heightened awareness. A designated artistic zone. It is not simply the art on the walls that is "in the zone," but the students as well. The museum is as much their space as it is the artists' space. In it they can make decisions about what they like and don't like, and may sit in front of an artwork and study it. There's a decorum that needs to be created inside a museum or gallery space—quiet, meditative. Somewhat introspective.

After students have found a particular piece that attracts them, the next step is to answer a series of provocative questions, such as:

How does my eye move when I look at this piece?

Does it move in a circle?

How many colors are in this work?

What is the quality of stone? Of bronze? Of plaster? Of string? Of wire?

What does it look like upside down? (Distort your narrative, linear, directional perspective.)

Is there any sensation in my body?

Do I have an immediate intellectual or emotional response?

What do I think the artist may have been thinking as he or she made this?

What words come to mind as I look at this?

How would I create an opera, a dialogue, a performance out of this painting?

How would I regard this if it were the first piece of art I ever witnessed?

If it were the last work I would ever witness?

What are my immediate associations?

What is the quality of the paint or other medium?

How, figuratively speaking, does the artwork taste, smell, feel?

Do I look for anthropomorphic shapes that relate to my human world?

What are the characters doing in this piece?

If a painting or sculpture could talk, what would it say?

If I were telling a story, how would this particular piece of "art"
    enter into it?

139

Only after the students have posed and responded to questions about the artwork should they check out who the artist is, read the title, date, or any description that gives context and depth to their understanding of the piece. After they have done this, they may write about why they think the artist chose that particular title for his or her piece, or why they think it was left untitled. Using the title alone can be very provocative to the writing practice. Ask them what they would call it. Have them write a poem about the artwork using the title as the first line. Have them compare their title to the original and discuss how the two are different.

There's a well-known painting by the French surrealist artist René Magritte entitled "The invisible world" (*Le monde invisible*), which shows a large porous gray rock sitting inside on a wooden plank floor in front of a window that looks out on a mildly stormy sea and sky. Why is this called *The Invisible World*? Is this rock meant to represent the secret self of the planet Earth? In another painting by Magritte, *The Waterfall* (*La Cascade*), the interior of a forest encloses a painting (sitting on an easel) depicting the exterior of the forest—but of course there is no waterfall in sight (although it might reside inside the forest). Magritte's titles often point to the unseen, and thus enlarge the scope of his paintings. In a way, the title/image relationship is like the third mind—the two combine to create a third element.

The final step in the museum experiment—perhaps back in the classroom—is to review the writing and try to shape it. One good exercise that works well with older students is to give them scissors and gluestick and ask them to cut up what they have written and then paste it back down in another order on a large piece of newsprint. From the new "collage," they can then find the seeds of a poem, story, dialogue, monologue, or even an essay. Have them type up their collages and read them back to other members of the class in small groups. This exercise challenges the sense that writing is somehow fixed. It encourages students to see words as things that can be moved around, played with, taken apart and put back together again.

The idea here is to conjure or trigger associations that might not naturally occur. We don't want our poetry or other kinds of writing to only rely on our feelings and autobiographical experiences. Emphasizing the visual adds new (visual) elements to the writing.

❖ ❖ ❖ ❖ ❖ ❖ ❖ ❖ ❖

Creative Writing Life Experiments

Here are some additional exercises I have successfully used with my students:

A John Ashbery Method: Create a title for a poem, then take a walk and come back to write.

Write a poem using the jargon of another field (anything but therapy): mechanics, fishing, boating, gemology, astronomy, psychology. Intercut with your own writing.

Through snail mail, email, or other means, start an epistolary collaboration, with a lot of Dear So-&-So's.

The William Burroughs Walk: Take a walk, notice everything blue (or red or white or green or gold), and make a list. Also notice what you are thinking when you see particular things or people. What is in your mind at the time. Combine what you see with what you flash on and remember.

The William Burroughs Fold-in: Take two different pages from an outside text (magazine article or book) and cut each in half vertically. Paste the mismatched pages together. Then create a new text. (See *The Third Mind* by William Burroughs and Brion Gysin.)

Try the same experiment horizontally, or cut up individual lines and place in a hat and pull out line by line à la Dada method of Tristan Tzara.

Write a calendar. A meditation for each month of the year. Try modeling your piece on a calendar from another culture.

Make a poem in the shape of a vehicle, a ziggurat, a double helix, a cloud, a storm, a person, a particular orchid.

Anne Waldman

The Talismanic Object Experiment: Everyone brings in an object with a story. Each one is displayed, discussed. The other students, in turn, ask questions, take notes, write. Pay attention to how the objects are being discussed, not simply the information they engender. Go around the group in a thorough fashion. You will have pages of words. Then refine or expand. Focus on one or more or all of the objects. Tell stories, or be very spare and abstract. It can be a detective story, a litany, whatever you desire the shape or form of the writing to be.

The Portrait Duet: Pair off. Sit with your partner and "sketch" each other with words, making a detailed description of the person's physicality and also what associations arise as well. Then start talking and interviewing each other with profound questions: What is your greatest fear? Things of that kind. Keep writing as you are both talking. Notice *how* things are being said. Then sit in silence again and review your writing. Shape it, edit it, expand it, or not.

However you utilize these ideas, be sure to remember that we all have untapped areas of *phanopoeia* as writers. It is instructive to design your own experiments and collaborative possibilities.

ACKNOWLEDGMENTS: Parts of this essay were derived from an interview with Lisa Berman entitled "Surprise Each Other: The Art of Collaboration" and the essay "Creative Writing Life," both of which appear in *Vow to Poetry*.

Bibliography

Artists' Books in the Modern Era 1870–2000. San Francisco: Fine Arts Museum of San Francisco, 2001.

Burroughs, William, and Brion Gysin. *The Third Mind.* New York: Viking, 1978.

Castleman, Riva. *A Century of Artists Books*. New York: Museum of Modern Art, 1994.

Haas, Robert Bartlett, ed. *A Primer for the Gradual Understanding of Gertrude Stein*. Black Sparrow Press, 1971.

Motherwell, Robert, ed. *The Dada Painters and Poets. An Anthology*. Cambridge, Mass.: Harvard University Press, 1981.

Rothenberg, Jerome, and Steven Clay, eds. *A Book of the Book: Some Works & Projections About the Book & Writing*. New York: Granary Books, 2000.

Stein, Gertrude. *Tender Buttons*. Los Angeles: Sun & Moon, 1991.

Waldman, Anne. *Vow to Poetry. Essays, Interviews, & Manifestos*. Minneapolis: Coffee House Press, 2001.

————, and Elizabeth Murray. *Her Story*. New York: Universal Limited Art Editions.

————, and George Schneeman. *Homage to Allen G*. New York: Granary Books, 1997.

————, and Lewis Warsh. *The Angel Hair Anthology*. New York: Granary Books, 2001.

————, and Susan Rothenberg. *Kin*. New York: Granary Books, 1998.

Conversations Beyond the Gallery

Teaching Art and Expository Writing to College Students

by Scott Herndon & Kristin Dombek

*i*T IS UNFORTUNATE THAT THE SPACES where art is displayed often feel like the least productive sites in which to enjoy, think about, and engage with it. Quiet and austere, museums and galleries intimidate us with their seriousness—and the fact that museum guards watch our every move in conspicuous silence doesn't help, either. When we wonder "What on earth is that?" or "What could this possibly mean?" we may feel too embarrassed to discuss these questions with our companions. We are supposed to know the answer. So, in silence, we observe the art from a distance, draw closer, then quickly move to the next piece.

This behavior is telling: in a bout with self-consciousness, we have unwittingly brought the habits of channel-surfing to bear in the space of the gallery. We act as though art should strike us immediately, or not at all. We simply catch a glimpse and consume another image.

Even when a piece of art does speak to us, typically our comments are careful and geared toward "getting it right." We try to make smart connections rather than expose our honest initial reactions: "Doesn't this remind you of So-and-so?" or "I believe these photographs are critiquing So-and-so." These gestures towards art history feel good because they alleviate our anxiety that others may think the artwork has escaped us.

Is it any surprise, then, that our students employ the same mechanisms when faced with art in the gallery?

In New York University's Expository Writing Program, where we teach, students are asked to write about art in their first-year writing workshop. We begin by sending students out to select and study works of art and respond to them in writing. We hope that students will develop essays inspired by a personal and conceptual relationship with the artworks they choose. But early in the writing process, a problem often arises: students' initial written responses are frequently not rich or complicated enough to provide the foundation for an effective college essay. Sometimes the students "choose" a work that is too easy and familiar—a Monet or Renoir image downloaded from the Internet, or a Robert Doisneau photograph on the poster in their dorm room. Then they write quick, clichéd descriptions of these well-known works. If they do go to a gallery or museum and take the time to sit with an original piece of art, their writing is often too careful, formal, and stilted. Thus the students fall into the same trap we do—and miss out on the kind of aesthetic experience that might lead them to new discoveries about art, writing, their world, and themselves.

It might be easy to attribute this problem to the ignorance of students, the scarcity of art instruction in primary and secondary education, or some other scapegoat, but students *are* capable of writing in creative and innovative ways about art if they take the time to experience it on its own terms—and, perhaps more importantly, on their own terms. Students must be given license to experiment, and they must come to view the apprehension and confusion they feel when challenged by an artwork as an asset, rather than a limitation. If we do not pay enough attention to the process they need to go through to arrive at engaged, provocative ideas, we inadvertently encourage them to write before they've entered into a conversation with the artwork itself.

What follows are some of the methods we've developed for helping students to write about art in a complex and rewarding way.

Although our end goal is to get students to select an artwork on their own and then begin to write outside the classroom, it is essential to lay some groundwork to help them cultivate their own strategies for viewing art.

Scott Herndon & Kristin Dombek

We view this experience as a rite of passage, constituted by three stages:

1) The initial encounter, in which the student first observes the artwork.

2) The liminal phase, in which the student experiences a collection of possible interpretations and meanings.

3) The end of the encounter, in which the student comes to a creative interpretation for the artwork.

Our classroom work with single art objects is designed to prolong the different stages of this encounter so that students have time to experience the piece of art on its own terms, entertaining many possible ways of thinking about it and then choosing the most productive way to engage with the work.

The Initial Encounter

Here are some principles we've developed for initiating the encounter:

- Bring a provocative work of art into the class. If not a painting, a poster or a photograph will do.
- Provide students with ample time to notice the artwork's features In a class, this means giving students enough time to list as many observable details of the artwork as they can. Urge them to be as creative as possible in what they choose to see. The details they find can range from perspective, color, and texture to figures and their poses, positions, and spatial relationships to one another.
- Create a space that is free of surveillance. Write along with your students, doing everything you can to demonstrate that you are not watching over them, and that everyone's opinion carries equal weight.
- After everyone has had enough time to write, ask each student to share a detail of the piece, mentioning some feature that no one else has described. Aim for multiplicity, rather than seeking one all-encompassing

description. Celebrate the unending range of elements that can be noticed and commented on. By writing with our students, we can be sure enough time has elapsed when we ask students to put their pens away.

Each of these steps is crucial to having students gain the confidence to be playful, creative, and rigorous in their responses to art. In time, students will learn to think and write with all types of art, regardless of whether they are figurative or abstract. We have discovered, however, that at this early stage students find that images with figures are more accessible and stimulating than non-representational works. We recommend following a general rule: always pick artworks by keeping in mind how they might stimulate the students' writing, rather than on the basis of your personal taste.

One painting that has worked very well for us is *A Strange Sense of Propriety (Twin Suns)* by Erik Johnson. This painting offers a range of recognizable objects and relations for students to notice and describe: clouds, two bursts of sunlight, a severed worm or snake, a flat island surrounded by water, foothills and snow-covered mountains, and many variations in shading, tone, and brushwork. We ask the class to write for ten minutes, describing as many details as they can observe, but without thinking about the relationships between them. This strategy keeps students from leaving the material art object behind in pursuit of a cursory interpretation.

The Liminal Phase

Thinking with art begins when we teach our classes to revel in the uncertainty created by excess and possibility. Developing this skill takes time: it requires that the class feel comfortable experiencing art without "expert" opinion or "critical" judgment. It requires that we as teachers be patient and playful with what may sound like "bad" or "silly" comments; a robust discussion will generate subtle and effective ideas in time.

The goal of the second phase is to create a set of potential, provisional connections among the various details in the artwork, and to speculate playfully about the significance of these connections. To initiate this, we have students write a list of questions about what they noticed in the piece only a few minutes earlier, and offer the following prompt before they begin writing:

In the next ten to fifteen minutes, ask as many questions as you can of the artwork. No question is too simple. Each question should revolve around a detail in the painting, as you wonder what it is, why it is there, how it relates to other details present in the piece, and so on. Ten minutes is a long time to ask questions about anything, so begin with the simplest questions you can imagine, and save the hardest ones for the end.

Scott Herndon &
Kristin Dombek

The liminal phase is a threshold moment, when students find themselves between observation and interpretation. Because of this, we instruct the class that any conclusive or declarative sentence is strictly forbidden during this exercise.

After several minutes pass and students write more and more difficult questions, we push them a bit further:

Now begin asking questions about how the details you see in the piece relate to one another. Is one detail more significant than another? Why is this so? Frame your questions in terms of how you interpret the painting, e.g.: Why am I concentrating on this detail rather than that one? Could it have something to do with a hypothesis I already have?

This last reminder encourages students to grapple with the issue of significance while maintaining their connection to the artwork. By linking their observations to questions, the students find themselves working in two directions simultaneously: forward toward a complex final interpretation, and backward to their impressions in the initial encounter.

By the end of this very simple exercise, then, students have begun to do something immensely complicated: they are noticing details, weighing them against each other for interpretive effect, and beginning to reflect on the power and presence of the artwork.

Of Erik Johnson's *An Allegory of Emotion(s)*, one group of students asked the following questions (see figure 14):

- Is the tornado coming toward the figure, or moving away?
- Are those male or female feet? Are they about to move?
- Is the snake bent into the shape of an infinity sign? Is it broken, or on the verge of forming?
- What are those feet doing? Is the tornado readying itself to strike this person? Is the snake? How is the infinity sign connected to this?
- Why are the feet more important to me than the rocks? Why am I con-

centrating on the darkness of the tornado rather than on the blue sky all around it?

- Why do those feet seem familiar? Why do they give me the creeps?

It makes sense to require that our students move from basic details to the problem of significance (and ultimately to their own experiences, elicited by the artwork) in a set of questions. If students can begin to interpret the work on the basis of these questions, they will be in a far better place to do the work we will ask of them in the final stage—work that aims not to explain once and for all what the artwork means but to generate new ideas for creative expression.

The Final Stage: Coming to a Creative Interpretation

If there is one positive thing to take from contemporary scholarship in the humanities, it is the widespread use of critical methods that not only invoke as many questions as answers but that also respect the great complexity of interpreting aesthetic experiences. The implications of these interpretive methods are immense for a pedagogy of writing about art.

For the philosopher Roland Barthes, the interaction between writing and visual art is often a "parasitic" one in which the writing serves to diminish the effect of the art, to explain it away, to make it *say something* that is authoritative and precise. In this sense, the photograph (for example) is used by the writer to stand for what he or she is trying to say: it becomes merely supporting evidence for his or her claims. For Barthes, if a photograph "means" anything at all, it means too many things, all at once. In his book *Image Music Text*, Barthes extends this line of thought, describing how the captions placed beneath press photos work to compromise the integrity of the image:

> The text constitutes a parasitic message designed to connote the image, to "quicken" it. In other words, and this is an important historical reversal, the image no longer illustrates the words; it is now the words which, structurally, are parasitic on the image. The reversal is at a cost—in the relationship that now holds, it is not the image which comes to elucidate or "realize" the text, but the latter which comes to sublimate, patheticize or rationalize the image. (Barthes, 25)

If the artwork always means and says more than any one interpretation of it does, why are those who write about art, students and professionals alike, always trying to explain what artworks mean?

Have we stumbled on a paradox here? Our answer is yes, but it is a paradox that actually provides fertile ground for student writing—and all writing about art. The trick is using the paradox to frame the writing. Slavoj Zizek offers one approach. Describing underwater photographs of the sunken Titanic in *The Sublime Object of Ideology*, Zizek focuses on how we as viewers experience the photograph. Zizek orients his questions around the "trauma" caused by these images, and how this "trauma" makes us leave the photographs behind, disavow them, interpret them away. What we really should do, Zizek argues, is examine how the haunting photographs make us feel spellbound, at a loss for words, fascinated and terrified at the same time. This move toward describing the multiple, complex, and even contradictory experiences that one artwork can generate allows for an interpretation of the images' meanings that does not "rationalize" them.

So by the final exercise, in which they will forge a creative interpretation of the work, our students have already generated their own experiences of the artwork itself and have gained an understanding of how the artwork has given rise to these experiences. Now it's time to turn this experience and understanding into ideas. We start with focused freewriting:

> In the next fifteen minutes, create a fictional scene, in which you do not mention the painting. Pick three or four details, whatever they may be, and use them to create a mood, a setting, and a story that resonates with your experience of the artwork. Write about these details as you would in an inside joke: so that anyone in the class will know where they came from, and why, but no one else will. Be as creative and imaginative as you can.

This freewriting exercise moves students still closer to examining their personal relationship to the artwork by playfully creating a fiction for themselves—a necessary step in using the artwork as a springboard into their own ideas.

Here are some excerpts from responses to *An Allegory of Emotion(s)*:

I like it on the beach except for having to see everyone's bare feet, so fragile, so easily sliced on rocks, stung by jellyfishes, bitten by who knows what bugs, burnt in the sand. I would like to run along the beach under the gaping empty sky, faster than a tornado between the pitched umbrellas and plastic chairs and dirty towels, knocking nothing over but distributing socks and bandages and flip-flops, wrapping everyone's feet in stolen hotel towels, and whispering in their ears to please wear boots or stay home.

In the West the sky is not one thing. You can see really different things going on in different parts of the sky at the same time. I love this. Women, someone said, are supposed to be scared of the spaciousness of the West but I love it here. I'm watching now as a storm moves across the sky to my left, with the biggest twister I've ever seen in it, and the sun shines to my right over the distant mountains. My pet snake Wilbur winds himself around my ankles and I think I can feel infinity in this immense sky because such different things can happen in it at the same time.

After our students have finished writing, we ask each of them to read aloud what they have written. We read what we have written as well. As they move from the classroom exercise to writing their own essay, our goal is to move students toward understanding the new thinking they're doing, to continue to use observation and conversation when writing their final essays, and to add thick descriptions that honor the materiality of the piece.

The Essay

After completing these three phases of classroom work, the students are more than prepared to do it on their own. We give students a list of galleries and museums and ask them to choose one, visit it, and select an artwork that particularly intrigues, excites, and/or puzzles them. The writing assignment duplicates the stages of the rite of passage. We help them mine for larger ideas and questions by eliciting memories of personal experiences connected to the artwork. We also recommend related texts that might prove helpful.

The following excerpt, taken from the middle of one student's final essay, reveals one way in which all our work together can provide a springboard into an original, rigorous essay. The first paragraph of this excerpt shows how Ted has lingered long enough in the initial encounter to be able to evoke the painting in a vivid way. He has also incorporated some of his initial description of the work, using carefully chosen adjectives and verbs from it. These foreshadow the ideas he will develop later in the essay:

Scott Herndon &
Kristin Dombek

> In one of Winslow Homer's more famous paintings, a fisherman alone in a dinghy is caught by a fast-moving storm, a cloud of fog crushing in from the horizon. The sun is being smothered, the whitecaps on the swells leaping eagerly, and the wave beneath his boat rocks it aside, about to slam it down into the next trough. The fisherman is not frantic, though. His oars are poised above the water, held steadily outward by strong, thick wrists. The man, in his drenched brown canvas jacket and pants, studies the clouds. His beard, his shoulder, his eyes, all point toward the horizon, toward the mucous-yellow light swallowed by a fog of purplish-gray. The fog steams off the water at the horizon, as if the sea is boiling out there and will soon scald the staring man in his errant boat. Out behind him, the larger fishing boat, from which he has launched his dinghy, streams away under full sail, threatening to disappear and leave him to fight the coming storm on his own with only his instincts and a pair of oars.

Ted stays very close to the original artwork, depicting it in a way that most any viewer would agree with. But in his next paragraph, he begins to raise questions inspired by the painting. His questions are mostly psychological—he wants to know what's going on in the man's head. Because the artwork does not provide him with easy answers, he begins to imagine possibilities. Here, we can see the remnants of the liminal stage, in which he entertained multiple interpretations:

> The wave that snatches the dinghy also pulls it away from the larger boat, in the opposite direction, and yet the man does not seem to take full notice; he is in awe of the instantaneous danger of the clouds. Does he even care about the menace of the storm? Face upturned into the bruising clouds, does he care about his death, or just the unexpected beauty of a natural, irresistible force? The fisherman watches the storm come to get him, waits for

a moment, taking stock of his enemy. He forms a clear image in his mind of the storm which will sink him to the ocean floor; he has paused a second too long. His chances of escape have dwindled to nothing as he stares stoically at the approaching clouds.

As Ted continues, he's inspired by a familiarity, a connection between the painting and his life. And so the questions raised by looking at Homer's painting begin to color his own memories, and he reproduces this movement for his readers as he leaves the painting behind. The foundation for this, of course, is the final stage that he practiced in class and on his own, dramatically personalizing the particular presence and power of the piece:

> It is my father's beard. The man in the boat has my father's beard; he strikes the pose of my father at his Sunday morning baseball games, watching a fly ball to right field from third base, neck turned almost ninety degrees, body still facing forward, ready to snatch a ground ball. There are other similarities. My father was cut adrift from his life, and it was just as much his fault as this fisherman's, who seems to have strayed too far in search of bigger fish. And now the two of them pause when they should act, take a deep breath when they should sprint or row. They should sustain the pace of that boat out there, that past enthusiasm for and dedication to being alive. But they are not, or have not yet started, and I cringe at the sight like the blonde cheerleader opening the closet door in any high school horror film. Now it is too late.

Ted goes on to investigate problems surrounding middle-aged masculinity, and the painting provides a touchstone. He weaves in the language of his initial description throughout, using boating, fishing, and being caught in a storm as metaphors for his father's struggles—and everyone's. This type of allegorical reading can backfire; it's tempting to read a painting only as an allegory for personal experience. But the preparatory work we've done in the classroom helps students to maintain a distinction between the artwork and themselves. Ted, for instance, had wrestled with and wondered about the Homer painting long enough to remain attentive to its composition and details, develop a range of possible interpretations of the scene, and vividly recreate for his reader the visual impact this powerful painting wields.

Our goal throughout has been to stave off the moment of interpretation until students have written something that is at once resolutely their own and a product of a conversation with a work of art. As a result, students have made a deep and rewarding inquiry into how the artwork came to affect their imaginations. They are much, much closer to more engaged, pleasurable, and challenging experiences in galleries and museums, on the one hand, and to more rigorous and imaginative writing, on the other.

Scott Herndon &
Kristin Dombek

Bibliography

Barthes, Roland. *Image Music Text*. Translated by Stephen Heath. New York: Hill and Wang, 1977.

Mann, Ted. "Fathers and Sons." Undergraduate essay, previously published in *Mercer Street*. New York University, 1999.

Zizek, Slavoj. *The Sublime Object of Ideology*. New York: Verso, 1989.

ACKNOWLEDGMENTS: The authors would like to thank the Expository Writing Program at New York University, in particular Pat C. Hoyll and the directors, for the ongoing conversations about teaching that made this essay possible.

The Verbal-Visual Nexus
Artists-in-Residence Teach Writing

by Tina Rotenberg

*d*URING MY FIRST YEAR AS THE DIRECTOR of Visual Arts/Language Arts (VALA), an organization I founded seven years ago, I took groups of young public school children from the East Bay to see an Imperial Chinese exhibit at the Asian Art Museum, a Mbuti exhibit at the UC Berkeley Art Museum, a Days of the Dead exhibit at the Oakland Museum, and a Guatemalan weaving exhibit at the Hearst Museum of Anthropology. It soon became clear to me that for these primarily African-American, Latino, and Asian-American children the visits provided an introduction to little-known or unknown cultures, histories, and literatures. Perhaps even more importantly, I realized that I was familiarizing these children with their own cultures. I decided to make it my objective, and VALA's, to expose public elementary school children to the arts and writings of different cultures not only so that they could learn something about diversity and art, but so that they could come away feeling a sense of pride and self-respect.

VALA now consists of fifteen artists, each hired to conduct five-week programs that typically involve either a visit to a museum or a performance in the classroom by the artist and/or by the children. The first three ses-

sions introduce the children to various artists, cultures, and art forms, and
the two final sessions are hour-and-a-half workshops focusing on hands-
on projects that bring together writing and art. A wide range of artists and
performers have worked for VALA: African-American jazz musicians,
Native American artists, a bookmaker, a sculptor, a ceramicist, a bilingual
artist who teaches Mexican folk dancing and music, a Mexican painter, and
two artists from PIXAR animation studios—to name a few.

VALA's strategy is to build programs that are thoughtful and challenging cross-cultural experiments and that explore widely diverse artistic fields, creatively employing resources in the community. It is our
intent to challenge artists, children, and classroom teachers. As a result,
each program is an original and distinct artistic-cultural-literary entity
(rather than a repetitive formula). The artists I've tended to hire are working professionals who are generally more accomplished as practicing
artists than as teachers of young children. Their sophistication and personal experience as artists, however, is an invaluable tool for articulating
complex, intricate, intuitive art-viewing and art-making processes to the
students.

Over the years, we have found that giving writing an important role
in the context of making art benefits both practices. Students who find
writing to be challenging are often freed up when they write in conjunc-
tion with drawing, painting, collage, and other more "free-form" art-making activities. Likewise, the students' artworks are usually much more
successful due to the inclusion of writing. Here are three profiles of VALA
teaching artists, which show some of the many possibilities for integrating writing into an art-based classroom.

Ben Shahn and Homelessness

Amy Trachtenberg is a visual artist from San Francisco who often crosses
into the disciplines of theater and literature. In her work with children,
she has focused on teaching a form of note-taking in the observed world
through drawing and writing. Amy's first VALA project confronted homelessness in a way that elicited very striking artwork as well as prose writing.
Amy began by introducing the children to her own work—by doing this
she established herself as a real working artist. The students took seriously
what she taught them about drawing techniques and observation strategies, and consequently they took their own artistic efforts seriously.

As the focal point for her program, Amy chose an exhibit of the Jewish artist Ben Shahn's posters at the Judah Magnes Museum in Berkeley. In the 1930s, Shahn emerged as a significant American painter and graphic artist dealing with the major social issues of his time: the Great Depression, union rights, and poverty. Shahn frequently emphasized strongly rendered images of hands to convey the plight and emotion of his politicized subject matter. From the start, Amy emphasized Shahn's commitment to and absorption in issues of social justice, stressing how Shahn used art as a tool for communication, not merely for self-expression.

The first project was a drawing exercise in which the students made charcoal and ink sketches of their hands. Amy demonstrated the ways charcoal could be handled—to create a smeared ground or atmosphere, or to draw a sharply defined line. Using both sides of the paper, the children did multiple drawings. As in all of her classes, Amy instructed the students to resist the temptation to trace their hands, and encouraged them to keep looking at their hands, as though their eyes were their pen.

Amy then focused on Shahn's poster designs and discussed how he took risks to make strong statements about social injustice. This led into a project that honed in on the issue of homelessness, a subject that the classroom teacher had spent some time discussing with the students before Amy arrived for her second session. The children began by writing first-person accounts about what they imagined it would be like to be a homeless person. Amy, the teacher, and I went around and read the children's writing, and helped each student pick out his or her most powerful statement: "I always wanted to start over" (see figure 15). "If a person ever told me to get off the streets, I would feel bad because every person deserves kindness, even a bug." The students then wrote their statements on strips of paper, using charcoal, ink, and tempera.

Meanwhile, Amy had taped up xeroxed photographs of people from different cultures—old, young, standing, reclining—that could serve as models for the student artists. Each student received a piece of 11" x 17" construction paper for creating their own images of homelessness. Amy discussed how artists use live models and photographs as well as the work of other artists. She stressed that these do not hamper the artist's imagination, but rather supply a variety of possibilities from which the artist can create new images. When they had finished their images, the students pasted their one-sentence strips on their posters. By the end of the session, each one of them had created a black-and-white poster with his or her own text.

In addition to being a singer and a printmaker, Debora Iyall, a VALA artist who is a member of the Cowlitz Tribe, is the set designer for ShadowLight Productions, a California theater group that combines Balinese shadow play techniques with traditional native storytelling. Although she joined VALA as a visual artist, she has put a great deal of effort into studying ways of including the language arts in her teaching, especially different poetic forms and exercises.

Tina Rotenberg

Last year, Debora worked with two fourth grade classes. She first presented a Native American story called "The Salmon Sisters." This story is part of a larger work called "Coyote's Journey," which is from the Karuk tribe and is narrated by Charlie Thom, a Karuk elder story teller. It is from the Indian oral tradition and often told by grandmothers to children. It presents a narrative of two rich sisters who kept all the salmon locked up in their house. All the animals held a council to decide who would go and free the salmon. Nobody wanted to go except for coyote, whom all the animals disparaged because he smelled so stinky. However, coyote successfully tricked the sisters by leading them away from their house to search for acorns—then he could free the salmon. After telling the story with the students' help, Debora wrote down a list of indigenous animals of the northern California coast. Finally, she gave some historical background to the story by discussing the negative impact of European contact and the Gold Rush on the indigenous human population.

In the second class, Debora showed the students how to draw animals from basic shapes, using different kinds of lines. After telling them that artists, like athletes, train regularly in order to develop and maintain their hand-eye coordination, Debora had the students do a warm-up exercise: using basic shapes, they drew the animals very large on loose, overlapping sheets of paper. These were then cut out and made into puppets, which represented different characters and scenes from the Salmon Sisters story. Every child wrote a line of dialogue on the puppet's back. This dialogue was inspired by the part of the story where all the animals get together and try to decide who will free the salmon from the two sisters.

In the third class, Debora and the students wrote a collaborative poem about animals. Then each child wrote an acrostic poem:

Owl

Owl flew off the tree,
Went through the woods, and
Landed back on the same tree.

—*Isaiah*

Jose's Owl Poem

Old
Wood
Land

—*Jose*

Elk

Energetic as a child
Like an iron wall
Keen as radar

—*Nick*

After they had written and illustrated their poems, they worked in groups on the landscape for their puppet show, and watched the ShadowLight video of the Salmon Sisters story.

In the fourth session, Debora told the Salmon Sisters story again, with the students' prompting. She went over each scene with them, writing it on the board. She assigned animal puppeteers, scenery puppeteers, and a narrator. The students went through the play with each group taking turns performing. The half of the class that was not performing worked on listening to the other half, learning to play "audience." Debora left the shadow screen and light for the teachers to work on with their students after she left.

This project involved the students in drawing and painting, and in writing both poetry and scripts; it also introduced them to aspects of theatrical production and presentation techniques closely related to film-making and active performance. By using ShadowLight techniques on a very basic level, Debora was able to use projected shadows to create "a new kind of theater which combines the power and scale of film with the immediacy of live performance."

Debora helped sustain her strong sense of a living spiritual and cultural heritage through her work with these children. Their involvement and enthusiasm for the project gave them insight into the imagination and a broader concept of how various cultures perceive the world.

Tina Rotenberg

Bookmaking

Alastair Johnston, a pioneer of the artist book movement in this country, apprenticed in letterpress printing and founded Poltroon Press with artist Francis Butler. As a VALA teaching artist, he incorporates poetry, storytelling, drawing, calligraphy, and traditional bookmaking techniques from around the world to create unique and challenging projects. A master of the creative genre called "word art," he is a poet and typographer, adept at putting others' words into typographic form. Alastair quite literally serves VALA's dual purposes—that is, he melds the visual and language arts together, teaching children how to make books and artful, ornate texts to go with them.

Recently, Alastair led two bookmaking workshops simultaneously: one with a fifth grade class at Cragmont School in Berkeley, the other with a fifth grade class at Lincoln School in Oakland's Chinatown. In the latter, all 30 children were Chinese and spoke Cantonese and Mandarin. He began both classes by explaining the drawn origins of our alphabet, using examples from ancient cultures. In the Oakland class, he drew Egyptian hieroglyphs for *water, sun*, and *rain*, and asked the Chinese children to call out the words in Cantonese and Mandarin. He went on to talk about phonograms and ideograms. In addition to hieroglyphs, he showed them how rebuses work (e.g., a picture of a bee for *be*; a picture of an eye for *I*) or numbers in place of letters ("L8R" for *later*). Alastair showed slides of Mayan and Egyptian hieroglyphs and explained the connection between pictures of objects and their symbolic and metaphoric connotations. He explained the magical properties of language and decoration in early illuminated manuscripts and explained how, with limited information, medieval scribes elaborated on tales of mythological creatures to create fantastical representations of these beings in the borders of their works. He showed an early printed book that recorded plagues and earthquakes, and showed fantastic creatures, such as mermen, mermaids, and freaks of nature (the *National Enquirer* of the sixteenth century!).

Alastair brought color photocopies of some of these mythological creatures from the medieval manuscripts. After passing them out, he asked the children to create their own mythological creature. Predictably, the boys began drawing Godzilla-type monsters, while the girls opted for more genteel Little Mermaid-type beings. Alastair, the classroom teachers, and their aides went around the room gently suggesting ways to create something more original. Alastair tried to get them to go more into the details of their story. For the boys whose creations were essentially robots of destruction, he tried to suggest ways in which their powers could be used for protection rather than harm. One student, J. Shawn, came up with "The Bone Collector" (the title of a recently-released movie) and made a drawing of a skull that had destructive powers. After one of the aides suggested that his skull might also protect people, he decided to refashion his text.

After revising their ideas, the children set happily to work creating their art. Alastair explained that the best way to do this for reproduction was to use strong black contours, leaving a border and keeping the image on the left half of the paper and the text on the right. He went around and helped the students with their titling, for which they used display letters based on the examples he had shown them. On the right, they each composed a description of the mythological creature. Alastair encouraged them to describe the creature physically and then to write about any special or magical powers it had. Here are three:

Caralamoo

Caralamoo has five heads, one human hand and four elephant legs. It can either walk or fly with its wings. He has a cloud castle that he lives in. When he is angry, his wings turn red and when Caralamoo is happy, his whole face smiles and turns white. Sometimes all of the heads argue with each other.

—Tangor

He is a mythological creature who loves to play tricks on humans. He loves to SCARE too! When he is mad he designs a big prank on everyone. He has two pairs of two hands, two legs sticking out of his sides, a tail and ears of a jaguar. He lives in the mountains. He does cartwheels to move. He gets his name from standing on his hands all the time.

Tina Rotenberg

—*Enkhee*

Neptune

Neptune lives in an underwater cave in the tropical part of the Caribbean. Although she does not need air, she comes just to look at what's there. She only comes up in the Bermuda Triangle because hardly anyone is there. She does not disappear in the Bermuda Triangle, and no one knows why.

—*Lovelyn*

In the interim, Alastair made twenty copies of each page that the children wrote and illustrated, reducing them on the photocopier. Before the final class, he printed a title page, then folded and collated all copies of the book, putting the images in alphabetical order by title, rather than by student. After collating the book blocks and covers, he punched five holes in each book. He gave each student thread and an upholstery needle and asked them to follow carefully as they stitched the books in a traditional Chinese manner. Two girls who finished early helped the others. The children then decorated the covers of their books and went around signing and inscribing their pages for each other.

During the program described here, the artist, drawing on his extensive knowledge of typography, writing, and bookmaking, became a kind of portable museum as he brought into the classroom an array of visual and verbal materials: slides, color xeroxes, and stories. Significantly, ancient and historical forms and methods were introduced side by side with examples from the immediate contemporary, or vernacular, environment. The students, even without being consciously aware of it, were encouraged to consider and observe their own present world (graffiti on a fence or a wall) in a nuanced, thoughtful way. From their first-hand experience in this class, students learned to associate value with things they do carefully and thoughtfully. The children were actively involved in making a collaborative art and writing project instead of being told in so many words that art is valuable and out of reach. The book ended up being not just a collaboration between the fifth graders, but a project in which they brought their imaginative skills together with Alastair's professional capabilities.

The students in Alastair's class each received a copy of the book they made to take home and keep. The project was successful in helping the children learn to value and care for the writing and artwork they do, instead of rejecting it.

Conclusion

One of VALA's goals is to inspire and energize classroom teachers to engage in new ways of teaching writing to their students on their own after the artists have left. There are a number of exemplary teachers who have adopted new approaches and techniques for teaching writing based upon their involvement with guest artists' programs this past fall. At Cragmont, for example, a fifth grade teacher has been using PIXAR animation artists' theater games for creating collaborative stories to motivate her students to write, and a first grade teacher has continued to use an elaborately designed method for teaching haiku that was introduced by a Filipino-Japanese brush painter and haiku instructor.

Even more strikingly, a third grade Chinese-American teacher from Lincoln contributed significantly to VALA artists' understanding of bilingual education and to their ability to teach writing to children whose first language is Chinese. At VALA's artist training workshop, she began her presentation with a five-minute description in Chinese, using hand movements to try to demonstrate how to make a pattern for a shirt, dramatically emphasizing the estranged and confused experience of students whose primary language is not English in a class where the instructor speaks only English.

Due to changing demographics, virtually *all* U.S. classrooms are multicultural and multilingual. Making art, looking at it, and listening to it provide essential resources for understanding other people, their cultures, and their ways of perceiving the world. Through art and writing, children who differ from each other make connections and encounter each other in fresh new ways that open up possibilities for richer related lives. I'm convinced that each of these creative media—art-making and writing—suffers from being sharply divided, and each benefits by being approached as a deliberate and exciting creative practice that children can learn to take pleasure in.

Tina Rotenberg

ACKNOWLEDGMENTS: Special thanks to Amy Trachtenberg, Debora Iyall, and Alastair Johnston. For information about VALA: Visual Arts/Language Arts, contact Tina Rotenberg at (510) 845-9610 or via email: tina@valaproject.org. The video of the Salmon Sisters story is available from ShadowLight Productions, 22 Chattanooga Street, San Francisco, CA 94114.

Ut Pictura Poesis

An Introduction to Surrealism

by Michael Theune

The surrealist poet in his use of words was approaching the painter's technique, and that is how a closer bond was established between poetry and art than ever before, and a greater gap between poetry and the literary forms that continued to have as their aim the expression of ideas.

—Anna Balakian, *Surrealism: The Road to the Absolute*

*i*T IS DIFFICULT TO INTRODUCE middle-school students to surrealism. In contrast to adults—who often admire surrealism for the temporary escape it affords them from the rules and regulations of daily life—young people frequently seek to distance themselves from all that is childlike and fantastical. Believing that art is serious and that to be serious is to be mature, many young writers use their creative writing as an opportunity to produce evidence that they can handle adult themes. The reticence young people display toward the bizarre and the strange reveals itself when, after having been creative, after having written something wild and new, they remove themselves from it by adding to their invention a clear sign that they were just kidding: "And then I woke up."

As a teaching writer in Houston's Writers in the Schools, I have found that young people need to be convinced of surrealism. To make surrealism appealing to my students, I try to attach it to specific pleasures and accomplishments. While I love using all manner of surrealist games (such as exquisite corpses and cut-ups), I have discovered that those activities are more successful when preceded by an exercise that involves writing poems based on surrealist paintings. The activity I have developed combines a survey of surrealist paintings with an introduction to the poetic form called the pantoum.

Michael
Theune

This activity begins with a brief discussion of the meaning of surrealism. I write "surreal" on the chalkboard, and then I ask if anyone knows what that word means. If someone does, I let him or her explain, adding to the conversation what I know. I break it down: "sur" means "above" or "beyond" and "real" means, well, the "real," the "common," the "everyday." Surrealism is art that is interested in things beyond the real: the imaginary, dreams and the unconscious, the part of the mind where dreams originate. In the first of his three manifestoes, André Breton, the leading proponent of surrealism, states, "I believe in the future resolution of these two states, dream and reality, which are seemingly so contradictory, into a kind of absolute reality, a *surreality*" (Breton, 14). Although I neither consider nor want what I say about surrealism to be an art history lecture, I believe enough should be shared about surrealism to make it seem like a movement, with an understandable worldview, and thus a fact young minds can attain. As a result, I'm always ready with a few details: that surrealism flourished between the two world wars, in the 1920s and the 1930s. The movement originated in France, but it was of international interest, and continued into the 1950s. Depending on the mood of the class, I may read and discuss the following quotation from Breton's second manifesto:

> The idea of surrealism aims quite simply at the total recovery of our psychic force by a means which is nothing other than the dizzying descent into ourselves, the systematic illumination of hidden places and the progressive darkening of other places, the perpetual excursion into the midst of forbidden territory. (Breton, 136–7)

While I make sure to provide students with enough information on surrealism to make surrealism itself seem real, the best way I've found to get students to consider the relevance of surrealism is by way of dreams. I ask: What are dreams? Where do they come from? After some speculation, I ask: Do dreams always make sense? No. Why not? Because they are filled with surprises; things show up where they usually aren't or shouldn't be. (The ballet dancer on the football field, the elephant in the underwear drawer). Even though dreams don't always make sense, can they make you happy? Can they make you sad? Or frighten you? Or give you ideas? Yes. Dreams, though often nonsensical, are powerful; their impressive images move us and stay with us.

Once the students have grasped that idea, I introduce them to my stack of postcards, a collection of about 100 images that change with almost every visit to a museum or used bookstore. The majority of the postcards feature art by surrealists and proto-surrealists, including Giorgio de Chirico, Salvador Dali, Max Ernst, René Magritte, Joan Miró, and Pablo Picasso. However, the stack also contains a number of images by "eternal surrealists," the name Breton gave to artists of many cultures throughout history who incorporated the exotic, the wild, and the strange into their work. These include William Blake and Vincent van Gogh.

Before distributing the individual postcards, I share one or two of them with the entire class. Because recognition leads to familiarity and increased comfort in dealing with the surreal, I try to use famous images like Dali's *The Persistence of Memory* for general discussion. Responding to initial reactions of "Huh?" and "Weird" and "I don't get it"—with the intermittent "Cool" and "Awesome"—I ask what's weird, what don't they get, what's cool. Student responses vary from "The clocks are melted" to "It looks like there's a closed eye on a melted face." Inevitably, there is a collective attempt to figure things out, and it is good to allow the class time to muse on what kinds of ideas the images convey.

This having been said, I think it's best to direct the conversation away from the analytical and the abstract. What's most important for the writing that the students are about to do is that they think about and respond to the images in specific, detailed ways. To demonstrate, I show them a postcard. Instead of focusing on the ostensible subject of the painting, I look in the background and create a detail from it. If I'm using de Chirico's *The Song of Love*, I might say "a green sky" or "a sickly sky" or "the dark beneath the doorway." I encourage them to imagine what's not there: "a missing hand," for instance, or "the silent speech of statues." If I'm using Miró's *The Nightingale's Song at Midnight and the*

Morning Rain (see figure 16), I might mention the "black and blue stars," "eyes rocketing through space," or, dreaming a little further "stars like thistles caught in the sky" or "a rough draft of the night sky." In order to give students practice, I ask them to think about a specific sense, perhaps that of touch: What would these objects feel like? Prickly. Great! A prickly galaxy. Bumpy. Yes! Bumpy waves. Sharp. Fantastic! The sharp blade of a star.

After the students seem to have the hang of it, I instruct them to make a list of the strange new details they discover in the postcards I proceed to distribute—typically each student receives two postcards. Every few minutes, I have them trade postcards. The feeling of this time is more energetic than meditative, and this is good. Students are creating and collecting images, not reflecting on them yet. And, because this is a prewriting time, I feel free to talk during it, checking in on their progress, encouraging them, and giving them additional ideas. After about ten or fifteen minutes, I tell the students to stop. We take a moment to share a few of their favorite lines before moving on to the final part of their writing assignment: the transformation of their detailed images into pantoums.

Officially, a pantoum consists of four or more quatrain stanzas in which the second and fourth lines of a stanza become the first and third lines of the following stanza. In the final stanza of a pantoum, the first and third lines of the first quatrain become the second and fourth lines. Additionally, there are a few tricks for pantoum writing. Lines one and three of the first stanza can be repeated either in their original order in the final stanza or else "flipped" so that line one becomes line four and line three becomes line two. To complicate matters further, the lines may be repeated exactly or by some close approximation (for example, punctuation may change). As you can tell, pantoums tend to be a form more difficult to understand in the abstract so I usually distribute copies of a pantoum to share with the class. Pantoums are plentiful and can be found in a number of places, including Ron Padgett's *Handbook of Poetic Forms*. Here is John Ashbery's "Pantoum":

> Eyes shining without mystery,
> Footprints eager for the past
> Through the vague snow of many clay pipes,
> And what is in store?

Footprints eager for the past,
The usual obtuse blanket.
And what is in store
For those dearest to the king?

The usual obtuse blanket
Of legless regrets and amplifications
For those dearest to the king.
Yes, sirs, connoisseurs of oblivion,

Of legless regrets and amplifications,
That is why a watchdog is shy.
Yes, sirs, connoisseurs of oblivion,
These days are short, brittle; there is only one night.

That is why a watchdog is shy,
Why the court, trapped in a silver storm, is dying.
These days are short, brittle; there is only one night
And that soon gotten over.

Why, the court, trapped in a silver storm, is dying!
Some blunt pretense to safety we have
And that soon gotten over
For they must have motion.

Some blunt pretense to safety we have:
Eyes shining without mystery
For they must have motion
Through the vague snow of many clay pipes.

I have found that the best way to address students' initial resistance to pantoums is to have them consider the pantoum form in much the same way they considered surrealism. I ask them to be clear about what interests them in the writing, about what is unclear, and about how this writing differs from other writing they have encountered. In doing so, I remind them that there's a long tradition of thinking about poems as pictures. Decades before the beginning of our last millennium, the Roman lyric poet Horace stated that "a poem is like a picture" (*ut pictura poesis*). The students are simply continuing the tradition.

While the pantoum may seem unintelligible as it creates a collage effect, promoting juxtapositions of images—Max Ernst claimed that one of the main interests of surrealism was "the fortuitous meeting of distant realities"—it helps introduce students to surrealism because it has easily identifiable rules. If, given a minute to look the pantoum over, students are asked to figure out the pantoum form, they can usually decipher it. The beneficial result of this is that the poem ends up seeming not only like a wild, bizarre text but also like a game, like a puzzle to be solved, a challenge to be undertaken and overcome. Students succeed just by figuring out the form.

Michael
Theune

Just prior to their pantoum writing, I make some suggestions and give some rules. I suggest that students consider combining some of their images to make sentences. For example, they could combine an image from de Chirico with one from Miró to make the line, "Black and blue stars hang in the sickly sky." I also suggest that students think a bit about their first and third lines as these are lines that will also serve to conclude the poem—what lines or images might work well to have both at the beginning and at the end of the poem? Then I give three rules. First, although students may add words to the pantoum that are not in their image list, they may not add too many; if allowed to write a pantoum not guided by the image list, students tend to write the specifics out of the poem. Second, students cannot use the words "dream" or "waking up" in their pantoum; surrealist images are already dreamlike and do not need to announce their dreamlike status. Third, although Ashbery calls his poem "Pantoum," students may not title their poem either "Pantoum" or "Dream"; titles are important parts of writing, and the creation of titles should be as creative as the decisions made about the images and structure of the poem. Then, the students write.

The above may seem like a lot of effort but really it isn't. In broad strokes, this writing project, which consists of image collection and organization, is rather simple. As some of the following pantoums show, this project can create strong poems with vivid images. The teachers with whom I worked even reported that a number of students were using pantoums for other writing projects they'd been assigned. In fact, one student ended up keeping a notebook by his television, jotting down clips of phrases he heard and describing images he saw, collecting the seeds of what later became a stunning poem.

I think much of the success of this project is due to the pantoum form itself. The pantoum form is a magical mix of contradictions and possibilities. It combines the enchantment of incantatory repetition with the energy of strange configurations, and it grafts onto its jolts of juxtaposition the satisfaction of circularity. At its supposed conclusion, the pantoum wakes up but it wakes up to itself, paradoxically and wonderfully continuing the dream. Additionally, the pantoum form is appealing because it allows students the sense that they are capable of writing beyond themselves. In reading over their own work, I think students encounter something amazing: a work that is personal, and yet was created by incorporating outside materials into a prescribed form. This enchanting contradiction, the inner and the outer unified, is the surrealist's dream—just as the hope the pantoum promises (that with a little orchestration something that begins in bewilderment can result in beauty) is the child's.

Answers

A taste of fiery water in the palm of my hand
Freezing fire floating
Birds flying into outer space
Crying, weeping, sobbing

Freezing fire floating
The blizzard blown to a tornado
Crying, weeping, sobbing
What to do? What to do?

The blizzard blown to a tornado
Kneeling on the floor
What to do? What to do?
The music screams my name

Kneeling on the floor
A taste of fiery water in the palm of my hand
The music screams my name
Birds flying into outer space

—*Cianne Jimenez*

Michael
Theune

The Tide

A horse gallops along a sandy desert
Sudden shouts, frantic footsteps
A wild chase begins
Sand flies up into the air

Sudden shouts, frantic footsteps
Past the stones with eyes
Sand flies up into the air
The tide is growing higher

Past the stones with eyes
Under large shadows of elephants in the air
The tide is growing higher
The ocean turns to rock

Under large shadows of elephants in the air
The hooves echo from the mountains
The ocean turns to rock
Horses float up, into the sky

The hooves echo from the mountains
A horse gallops along a sandy desert
Horses float up, into the sky
A wild chase begins

—*Josh Barr*

Ut Pictura
Poesis

A woman feeds a city of knowledge to a hungry child.
A dog stands on a mountain of dreams.
An animal bends to see the other side of life.
The sun is followed by a stream of pitch-black darkness.

A dog stands on a mountain of dreams.
A ladder reaches into the heavens.
The sun is followed by a stream of pitch-black darkness.
A bird screams out for a little help in life.

A ladder reaches into the heavens.
A pair of eyes peer into a new world.
A bird screams out for a little help in life,
Looking like it could use all the colors of a rainbow,

A pair of eyes peers into a new world.
A woman feeds a city of knowledge to a hungry child.
Looking like it could use all the colors of a rainbow,
An animal bends to see the other side of life.

—Chondra Dickerson

As these final poems show, not all of the poems employed a large number of surreal images, but, with the help of the pantoum form, all acquired a considerable emotional force.

This Is Different

My head is like hairspray.
It is hard
And tough.
I do what it tells me to do.

It is hard—
My thoughts are distant.
I do what they tell me to do.
I wait, listen.

My thoughts are distant.
It's weird.
I wait, listen.
This is different.

It's weird:
My head is like hairspray.
This is different
And tough.

   —Amanda Nelson

Michael
Theune

   Instead of combining various images from different surrealist works, the following poem focuses on one image—Dali's *Archaelogical Reminiscence of the 'Angelus' by Millet*—for its lines. It is a tribute to the importance of sometimes bending the rules, of skirting the edge of the project's guidelines.

View

I was holding my father's hand.
We lifted our necks high into the air.
The sculpture was so high.
We gasped in amazement.

We lifted our necks high into the air.
Your mother would have loved to see this, he said.
We gasped in amazement.
It was a breathtaking view.

Your mother would have loved to see this, he said.
My neck hurt.
It was a breathtaking view.
I looked down to ease the pain.

My neck hurt.
I was holding my father's hand.

I looked down to ease the pain.
The sculpture was so high.

—*Kadie Palma*

Bibliography

Balakian, Anna. *Surrealism: The Road to the Absolute.* Chicago: University of Chicago Press, 1986.

Breton, André. *Manifestoes of Surrealism.* Translated by Richard Seaver and Helen R. Lane. Ann Arbor: University of Michigan Press, 1969.

Padgett, Ron, ed. *The Teachers & Writers Handbook of Poetic Forms.* Second edition. New York: Teachers & Writers Collaborative, 2000.

Her Umbrella Was Made of Leaves

Teaching Photography and Writing at the Boys and Girls Club

by John & Julie Moulds Rybicki

*i*F YOU WANT TO SEE A CHILD LIGHT UP, give him or her a camera and say: Go, show me the world. Recently, my wife and I were lucky enough to co-teach a series of four-week photography and writing workshops with photographer Mary Whalen. The workshops, held at the Boys and Girls Club of Greater Kalamazoo, were sponsored by the Voices arts program. We knew full well that our students, ages eight through sixteen, did not register for each workshop because they were dying to write; it was the camera that lent glamour to the class. But through the lure of the visual medium, we discovered ways to inspire the students to ignite the page with their writing.

At the start of each course, Mary Whalen led students on one or two days of intense shooting. She guided students to look deeper into the world, to try to catch on film in shadows and light something that might awaken the viewer to a new way of seeing. In other words, we snapped a lot of black-and-white pictures hoping one of them would be something large and transcendent; a single photo that was a novel, a short story, or a poem. (Before students started shooting, Mary always had each student take a photo of his or her face, an easy way to identify who shot each roll of film.)

One of our most exciting course excursions took us 150 miles east of inner-city Kalamazoo into inner-city Detroit, where artist and visionary Tyree Guyton was up to something large indeed. Guyton had taken an entire city block of abandoned houses and automobiles and turned it into a wonderland of urban art. His Heidelberg Street landscape was replete with tennis shoes dangling like ornaments from the trees; a polka-dot house over here; old car hoods over there, leaning against the trees like medieval war shields a giant might use, each hood painted with the faces of children, what Guyton calls "the Faces of God." Picasso-esque in its fractured form and use of color, Guyton's art can haunt your every waking step and change you for good.

As the group of high school boys tumbled from our van with their cameras in hand, they were wonder-struck, as if they had just landed on the moon. They plunged into Guyton's vast garden of art, snapping pictures of the junked cars and tennis shoes, toilet seats and mirrors.

The next week, at the Boys and Girls Club in Kalamazoo, Mary introduced the students to the darkroom. They dunked their photos into developing solution, watching them appear magically as art. While half of the boys learned to print, Julie and I gathered the other students around a table. Before class, Mary had developed each boy's black-and-white film, printed contact sheets for each, and marked the most promising photos. We used their proof sheets as a focal point for inspiration, having the students write titles and pieces about the marked photos.

Julie and I begin each of our writing classes by having students compose, one at a time, out loud. Even a child with remedial writing skills can often speak a beautiful river of a sentence. When he or she does, we ring out with, "Write that down!" This way, almost every writer has already succeeded. We also encourage students to forget about spelling and punctuation in their first drafts, and to let their ideas flood out onto the page. We urged this group of kids to find something in their Heidelberg Street photos that triggered their senses or some emotion up from the heart's core. We asked them to break the laws of nature in their writing, to speak as if they were objects on that street: "What do you see or feel or fear?"

After three sentences, some of the kids felt their pieces were done. We posed a series of questions to keep them going: "What might your personified object do at night? In the rain? In the cold? What other objects on the street struck you? Why not have them come to life in your writing and enter the drama? What are the other objects on the street doing? Give them a voice." Thus, brief pieces came to fill a paragraph or page. One student in the class, Sammie Gray, was so mesmerized by the bus he photographed on Heidelberg Street—a replica of the one Rosa Parks rode on—that he became the bus, and this triggered a haunting torrent of language:

John & Julie
Moulds Rybicki

Heidelberg Street Bus

I am a bus on Heidelberg Street. I am too old to move, and I can't open my eyes. At night I come to life and ride to the bad neighborhoods and pick up the homeless, let them sleep on my floor. When I ride through this neighborhood, I honk at the shoes and they start dancing in the trees. The toilet seat dangling from the tree just hangs there. That's it, it's just hanging out. Sometimes I watch the bathtub drive the shoes and the teddy bears around. That's their car.

Some nights the shoes line up like soldiers and the captain of the shoes marches them to the Detroit River. The shoes swim in the river and take baths. They go and look for homeless people. They also look for people who wore them long ago. They see all the beautiful lights over in Canada and walk on water and start looking for their owners over there. They slip onto people's feet to check if that's their owner. If it doesn't feel right they slip off again. What the shoes want most of all is to be back with their owners—they want to be wanted.

Jeremy Russel had photographed a mirror amidst the objects littered across an empty lot on Heidelberg Street. In his writing, he entered the mirror world:

Mirror of Heidelberg

I am a mirror on the street in the Heidelberg Project. I have so many companion things. I often party with the shoes at night, but someone just told me something that made me think. I can see everything. I can reflect anything but I have no face. You can look in my direction but all you see is yourself. It hurts me so bad, I have nothing to offer. All I can tell you is the story of others. I feel as though I should give up. But I never quit. I symbolize persistence because I never stop reflecting constantly, shining the stories of others. So remember me and never give up.

Titles, Narratives, and Revision

At the end of each class, we had an art opening. At these exhibitions, we wanted the two media, photography and writing, to harmonize. Our first step toward creating harmony was to create strong titles. We asked the kids to come up with three possibilities for each photo in the show. Usually one of the titles worked, but often a student would use a combination. For instance, Emeshia McMillian's long and lively title—*All That and Everything Vaneisha: Her Umbrella Was Made of Leaves*—put together two of her titles. If students were still having trouble titling their works, we asked the kids questions to elicit more options. When we encouraged them to look away from the page and speak their ideas, the roadblocks would nearly always vanish. Some of our favorite titles included these by Brian Robinson, Aaron Menter, Dante Robinson, and Emeshia:

> *A Cage on the Sun* (a jungle gym on a playground)
> *The Sleeping Frog Had a Belly Button* (a ceramic frog)
> *Paper and Boy* (a newspaper boy)
> *Lookgood Martin* (a handsome basketball player)

Once the photographs were titled, we moved on to writing prose narratives about the photographs. We dared children both to summon up literal experience and tell a glorious lie, using their imaginations to make the kinds of intuitive leaps that might seem breathtaking to the reader. Emeshia, a student in nearly every photography class we taught at the Boys and Girls Club, wrote:

> Vaneisha was hiding out because it looked like it was going to rain. Even if it did rain, she would still get wet, because the umbrella was made of leaves. If all the umbrellas in the world were made of leaves, I would put shirts over them.

Another favorite of ours was by Mya Shepard, whose lovely photo of three young cousins huddled together was entitled *Ring Around the Girls*:

> Three girls are enjoying the basketball game, Edison versus Woods Lake. The game is going to be the bomb and the girls are going to cheer Edison on. They're going to go "Yea! Yea!" The girls are my cousins. They are related to my grandmother. Half the kids in Kalamazoo are my cousins.

John & Julie
Moulds Rybicki

If the young writers faltered, producing lukewarm lines or hazy images, we asked questions in an effort to trigger some breakthrough in the writing. For example, Mya expanded her piece after she was asked, "What teams were playing? Who are these girls? What are they yelling?"

As before, the children's stories often involved personifying the objects in their photographs. Nine-year-old Marcus Robinson wrote the story below about his camera after we asked him if it had magic powers. We went on to ask him, "Where does it like to go? What does it like to eat? What makes it mad? What is it afraid of?"

My Camera

> My camera is black. He has one eye on top and has a nose that can go in and out. If I take a picture with my camera, he will make you look better. My camera can make you have different clothes on. My camera goes on vacation in Camera World. He goes to see his camera mom and camera dad. He likes peas and tomato juice and vegetables. He doesn't like marshmallows. He gets mad if you mess with him. My camera is afraid of fire, afraid he might melt and burn. If you erase my camera with an eraser, he will disappear.

After a while, students internalized this method of questioning, and started asking themselves and other students the questions that would expand their pieces.

Sports Poems

We also sent the students out into the community to photograph local organizations, personalities, and events. One group of teen boys wrote a series of sports poems after visiting a minor league baseball team, the

Kalamazoo Kodiaks. The boys were invited to meet and interview the players and act as photographers for the game. They peppered the players with questions and snapped dozens of shots—a bat over some slugger's shoulders as he eyed the distance; a spray of dust as a player slid into home plate. Their photographs seemed to capture the dreams these players had of someday making it to the big leagues.

With this group of boys, we focused on writing poems to complement the strongest photos they had taken. We encouraged them to reach for something transformational and large that would spark powerful words to tumble onto their pages. As models for the baseball poems, we used two pattern poems: "He," by John Ashbery, a poem that begins each line with "He is . . ." and "Of 1826," by John Berryman, a "Dream Song" that begins each line with "I am. . . ."

Chris Betke wrote this baseball dream piece to accompany his photos of a pitcher:

> The pitcher dreams of a naked woman holding a bat. The pitcher goes to church with his baseball bat and baptizes it. At night, he sleepwalks across the baseball field where he meets a lot of women. The bases start to float in the sky and fly in circles. Baseball bats start slapping at the pads while the women smile at the pitcher with red lipstick on their lips. They're cheering for him and the stadium lights are flickering on and off in different colors, while the moon turns bright purple and sweats candy onto the field.

In another sports-themed course we taught with Mary Whalen, we had students write letter poems to and from their skateboards, their feet, and their double-Dutch jump ropes.

Marcus Robinson wrote from the point of view of a basketball hoop: "If I were a basketball rim, I wouldn't like things going through my head."

Portraits

Near the end of the Voices program, some of the students were ready for more advanced training. To cap off the year, Mary held two more technical workshops, one focusing on shapes, one on light and shadow. To inspire students to look more critically at shapes in their photos, Mary had them find the letters of their names in objects in the outside world. For instance,

John & Julie
Moulds Rybicki

Ondreya Anderson found the letter "O" in the circle at the bottom of a basketball net. To complement Mary's teaching goals for this session, we used that old standby, the acrostic poem. We both generally dislike this activity, but here it suited our needs perfectly, as shown by Ondreya's acrostic (see figure 17):

O ne day, on a

N ice day, a girl named

D ominique was riding her

R aggedy bike and

E verybody always

Y elped and made

A nna, Dominique's friend, leave.

The final combined photo-poem results of this activity, professionally framed by Mary, were much admired on the walls of the Boys and Girls Club.

In every class, Mary took a portrait of each student. When the student's work was displayed or published, people could connect the child's face with his or her work; viewers enjoyed this extra connection to the creators of the pieces. To go along with this practice, we adapted several "self-portrait" writing activities that merged well with the student portraits on display. To begin, we had students draw the elements of their faces one at a time: hair, eyes, ears, mouth, nose, head, chin, etc. The simpler the illustration, the better.

After the students made their drawings, we had them come up with four or five images that their pictures reminded them of. For instance, one boy who drew his close-cropped hair saw it as a row of soldiers, a lawn, a comb, and a long line of baseball bats. A girl with braids saw her hair as snakes, ropes, a road, and braided bread. A curly-haired boy saw his hair as tires, plates, moons, and Frisbees.

First we had students go through at least four or five characteristics of the face and generate a list of images, and then move on to the body. A good example came from Marcus Robinson:

My eyebrow looks like a cattail, a waterfall, and a bird.

My finger looks like a hat, a Mr. Potatohead, and a football.

My belly button looks like a drawer, a circle, a lens in a pair of glasses.

My arm looks like a spider, a hill, a hook, and a slide.

After that, we encouraged the students to extend the images. India McElrath expanded upon her original list nicely, dropping lines she was less interested in:

My mouth looks like a big old kiss that is shaped like a heart.

My eye looks like a cloud shaped like a piece of meat.

My hair looks like some water splashing on a radish.

My ear looks like a rainbow or a tablemat.

Young writers are so close to the imagination, but it remains important for teachers to remind them that emotion adds essential heat to any piece of writing. We need to urge students to use their physical images to trigger emotional statements; take, for instance, this self-portrait poem by Leshaye Nelson, a fifth grader at Pelham Magnet Middle School in Detroit:

My hair looks like a shadow
in the sky. Should you ask why,
a shadow in the sky?

My ear looks like the three
layers of water in the quietness
of the city. Out of all the goodness
of me, the quietness of the city
is the love kind to me.

My hair looks like a shadow
in the sky. Should you ask why
a shadow in the sky?

The Kalamazoo students then superimposed their poems onto their black-and-white portraits. Julie and I typed up the portrait poems and Mary photocopied them onto sticky-backed, clear acetate paper. We then let students cut and arrange lines of poetry on their photographed faces.

In other classes, we had students recopy self-portrait poems with special metallic pens that write on photographs. Children transcribed the lines celebrating their nose around their nose, etc., and then colored in their faces with a rainbow of regular markers. These wildly colored photos with poems spiraling around their borders were striking and sometimes quite beautiful. This activity also worked well with photocopies of photographs, on which students could use crayons and colored pencils.

Another exercise complementary with student portraits was "Self-Portrait as an Animal," based on Donald Hall's poem "Self-Portrait, As a Bear." The samples below were written by a group of young mothers in the "My Life, My Lens, My Child" program, which used the Boys and Girls Club's darkroom. The teens chose from hundreds of animal photos torn from a wildlife desk calendar. Studying her chosen photo, each young woman imagined herself as a wolf, a rabbit, or a tiger. Some of these pieces were like spiritual biographies. Cristen Nesius, a student at Comstock High School, described herself as a mommy duck:

> I swim here in the pond with my newly hatched ducklings. I am a mommy duck, and my biggest problem now is to keep my babies from harm. They need to be taught and they need to be raised. This fall they must fly south and the flock has to show them the way. Next year they will be back in this spot and having ducklings of their own. Until then, I must teach them right, and keep them safe from harm, so someday they may make me proud.

The resulting self-portraits were displayed for a month at a local café, after an opening replete with sheet cake and an Irish fiddle trio.

Student Exhibitions

Two aspects of the photo-poem project made it special—and fun—for the kids. The first was the "photo shoot" field trips. These trips, usually low-cost, included attending a semi-pro baseball game, a zoo, an art gallery, and a women's volleyball practice. The club supplied a van and a driver, usually arts director and playwright Lisa Miller, who was critical to the program's success.

Other photo shoots were on-site—at the club itself, at Edison Elementary School next door, or in the neighborhood surrounding it. At their school gym, the kids "covered" a sixth grade boys' basketball game, running down the sidelines like sports photographers. Another day, students posed for shadow photos behind thin cotton backdrops on the school stage, using theatrical props and lights supplied by a lighting technician from the local university.

Perhaps most rewarding for the students was the joy of having their photography and writing displayed at more than one art opening. A month before each event, Toni Baldwin, Voices program director (also a visual artist), sent press releases to reporters and local dignitaries. A week before the exhibit, students filled out six invitations at the club, to be given to parents and relatives. Julie and I typed up all the poems. Mary framed each child's best photos, using museum quality frames and mattes, and dry-mounted the writings.

On opening night, family and community leaders arrived to *ooh* and *ah* over the show and to consume juice and baked goods. The students were celebrities for the day, mobbed by people commending them for their artistic achievements. The teen boys even made postcards from their photos and sold them. The kids went home filled with cake and glory, but it did not stop there.

Newspaper reporters covered the exhibits, using child-created poems and photos in their articles. Several students were interviewed about the program on Ann Arbor's National Public Radio station. Voices eventually sponsored an end-of-program traveling exhibit that brought the club's photos to schools, libraries, and malls in the area. The exhibition succeeded in bringing much well-deserved attention to an organization, the Boys and Girls Club, which does much good in the Kalamazoo community. Though the Voices program is now completed, the photographs and writings created by Boys and Girls Club members still decorate the building's activity room and boardroom.

For Julie and myself, a great satisfaction also came from team-teaching with Mary Whalen. The three of us quickly saw how naturally photography and creative writing could work together. When we met to discuss each course's themes (my neighborhood, sports, acts of art, light and shadow), the writing activities emerged organically. We urge all teachers of art and creative writing to try collaborative projects like this one.

Ashbery, John. "He." In *Selected Poems*. New York: Penguin, 1985.

Berryman, John. "Of 1826." In *The Dream Songs*. New York: Farrar, Straus & Giroux, 1969.

Fleming, Gerald. *Keys to Creative Writing*. Boston: Allyn & Bacon, 1991.

Hall, Donald. "Self-Portrait, As a Bear." Quoted in *The Poetry Connection* by Kinereth Gensler and Nina Nyhart. New York: Teachers & Writers Collaborative, 1978. Reprinted from *The Alligator Bride*. New York: Harper & Row, 1969.

ACKNOWLEDGMENTS: The photo-poem courses at the Boys and Girls Club were part of the Voices program, funded by a Federal Law Enforcement Grant and administered by the Kalamazoo Institute of Arts from June 1997 through September 1998. Special thanks to Bob Ezelle of the Boys and Girls Club of Greater Kalamazoo, and to the InsideOut writing program, for allowing Leshaye Nelson's self-portrait poem to be reprinted. Thanks also to Family and Children Services of Kalamazoo and Comstock Alternative High School for their sponsorship of the "My Life, My Lens, My Child" photography classes, and to Jaimy Johnson at the Kalamazoo County Juvenile Home Day Treatment Program.

For information on Tyree Guyton's Heidelberg Project, visit his website at heidelberg.org or write to the following address: The Heidelberg Project, P.O. Box 19377, Detroit, MI 48219.

John & Julie
Moulds Rybicki

Tim Rollins + K.O.S.

The *Amerika* Series

by Michele Wallace

*i*N 1981, TIM ROLLINS WAS A TWENTY-SIX-YEAR-OLD white artist from Maine who had studied with Joseph Kosuth at the School of Visual Arts; had co-founded Group Material, an alternative space and advocacy group for socially committed art; and who taught art as part of the special education program at I.S. 52 in the South Bronx. At the time, he made the highly unconventional and radical decision that he would combine his own art-making with the teaching of art to black and Puerto Rican public school children. This decision led to the founding of K.O.S., which stands for Kids of Survival, and the Art & Knowledge Workshop.

Together with a small, evolving group of "learning disabled" and "emotionally handicapped" kids from the South Bronx, Rollins began a process of political art-making which had the dual purpose of educating kids in the South Bronx about the world outside and educating the world outside about the South Bronx. But the real breakthrough in methodology came when Carlito Rivera, one of the kids in the Workshop, drew on one of Tim Rollins's books. "I wanted to kill him at first," Rollins says, "but boy, it looked great. And it was wild because here you have this dyslexic kid who couldn't read a word of the book, but in the drawing on the page—boom! there it was—all in an image. How did this kid know that this was the essence of the book?"

It was a breakthrough precisely because the heartbreaking struggle around literacy and reading was so central to the problem of critical and pedagogical resistance among radical teachers like Rollins and the counter-resistance it inevitably aroused among poor black and Puerto Rican kids in the South Bronx and other urban ghettos. At the heart of the difficulty were the so-called "learning disabled" and "emotionally handicapped" kids Rollins was working with; these categories of students are endlessly expanded by the Board of Education in order to accommodate the increasing numbers of children of color considered ineducable. Painting on text—moreover, the classical text of European art and literature—became a way of simultaneously staging a protest against the failure of our educational system as it is conceptualized by the dominant discourse, and of de-territorializing the still-remaining instructive vitality of high modernism.

"The making of the work *is* the pedagogy," Rollins explains. "The art is a means to knowledge of the world. That's why our project is so different from regular school—the kids are immersed in production—cultural production." The destruction and the construction of the text are held in a precarious balance as Rollins pays homage to his education (a B.F.A. from the School of Visual Arts and an M.A. in Art Education from New York University) by taking the kids to museums, reading to them from the "classics," and by teaching them the mechanics of art-making; and the kids pay homage to their education in prison-like schools and in the streets of a crack- and AIDS-ridden South Bronx by sharing with Rollins their emotional and aesthetic sensitivities. They join forces in their mutual instrumentalization of the text in the realm of the visual. Often the roots of their common understanding of images draws upon the abject in popular culture, for example, in horror movies and monster comic books such as Marvel Comics' *X-Men. X-Men*, which began as a comic book series in the 1960s, is about a group of teenage mutants whose deformities give them superpowers to fight evil in the world. Their spiritual and intellectual leader is a bald-headed professor who communicates with them by telepathy.

Although Rollins is nothing like the bald-headed professor in the comic book, the members of K.O.S. like to think of themselves as the X-

Men, and *X-Men* comic books are listed first on a Workshop bibliography—which K.O.S. distributes in its fairly frequent public appearances on panels—that "may help you develop a deeper understanding of our work." That bibliography also includes Paulo Freire's *A Pedagogy of the Oppressed*, Ralph Waldo Emerson's essay on "Self-Reliance," Henry David Thoreau's *Walden*, Gilles Deleuze and Félix Guattari's *Kafka—Towards a Minor Literature*, Robert Coles's *Children of Crisis*, George Bataille's *Literature and Evil*, Lionel Trilling's *Beyond Culture*, Dr. Seuss' *The Cat in the Hat*, Tillie Olsen's *Silences*, and *The Autobiography of Malcolm X*.

It is doubtful whether many of the students have read these works. At different times, some of the members of K.O.S. have been dyslexic, which makes it difficult for them to read. Those members of K.O.S. who can read admit they find it boring. But the object of this exercise is more the critical pedagogical environment which the bibliography, the production of the work, and the process have created. That workshop participants should aspire to intellectual growth is implicit in all their work. If they haven't read the books, the books are there for them to read, and the encouragement is there as well. More to the point, Rollins says, "The work is about survival—survival as individuals, as a group, as a people, a nation, a species. And it's about the survival of the books themselves, literature, language, culture. That's why knowledge is so important, because without knowledge about how the world works and where our ideas and hopes come from, there can be no freedom, there can be no democracy. Knowledge isn't power in itself—it's what you *do* with information that makes a difference. Our artworks are teaching machines."

But even more to the point, Rollins embraces the pedagogical philosophy of Paulo Freire, the renowned Brazilian educator who maintains that progressive and liberatory education is, necessarily, dialogical. By this Freire means that the dominant model for education should not be a passive transfer of knowledge from teacher to student but rather the active dialogue of teacher and student. Of course, the problem here is that dialogue is the hallmark of the elite, private school education. In contrast, public school education de-emphasizes personal contact and exchange between teachers and students because small classes are too expensive. Also, the pedagogical ideal tends to be authoritarian, perhaps partly in order to make a preference out of a necessity. (A lot of teachers are simply concerned with maintaining "control" in the classroom.) But the gravest

obstacle of all to the dialogic, multicultural classroom, which confronts
even the most radical and committed teacher today (even if that teacher is
a person of color), is finding a common language in which dialogue and
the production of knowledge can take place. "I don't believe in self-liber-
ation," Freire says in *A Pedagogy for Liberation*. "Liberation is a social
act. Liberating education is a social process of illumination....Even when
you individually feel yourself most free, if this feeling is not a social feeling, if you are not able to use your recent freedom to help others to be free
by transforming the totality of society, then you are exercising only an
individualist attitude towards empowerment or freedom."

Even if the revolutionary austerity of such a program is not entirely
appealing, Freire is still making a crucial point here about how one might
teach critical literacy, not only to the children of the middle class and children who can already read, but also, crucially, to the increasing numbers of
children, particularly children of color, who are being trained and prepared only to linger on the margins of the status quo.

As for the common language in which a dialogue can take place
between teacher and students, and not just any dialogue but a dialogue
which moves the student toward critical engagement with the text of Western culture, Rollins has come up with a very special answer. "We make art
with books, and we turn books into art," Rollins says. In response to which
Richard Cruz, one of the Workshop members, says, "I guess art is one of
the only ways we show our point of view about how we see the world." "Our
paintings are us," Annette Rosado adds, "and we're showing ourselves to
people like an open book." Which seems, at least, a beginning.

Ironically, these "teaching machines" have propelled K.O.S. to the
tangible art-world success of having a dealer and having their work
included in the collections of The Museum of Modern Art, Charles
Saatchi, and The Chase Manhattan Bank. So far the income has gone right
back into K.O.S.'s foundation, which has allowed the Workshop to become
independent from the censorship-prone machinations of federal funds for
the arts and from the bureaucracy of the public school system, which
would prefer that they emphasize quantity over quality. As is conventional
in art education programs, the focus would then be on training good art
consumers, not astute cultural producers. The foundation pays salaries and
stipends and underwrites the trips that the Workshop has made around the
country and around the world to see and to make art. But the most impres-

sive form of their success so far has been a critical pedagogical process which daily seeks to transform the lives of Workshop participants as well as the community around it, for it is a model that might be adapted for use in a variety of educational settings.

✢ ✢ ✢ ✢ ✢ ✢ ✢ ✢ ✢

The first *Amerika* painting I ever saw was *Amerika—For the People of Bathgate, 1988*, which appears on the wall of Central Elementary School 4 on Bathgate Avenue in the South Bronx. I was in a taxicab with Tim Rollins on a cold Saturday morning in February riding into a desolate neighborhood which is apparently abandoned on the weekends—no people, just that inexorable urban grayness—when we turned the corner of Bathgate Avenue, and there it was looming above us. Right away I had to smile. The painting made no pretense of being anything but paint; yet a series of golden horns as abstract and wild in variation as characters in Dr. Seuss seemed to be flying about in space, raising a joyous, clattering, anarchic racket in the morning light. I could almost hear it. Moreover, I could not stop wanting to look at it.

The reproductions and transparencies I had seen of the *Amerika* series the week before in The Dia Foundation's SoHo offices had scarcely prepared me for such pleasure. While they seemed both agreeable and amusing, I must admit that I am no longer easily impressed by paintings. For me, the way the paintings are made and what is to be made of the paintings have to be at least as important as any reading I might have of their intrinsic quality. For "painting" does not merely signify my grandmother's Sunday painting for her own amusement, or even my mother's successful painting as a feminist artist, but rather the endless reproductions of Leonardo da Vinci's *Mona Lisa*, which toured the U.S. when I was a child, or Vincent van Gogh's *Sunflowers*, which was sold for millions of dollars.

Therefore, it seems appropriate to include "the painting" in what Walter Benjamin refers to as "cultural treasures," which he advises us to view with "cautious detachment." His famous statement that "there's no document of civilization which is not at the same time a document of barbarism" can also be interpreted to mean that European high culture not only reconsolidates white dominance of the political and economic spheres, but also repetitively restages the barbarism of the original conquests of imperialism and colonialism by excluding people of color, poor people, and third world people from the production of "cultural treasures." In particular, the individual "painting" executed by the individual "artist" has become a symbol of the intense reification and alienation which plagues and deforms the utopian potential of cultural production in the West. Moreover, the history of fine art in the West seems calculated to render the art of the "other" as the exotic, primitive exception to their usual systematic exclusion. In the art world, white is still right, and the issues of race, class, and cultural diversity are eternally mystified behind the rhetoric of "quality" and "standards" and "high culture".

So, it was the process of Tim Rollins + K.O.S., the idea of a multicultural collaboration which would focus as much on the political and cultural transformation of the people involved as on the vagaries of the art market, that attracted me. Accordingly, it was just as well that the first *Amerika* painting I saw was the Bathgate mural, for it is perhaps the consummate public work. So perfectly and subversively discontinuous with its lifeless public space, it gave me a chance to realize that, in fact, the collaborative and inclusive mode of production of Tim Rollins + K.O.S. does make a difference in the end result of the work itself. Not only does the "Amerika" series find its perfect venue, in a sense, on the wall of a South Bronx public school, it is also successful at transforming that space at the level of the visual. As in the live performances of New Music groups like Sun Ra, Ornette Coleman, or the World Saxophone Quartet, the formal unity of vision we so deeply desire in art had somehow been seduced into a truce with the articulation of diverse "visions" and "voices." I refer to "voices" and "visions" even as *Amerika*'s golden horns seem to be laughing at the possibility of mimesis. The visualization of musical instruments so bizarrely deformed raises the question of music and harmony even as it bypasses the literal response.

The most fascinating thing of all was that it was somehow obvious that more than one person had a hand in *Amerika—For the People of Bathgate*. An aura of improvisation associated with jazz and ordinarily inconceivable in the concrete and material terms of the visual sphere seemed present as well. "Difference" is held "in a state of balance," Jean Fisher has aptly said of the *Amerika* paintings, in a "celebration of cultural heterogeneity." I now like to think that just seeing the Bathgate mural would have also given me some inkling of the history of the extraordinary collaborative and pedagogical process employed by Tim Rollins + K.O.S. in the making of the *Amerika* series (see figure 18).

✧　✧　✧　✧　✧　✧　✧　✧　✧

But in addition to the important accomplishments growing out of this collaboration, there are problems for me, as well, with the success story of
Tim Rollins + K.O.S., the first and most obvious of these being their name
and the fact that of the group only Rollins (because he's white, male, and
educated?) has had an individual identity in the art world. The other two
difficulties are actually two sides of the same dilemma. On the one hand,
there is their critical and irreverent approach to "modernism" and "high
culture." This seems to be Rollins's choice, stemming from his background
in conceptual art, his admiration for the ideas of Joseph Beuys, and his
role as co-founder of Group Material. On the other hand, there is their failure to be significantly engaged by multicultural texts or issues.

These form two sides of the same problem because the preoc-
cupation with demonstrating a critical approach to modernism tends to
render superfluous and unsophisticated the exploration of various ethnic
or even sexual specificities. This conflict has always prevented a white,
male, political avant-garde in the arts from becoming seriously and critically engaged by non-white and/or non-male, political avant-gardes in the
arts—especially since not infrequently texts and art by people of color are
actively involved in constructing modernist aesthetic and philosophical cri-
teria of their own.

Despite the widespread notion among white scholars and critics that
modernism is exclusively high European and, therefore, lily white and,
therefore, something that should pass like apartheid, there has emerged
among black critics in literary criticism at least (and it seems to me relevant to discussions of black cultural production in music, dance, theater,
and the visual arts as well) a parallel notion of black modernism (or black
modernisms). The term *modernism* is used not in order to periodize but in
order to describe sometimes ongoing aspects of cultural production in the
Third World and the cultural production of what Gayatri Spivak refers to
as "internal colonization" in the so-called First World (which would appear
to include almost all "minority" cultural production).

I do not want to get into a discussion here about the features of modernism except to say that they would obviously include some of the most
widely held and thoroughly institutionalized values about what art "is"

and ought to be in the present. By borrowing the term "modernism" in
order to describe some varieties of "minority" art practice, I not only
mean to choose this way to name those features that mark intense European or white American influence in black or "minority" cultural production (such as the very concepts of the individual artist, the novel, the
painting, or the symphony), but also to identify where black or minority
cultural production has borrowed from "white" modernism in order to
reinvent, revise, reclaim, redefine those notions concerning the spiritual
and/or ethical value and purpose of art.

I am thinking particularly of the idea of art as transcendent, as in
Walter Pater, or the idea that art will cure what ails "civilization," as in
Matthew Arnold, even as such ideas are increasingly accompanied by their
constant and incessant problematization as in Kafka, T. S. Eliot, James
Joyce, Gertrude Stein, and others. This is so much the case that much of
modernism inadvertently memorializes the failure of art to transcend the
material. But there is also the setting up of a dichotomy between the cyn-
icism and demoralization of realizing art's failure to cure "civilization"
and the notion that something—the "other," "Nature," "the unconscious"—lies beyond both "civilization" and "art" and can, therefore, offer
salvation.

Most significantly in the case of modernists like Gauguin or Picasso,
it is a "primitive other" which is made to signify the possibility of moving
beyond. Of course, we've come to understand that such a dichotomy is the
raw material of "racism," "neo-imperialism," "neo-colonialism," and the
passive-aggressive course of appropriation that has accompanied the rise of
transglobal capital. It is perhaps necessary to recognize as well that as
whites were using such ideology to turn their backs on the cultural production of people of color, artists of color were picking up the pieces, borrowing, re-appropriating that which had been appropriated, constructing a
dialogue with white modernism (one-sided and unheeded by white modernists), and, significantly, a dialogue with a silent, inarticulate "primitive
other" whom they saw as their former or their undiscovered selves. The
more educated and the more schooled artists of color were in the precepts
of European art, the more middle class they were—and they really needed
to be both in order to survive—the more likely they were to join white
artists in conceptualizing a "primitive other" as unfathomable, even as they
might refer to it as a better, wiser, truer self. As black artists and artists of
color whom I would describe as modernists—Jean Toomer, Langston

Hughes, Richard Wright, Ralph Ellison, Zora Neale Hurston, Jacob Lawrence, Romare Bearden—tried to close the gap between their educated "white" selves and their primitive "black" selves, they were nevertheless, involuntarily or voluntarily, engaged in a relentless critique of such unities as the self, the primitive, and the natural through their enunciation of how these categories have been used to render blacks "invisible." So to return to my earlier point, if modernism is viewed as a network of diverse, heterogeneous, and still open-ended approaches to the problem of cultural progress, then it becomes possible to talk not only about European modernism in the past, but also the rise of modernist strategies (among others) by emergent global cultures of the Third World, as well as minority cultures in the "First World."

The relevance of all of this to Tim Rollins + K.O.S. involves only speculation on my part, since what they're doing doesn't really fit any of the familiar categories. It seems to me quite clear that while Rollins's own inclinations as an artist would generally place him among postmodern strategists, he has often remarked that his relationship to K.O.S. has been pulling him toward a reevaluation of modernism and modernist strategies as abstract painting. My theory is quite simply that aspects of modernism—for instance, Picasso's *Guernica* or Georgia O'Keeffe's Southwest—make more sense to the young artists of color in K.O.S. than they do to Rollins, and as such, they are moving him toward their practice. I want to emphasize that by this I do not mean that they are coming up with a rehash of obsolete, white modernist strategies, but rather that Rollins is engaged with them, perhaps somewhat unknowingly, in the formulation of yet another multicultural strain of modernism. It is more streetwise, democratic, and inclusive than the old "white" modernism; it is less naïve and/or "ethnic" than the old "black" modernisms; yet, at the same time, it is more utopian and hopeful than any kind of postmodernism heretofore. It is doing in art something like what you might get in dance if you crossbred the Alvin Ailey Dance Company with Pina Bausch.

But the problem of the absence of multiculturalism at the level of content remains. When asked why K.O.S. doesn't read Toni Morrison's *Song of Solomon*, Rollins is dismissive. "We're too close to it," he'll say, or, "We prefer to work with dead art," like Kafka and Flaubert. Novels and paintings are dead forms, so what more fitting tribute to the failure of modernism than painting on a novel? People of color and their deployment of novels and paintings simply don't enter into it.

While it is true that the examination of the work of a black female writer like Morrison does run counter to the critical purpose of the group as defined by Rollins. I can't help but wonder if *Song of Solomon* is really that much more readable to these mostly Puerto Rican teenage boys. My perception in teaching such novels at universities is that even young black girls don't have any special access to Morrison's language. They have to be taught to read her. In particular, they have to be taught to read her critically. But if Morrison is, however, more readable to K.O.S., then wouldn't that make it precisely the text to make reading less "boring"?

Yet a further question remains whether or not there would be the same interest in the art market for a K.O.S. that painted on the text of Toni Morrison or Toni Cade Bambara, or even *The Autobiography of Malcolm X*, as they did at an earlier stage. Which brings us back to the emphasis in a white art world on a white male Tim Rollins at the head of K.O.S. Isn't it also true that if Rollins were black and a woman and the texts were black or Puerto Rican, with the "kids" being black or Puerto Rican as well, that we would be talking about something much less marketable, something infinitely more obscure?

✤ ✤ ✤ ✤ ✤ ✤ ✤ ✤ ✤

While the group began its existence in 1982, with a rapid turnover in the kids who made up the group, the first real success came with the first *Amerika* painting done during the school year of 1984–85. Rollins's classroom on the third floor of I.S. 52 was where all the difficult kids congregated when they had nothing else to do. The canvas covered with the pages from Franz Kafka's novel *Amerika* hung in the room for a year. Rollins told the evocative story of Karl and The Nature Theatre of Oklahoma and perhaps forty kids, only one of whom is still in K.O.S., took a serious shot at designing golden horns. "Shots" seems not an entirely metaphorical way of describing what was happening in a classroom in which throwing things was not uncommon. The result was *Amerika I*, first exhibited in "The State of the Art: The New Social Commentary" at the Barbara Gladstone Gallery. It was subsequently sold to The Chase Manhattan Bank, and undoubtedly was important in securing for them a National Endowment for the Arts grant. This money was used to pay for a studio of their own to go to after school, the first step toward independence, autonomy, and an art-world identity for the Workshop.

Michele Wallace

Twelve other *Amerikas* would follow. Among these were *Amerika IX, 1987*, a collaboration with kids in Charlotte, North Carolina; *Amerika XI, 1988*, a collaboration with kids in Minneapolis, Minnesota; and *Amerika: For Thoreau, 1988*, a collaboration with teenagers from the Dorchester and Roxbury areas in Boston, Massachusetts. The mural *Amerika—For the People of Bathgate, 1988*, was made in collaboration with the faculty and students of Central Elementary School 4 in the South Bronx.

The process for Tim Rollins + K.O.S. is a lengthy one, sometimes a year and often much longer. When making an *Amerika* painting—or any of their other projects such as the *Temptations of St. Anthony* series, or *The Red Badge of Courage* series in which they painted wounds, or *The Scarlet Letter* series in which they made elaborate calligraphic *As*—K.O.S. will select and study the relevant works of other artists in museums and in art books, and images from popular culture. They will do thousands of drawings, which they call "jamming." Then they'll begin to do painted studies on individual pages of the text itself. They sometimes do a large painting as a study. Only at the end of this process is the full-scale work made.

Kafka never finished the novel *Amerika*, and he never intended that it should be published, having left instructions with Max Brod, his best friend, to burn all of his manuscripts. Nor did he ever visit the U.S., although it is reported that he thought of Americans as "healthy and optimistic." Yet that isn't the picture Kafka actually paints of Amerika. In the book, Karl, the protagonist, forced to leave his native land at sixteen because he has made a servant girl pregnant, comes to Amerika on a boat. A wealthy and powerful uncle appears at the boat to take Karl in. After a brief period of language instruction and horseback riding lessons, he is rather arbitrarily disinherited for disobeying the uncle's advice. Karl then embarks on a series of adventures during which he encounters a variety of unscrupulous characters, all of whom take advantage of his youth and his lack of family in order to exploit and abuse him. Nevertheless, the novel ends on an upbeat note with a gap in the text and then the final chapter called "The Nature Theatre of Oklahoma."

It is this chapter which concerns Tim Rollins + K.O.S. Rollins narrates the story: "At the end of the year, he's ready to go home. He says to himself, 'I can't handle it, I'm a failure, I can't make it in Amerika.' And so just as he's about ready to get back on the boat and go home, he hears this sound. It sounds like a Salvation Army band. They're all carrying these placards. And the placards say, 'Come join the Nature Theatre of Oklahoma! The Nature Theatre of Oklahoma, where anyone can be an artist and everyone is welcome!' And Karl looks at this and thinks, 'I have been lied to, I have been cheated, I have been robbed, and I am sure this is just another situation where I'm going to get ripped off. But then again, that one sign says "Everyone is welcome." Even if it is bullshit, I'm going to try it. I've never seen that in Amerika before.' So he joins.

"Then they say, 'Well, we're leaving for Clayton tonight on a train. We're all going to go at midnight so you've got to get registered at the race track. You have to register before midnight because that's when the train goes, and you lose your chance forever.' So he goes to the racetrack, and as he approaches the racetrack, he hears this incredible sound of a traffic jam, and it's hundreds of horns like a jazz orchestra or something. And as he walks into the racetrack he sees an incredible scene of hundreds of people standing on pedestals, dressed up like angels blowing whatever they want to on these long golden horns. There's a big fat person who's making little noises, and a little skinny person making big noises, and it's this big kind of mess. All these sounds together.

"And Karl asks the old man who brings him in, 'What is this?' and the guy says, 'This is Amerika where everyone has a voice and everyone can say what they want.' That's it. Then I say, 'Now look, you all have your own taste and you have different voices. If you could be a golden instrument, if you could play a song of your freedom and dignity and your future and everything you feel about Amerika and this country, what would your horn look like?'"

In the case of the *Amerika* series, the variety of horns that have emerged has been simply stupendous—from letters to body parts to animals to piles of shit, floating sperm, baseball bats, and animals—yet none of the images engages in direct representation. Everything looks a little like something but not quite enough to call it that. The group has drawn its inspiration from a wide variety of sources: Marcel Duchamp, Francisco Goya, Mathias Grünewald, Georgia O'Keeffe, Pablo Picasso, Joan Miró, Paul Klee, William Morris, Paulo Uccello, and African and Native American art, Dr. Seuss, medical textbooks, comic books, and newspapers, just to name a few. Perhaps the most successful painting in the series that unites their political concerns with the visual effect has been *Amerika VI*, which was done as a memorial to the racial incident at Howard Beach. All of the paintings share a compelling and sophisticated beauty.

For me, however, a bittersweet note in all of this is the idea of Oklahoma being the home of the Nature Theatre where anybody can be an artist. Kafka could have scarcely had any idea of what the real Oklahoma was like as the final destination to which the so-called "Five Civilized Tribes" of the Southeast were driven in a series of forced marches called "The Trail of Tears." Yet his vision of the Nature Theatre seems to bear traces of foreboding as well as utopian hopefulness.

Not surprisingly, these traces of foreboding appear in particular in two details of the story which are often overlooked. First, the hundreds of angels with horns are not just people but "women" on pedestals and, second, Karl calls himself "Negro" when he signs up for work at the Nature Theatre in a typically Kafkaesque scene in which it is repeatedly insisted that "Negro" could not be his real name, although no one says why. Few Americans have any idea of Oklahoma in history or in the present except that it's the place they never want to go. Perhaps because of the fame of the musical *Oklahoma*, today's urban dwellers think of Oklahoma as the home of rednecks and oilmen. But, in fact, after the Civil War blacks thought of it as the land of opportunity, and there was talk of its being designated a black state or a Native American state around the time that it entered the union. Now black and Puerto Rican kids in the South Bronx, who can read neither Kafka nor the history of Oklahoma (although they can imagine both), are painting golden horns on the pages of a German novel which invokes the name of Oklahoma in the spirit of hope, freedom, democracy, and art. Only, as the children of neo-imperialism, they know there isn't any frontier, and they'll have to invent their own.

Note

The author would like to acknowledge that since this article first appeared, Rollins and K.O.S. *have* worked with texts by writers of color, including Linda Brent's *Incidents in the Life of a Slave Girl*.

Ahmad, Aijaz. "Jameson's Rhetoric of Otherness and the 'National Allegory.'" *Social Text* 17 (Fall 1987).

Aronowitz, Stanley, and Henry A. Giroux. *Education Under Siege: The Conservative, Liberal, and Radical Debate Over Schooling.* South Hadley, Mass.: Bergin & Garvey, 1985.

Baker, Houston. *Modernism and the Harlem Renaissance.* Chicago: University of Chicago Press, 1987.

Benjamin, Walter. *Illuminations.* New York: Schocken Books, 1968.

Burner, Eric R. *And Gently He Shall Lead Them: Robert Parris Moses and Civil Rights in Mississippi.* New York: New York University Press, 1994.

Foster, Hal. "The 'Primitive' Unconscious of Modern Art, or White Skin Black Masks." *Recodings: Art, Spectacle, Cultural Politics.* Seattle: Bay Press, 1985.

Gates, Henry Louis. *Figures in Black: Words, Signs, and the "Radical Self."* New York: Oxford University Press, 1989.

Giroux, Henry A. *Schooling and the Struggle for Public Life: Critical Pedagogy in the Modern Age.* Minneapolis: University of Minnesota Press, 1988.

Jameson, Frederic. "Third World Literature in the Era of Multinational Capitalism." *Social Text* 15 (Fall 1986).

Lemann, Nicholas. *The Big Test: The Secret History of the American Meritocracy.* New York: Farrar, Straus and Giroux, 1999.

Kruger, Barbara, and Phil Mariani, eds. *Remaking History.* Seattle: Bay Press, 1989.

Nasaw, David. *Children of the City: At Work & at Play.* New York: Oxford University Press, 1985.

———. *Schooled to Order: A Social History of Public Schooling in the United States.* New York: Oxford University Press, 1979.

Ravitch, Diane. *Left Back: A Century of Failed School Reforms.* New York: Simon & Schuster, 2000.

Schor, Ira, and Paolo Freire. *A Pedagogy for Liberation: Dialogues on Transforming Education.* South Hadley, Mass.: Bergin & Garvey, 1987.

Spivak, Gayatri. "Can the Subaltern Speak?" *Wedge: The Imperialism of Representation/The Representation of Imperialism* 7/8 (Winter/Spring 1985).

Michele Wallace

Writing Programs in Art Museums

by Kathy Walsh-Piper

*t*EACHING STUDENTS TO WRITE means teaching them to slow down, see carefully, observe, and respond. One great way to spark new awareness is to take students to a museum, a place set aside for looking and contemplation. Many art museums offer programs to encourage writing in their galleries: poets-in-residence, teacher in-services, curriculum programs, and programs for adults. Here is a sampling of what is happening in museums across the country.

Chicago

The Art Institute of Chicago's programs for teachers, students, and adults all incorporate writing. **Looking to Write/Writing to See** is a program that brings teams of visual art and language arts teachers together to develop interdisciplinary curricula. The museum also offers art and creative writing tours for middle school and high school students. In another AIC program, **Voices**, famous authors read works on or inspired by artworks from the museum's collections, and professional actors dramatically present the writings along with slides of the works. Writings on the AIC's permanent

collection by authors such as Saul Bellow and Susan Sontag were collected
in the book *Transforming Vision: Writers on Art*, a wonderful inspiration
for those interested in connections between writing and art.

Kathy
Walsh-Piper

Dallas

At the **Dallas Museum of Art**, creative writing workshops are available to
adult learners from the community. The original two-hour sessions, which
were offered in connection with special exhibitions, were so well-received
that they are now regular monthly offerings.

The program has had some surprising results. At the very first session, a group writing in the modern galleries was asked to make a list of
sounds and movements in a painting. A professional jazz singer working
from a Mondrian abstraction burst out with "I can't write it—I'll sing
it!"—and his song was stunning. During a session focused on the art of
Thomas Moran, a painter of the Western landscape whose work helped
influence the formation of the National Parks, the class was asked to write
about Moran's unusual colors in ways similar to how Rudyard Kipling
described certain colors ("honey splashed with port wine"). A guard in the
gallery was quietly writing along with the group, and shared her descriptions, astounding them all. Similarly, after a writing exercise on Georgia
O'Keeffe, a professor who brought her art education students from Texas
Women's University told the staff that one of the students who participated had never spoken before!

As Carolyn Bess, who runs the programs, explains, "It's a great way
to get participants to discover works of art from a different perspective, to
slow down and look carefully and think about personal reactions to a work
of art." Tracy Bays, another staff member, remarks: "People can be naturally poetic. In the situation of writing in the galleries, they can channel
those abilities." The writing, sharing, and group support "creates a way for
them to feel confident when they might not think they know enough."

Detroit

The Detroit Institute of Arts and the Detroit Public Schools co-sponsor
Students Writing About Art. The art museum selects ten works of art and

30 schools per year. Each teacher is sent a package of slides and information and brings the students to the museum, where they write poems. Later, the poems are submitted to a juried contest. A selection of winning poems is posted in the galleries next to their respective works of art, to be enjoyed by the public. The winning poems are read at a concluding celebration.

Houston

For the past seventeen years, Houston's **Writers in the Schools (WITS)**, a nonprofit organization, has been sending professional poets, fiction writers, and playwrights into the classrooms to lead creative writing workshops for children in grades K–12. Each writer visits three classrooms for 28 weeks throughout the school year and has the opportunity to bring students on writing tours of The Menil Collection, a Houston art museum. This year alone WITS scheduled more than 85 tours for more than 8,000 students. Tours are followed by an in-class art project led by a visual artist.

WITS Executive Director, Robin Reagler, stresses the value of visual art in a writer's residency: "Sometimes kids who don't respond to the written prompts that writers bring to the classroom will suddenly come alive at the museum. Visual cues can help many children find their way to language. Our writers keep journals as they teach, and time and again we hear of the amazing response they get from students in the museums, using art as a catalyst for writing."

Los Angeles

The J. Paul Getty Museum in Malibu, California, offers **Art and Language Arts for Teachers**, a professional development program for educators in the Los Angeles Unified School District. The two-year program includes curriculum development. One assignment is to design a lesson based on an artwork in the Getty and to link it to required curricula, usually in language arts or social studies. Teachers consider what is important about the work and what they want students to glean from it. As Jenny Siegenthaler, who works with the teachers, says, "The program gives teachers ownership; they come up with things that really work for their students."

The **Poets in the Galleries** program at the Fine Arts Museum of San Francisco also uses poets and other writers to connect poetry and art for students. The original concept, developed in response to the 1987 English/Language Arts Curriculum for the State of California, was to give teachers an alternative to the typical "art appreciation tour." Students, fourth grade and up, visit the museum twice, where they attend 90-minute sessions with a poet. They may or may not have had comparable poetry writing experience in the schools. The presentation focuses less on art history, than on personal response.

Kathy
Walsh-Piper

As I observed the program, poet Devorah Major told a group of seventh graders: "I am a writer, I write whatever and however I want to write. I will give you suggestions, but you will do your own thing." She challenged students as they looked at a painting of a man by Nicolas Poussin. "This is a portrait. Would you say that this is a man?" Through the ensuing discussion, the students explored the distinction between an *image* of a man and an *actual* man. Major compared a painting to the image in a mirror—a reflection—and explained that poets and painters both work with images.

She then skillfully drew the group into considering color by reading a richly textured poem about *black*, using words such as *sweet*, *dark*, *rich*, *raisins*, and *molasses*. She urged the students to immerse themselves in one color in a painting and to translate it by using their senses. Using a landscape by Martin Johnson Heade, students paired color words for *red*: *fire red*, *sunset red*, *heat red*, *love red*, and *cranberry red*. "You have to make it yours, to describe your own images of it." She asked students to "go inside" the picture, and to pair words in order to describe it: *rolling tide*, *warm sunset*, *fading pink*.

Santa Barbara

At the **Santa Barbara Museum of Art**, April is designated "Poetry Month." English classes come for writing tours in which students work together to compose a collaborative poem about a work of art—using a cookie sheet and magnetic words to get ideas flowing. Then students have individual time to draft poems and take notes, which they complete and polish back in the classroom. The Santa Barbara Museum also has a cross-generational program, in which junior high students work with senior citizens on subjects such as holiday recollections. Sometimes they brainstorm and write together; other times a student takes notes as the seniors speak, and then translates the ideas. On occasion, they all work together to create a series of chorus-like responses. The results are read at a reception at the retirement home and demonstrate the richness of one generation understanding another.

Washington, D.C.

Many of the programs that combine art and creative writing are joint projects between museums and schools. The National Gallery of Art in Washington, D.C., has a multiple-visit program called **Art Around the Corner**, an eight-year partnership with local District of Columbia public schools. Art Around the Corner brings nearly 400 fifth and sixth grade students from four inner-city schools to the Gallery eight times during the school year to view and discuss works of art. All tours tie into the District of Columbia curriculum.

Creative writing exercises prepare students for their visits to the museum. Specific writing exercises—such as journal writing and a combination of sketching and writing—have been incorporated into the museum visits, either at certain stops on the tour or in the last 20 minutes of each 90-minute visit. The teachers and docents involved with the workshops practice all the writing assignments that will be given to the students. Paige Simpson, program assistant, explained, "We can suggest writing activities based on art and put them in the lesson plans, but until the teachers and docents actually do them and realize how much fun they are and the potential they have, it doesn't sink in."

Winston-Salem

In the Reynolda House, Museum of American Art in Winston-Salem, North Carolina, the works of art are arranged comfortably throughout an historic home. Camilla Wilcox and the late Neil J. Wilcox developed the **Young Writer's Workshop** and taught it for more than fourteen years. Since 1998, the intensive summer writing program—now known as **Writing Adventures**—has been expanded to four week-long sessions for students in grades 3–5 and 6–10. Each week concludes with a public reception and reading accompanied by an exhibition of art created by the writers during the program. Neil and Camilla both discovered early on that working from art was useful because it helped students learn to visualize before beginning to write.

Kathy
Walsh-Piper

In a recent session, a new lesson was taught each day based on the students' favorite piece of art in the Reynolda House collection, or, more exactly, the one that "captured their imaginations." The students were first asked to look for a landscape painting so they could write a story about it. They were encouraged to allow an element (e.g, a tree) in the painting to speak and tell all that it sees and hears. The next day they searched for figures in the artworks, and were asked to pick one that inspired them and write a dramatic monologue about what the figure might be saying to or feeling about another figure in the painting or the observer. They then looked for still-life pieces, and wrote haikus or poems based on specific objects depicted in the paintings. The last day, each student wrote a final description of his or her favorite painting, using all the elements of writing they had practiced all week. The students then gave the description to their parents and had them find the painting described.

✦ ✦ ✦ ✦ ✦ ✦ ✦ ✦ ✦

The programs described above take place in both large and small art museums. A small museum or art gallery can provide an intimate setting for writing. And if you are a teacher in a locale without a museum, don't despair—color slides, posters, prints, or postcards can work well. In addition, many museums offer free loan materials. Consult the list of resources below.

The Art Institute of Chicago: Art and Stories Class; Art and Creative Writing Tour. A description of the tour and the materials used by the students is available to teachers. Contact: The Art Institute of Chicago, 111 South Michigan Avenue, Chicago, IL 60603; tel. (312) 443-3691.

The Detroit Institute of Arts: Student Writings About Art. The *Visitor's Guide* includes many self-directed learning strategies and also provides a short bibliography. Contact: Jennifer Williams, Assistant Curator, Department of Education. The Detroit Institute of the Arts, 5200 Woodward Avenue, Detroit, MI 48202; tel. (313) 833-7900.

The Fine Arts Museum of San Francisco: Poets in the Gallery. A poetry anthology is produced every year highlighting student work. Contact: Jeannine L. Jeffries, Assistant Director of Education, The Fine Arts Museum of San Francisco, California Palace of the Legion of Honor, Lincoln Park, 100 34th Avenue, San Francisco, CA 94118; tel. (415) 750-7692.

National Gallery of Art: Art Around the Corner. A packet on the multiple-visit program is available; call (202) 842-6880. In addition, teaching packets, color-slide programs, films, videocassettes, and videodiscs are available as free loans to schools, libraries, community organizations, and individuals across the country. For a free catalogue describing materials and ordering procedures, call (202) 842-6263, or write to Department of Education Resources, National Gallery of Art, Washington, DC 20565.

Reynolda House, Museum of American Art: Writing Adventures. For more information or educational materials, contact Kathleen Hutton, Curator of Education, Reynolda House, Museum of American Art, P.O. Box 11765, Winston-Salem, NC 27116-1765; tel. (336) 725-5325 or (888) 663-1149.

Santa Barbara Museum of Art: Poetry Month. Contact: Patsy Hicks, 1130 State Street, Santa Barbara, CA 93101; tel. (805) 923-4364.

Writers in the Schools (WITS). Contact: Robin Reagler, Executive Director, 1523 West Main, Houston, TX 77006; tel. (713) 523-3877; fax (713) 523-3877.

Bibliography

Bunchman, Janis, and Stephanie Briggs. *Activities for Creating Pictures and Poetry.* Worchester, Mass.: Davis Publications, 1994.
Carr, David, et al. *The Museum as a Place for Learning.* Ithaca: Herbert F. Johnson Museum of Art, Cornell University, 2001.

Department of Museum Education, Art Institute of Chicago. *Looking to*
    Write/ Writing to See: A Course in Visual and Language Arts.
    Chicago: The Art Institute of Chicago, 1996.
Koch, Kenneth, and Kate Farrell, eds. *Talking to the Sun.* New York: The
    Metropolitan Museum of Art/Henry Holt, 1985.
Lim, Genny, ed. *Eyes of the Wind: An Anthology of Poems.* San
    Francisco: Fine Arts Museum of San Francisco, 1992.
————, ed. *Through Our Voices: An Anthology.* San Francisco: Fine Arts
    Museum of San Francisco, 1990.
————, ed. *Unsilented Voices: An Anthology.* San Francisco: Fine Arts
    Museum of San Francisco, 1991.
————, and Jeannine Jeffries, eds. *Sunlight and Shadow: An Anthology
    of Poems.* San Francisco: Fine Arts Museum of San Francisco,
    1993.
Major, Devorah, and Jorge Argueta, eds. *Who Has Looked In Your Mirror?*
    San Francisco: Fine Arts Museum of San Francisco.
Paschal, Huston, ed. *The Store of Joys: Writers Celebrate the North
    Carolina Museum of Art's Fiftieth Anniversary.* Winston-Salem,
    N.C.: North Carolina Museum of Art, 1997.
Transforming Vision: Writers on Art. Selected and introduced by Edward
    Hirsch. Boston: The Art Institute of Chicago/Little, Brown, 1994.

Kathy
Walsh-Piper

ACKNOWLEDGMENTS: Many thanks to all the writers and museum educators who participated in this project and the kind support of the Robert H.
Smith Fellowship from the National Gallery of Art, which originally
funded travel and research for this project.

Select Bibliography

Creative Writing and Visual Art Sources

Adams, Pat, ed. *With a Poet's Eye: A Tate Gallery Anthology*. London: Tate Gallery Publications, 1986.

Altieri, Charles. *Painterly Abstraction in Modernist American Poetry*. University Park, Pa.: Pennsylvania State University Press, 1990.

Becker, Andrew Sprague. *The Shield of Achilles and the Poetics of Ekphrasis*. Lanham, Md.: Rowman & Littlefield Publishers, 1995.

Buchwald, Emilie, ed. *The Poet Dreaming in the Artist's House*. Minneapolis: Milkweed Editions, 1984.

Carpenter, John. *Creating the World: Poetry, Art, and Children*. Seattle: University of Washington Press, 1986.

Caws, Mary Ann. *The Art of Interference: Stressed Readings in Verbal and Visual Texts*. Cambridge, England: Polity Press in association with B. Blackwell, 1989.

Childers, Pamela B., Eric Hobson, and John A. Mullin. *Articulating: Teaching Writing in a Visual World*. Portsmouth, N.H.: Boynton-Cook, 1989.

Collins, Judith, and Elsbeth Lindner. *Writing on the Wall: Women Writers on Women Artists*. London: Weidenfeld & Nicolson, 1993.

Gorrell, Nancy. "Teaching Empathy through Ecphrastic Poetry: Entering a Curriculum of Peace." *English Journal* 89, no. 5 (May 2000).

Grossberg, Lawrence, et al., eds. *Cultural Studies*. New York: Routledge, 1992.

Heffernan, James A. W. *Museum of Words: The Poetics of Ekphrasis from Homer to Ashbery*. Chicago: University of Chicago Press, 1993.

Hines, Thomas Jensen. *Collaborative Form: Studies in the Relations of the Arts*. Kent, Ohio: Kent State University Press, 1991.

Hollander, John. *The Gazer's Spirit: Poems Speaking to Silent Works of Art*. Chicago: University of Chicago Press, 1995.

Johnson, Paul. *Literacy through the Book Arts*. Portsmouth, N.H.: Heinemann, 1993.

Koch, Kenneth, and Kate Farrell, eds. *Talking to the Sun: An Illustrated Anthology of Poems for Young People*. New York: The Metropolitan Museum of Art/Henry Holt and Company, 1985.

Kress, Anne, et al. *Teaching Seeing and Writing*. Boston: Bedford/St. Martin's Press, 2000.

McQuade, Donald, and Christine McQuade. *Seeing and Writing*. Boston: Bedford/St. Martin's Press, 2000.

Méndez-Ramírez, Hugo. *Neruda's Ekphrastic Experience: Mural Art and Canto General*. Lewisburg, Pa.: Bucknell University Press, 1999.

Mitchell, W. J. Thomas. *Picture Theory: Essays on Verbal and Visual Representation*. Chicago: University of Chicago Press, 1994.

Persin, Margaret Helen. *Getting the Picture: The Ekphrastic Principle in Twentieth-Century Spanish Poetry*. Lewisburg, Pa., London, and Cranbury, N.J.: Bucknell University Press/Associated University Presses, 1997.

Rogers, Franklin R., with Mary Ann Rogers. *Painting and Poetry: Form, Metaphor, and the Language of Literature*. Lewisburg, Pa., and Cranwell, N.J.: Bucknell University Press/Associated University Presses, 1985.

Rothenberg, Jerome, and Steven Clay, eds. *A Book of the Book: Some Works & Projections About the Book & Writing*. New York: Granary Books, 2000.

Scott, Grant F. *The Sculpted Word: Keats, Ekphrasis, and the Visual Arts*. Hanover, N.H.: University Press of New England, 1994.

Transforming Vision: Writers on Art. Selected and introduced by Edward Hirsch. Boston: Art Institute of Chicago/Little, Brown, 1994.

Williams, Susan S. *Confounding Images: Photography and Portraiture in Antebellum American Fiction.* Philadelphia: University of Pennsylvania Press, 1997.

Visual Art Sources

Ashbery, John. *Reported Sightings: Art Chronicles, 1957–1987.* Edited by David Bergman. New York: Knopf, 1989.

Atkins, Robert. *ArtSpeak: A Guide to Contemporary Ideas, Movements, and Buzzwords.* New York: Abbeville Press, 1990.

Barthes, Roland. *Camera Lucida: Reflections on Photography.* Translated by Richard Howard. New York: Noonday Press, 1982.

Berger, John. *About Looking.* New York: Pantheon Books, 1980.

———. *Ways of Seeing.* New York: Viking Penguin, 1977.

Chasman, Deborah, and Edna Chiang, eds. *Drawing Us In: How We Experience Visual Art.* Boston: Beacon Press, 2000.

Henri, Robert. *The Art of the Spirit.* New York: Harper and Row, 1951.

Hicok, Bob. "Rivera's Golden Gate Murals." In *The Legend of Light.* Madison: University of Wisconsin Press, 1995.

hooks, bell. *Emma Amos: Changing the Subject: Paintings and Prints, 1992–1994.* New York: Art in General, 1994.

Kandinsky, Wassily. *Concerning the Spiritual in Art.* New York: Dover Publications, Inc., 1977.

Karp, Ivan, and Steven D. Lavine. *Exhibiting Cultures: The Poetics and Politics of Museum Display.* Washington, D.C.: Smithsonian Institution, 1991.

Langer, Susanne. *Feeling and Form.* New York: Charles Scribner's Sons, 1953.

Lippard, Lucy R. *From the Center: Feminist Essays on Women's Art.* New York: Dutton, 1976.

———. *Mixed Blessings: New Art in a Multicultural America.* New York: Pantheon Books, 1990.

Oates, Joyce Carol. *George Bellows: American Artist.* Hopewell, N.J.: Ecco Press, 1995.

Our Land/Ourselves: American Indian Contemporary Artists. An exhibition organized by the University Art Gallery, University at Albany, State University of New York. Albany, N.Y.: University Art Gallery, University at Albany, State University of New York, 1990.

Rilke, Rainer Maria. *Letters on Cézanne*. Edited by Clara Rilke. Translated by Joel Agee. London: Jonathan Cape, 1988.

Rollins, Tim. *Amerika: Tim Rollins + K.O.S.* Edited by Gary Garrels. New York: Dia Art Foundation, 1989.

———. *The Temptation of Saint Antony, XV–XXXIV: The Solitaries.* San Francisco: Crown Point Press, 1990.

Sontag, Susan. *On Photography*. New York: Farrar, Straus and Giroux, 1977.

Stone, Myrna. *The Art of Loss*. East Lansing: Michigan State University Press, 2001.

Strand, Mark. *Hopper*. Hopewell, N.J.: Ecco Press, 1994.

Walker, John A. *Visual Culture: An Introduction*. Manchester, England and New York: Manchester University Press/St. Martin's Press, 1997.

Winterson, Jeanette. *Art Objects: Essays on Ecstasy and Effrontery.* London: Jonathan Cape, 1995.

Sources on Collaboration

Agee, James, and Walker Evans. *Let Us Now Praise Famous Men*. New York: Mariner Books, 2001.

Artists' Books in the Modern Era 1870–2000. The Reva and David Logan Collection. San Francisco: Fine Arts Museum of San Francisco, 2001.

Ashbery, John. *Self-Portrait in a Convex Mirror*. With original prints by Richard Avedon, Elaine de Kooning, Willem de Kooning, Jim Dine, Jane Freilicher, Alex Katz, R. B. Kitaj, and Larry Rivers. San Francisco: Arion Press, 1984.

Berssenbrugge, Mei-mei, and Kiki Smith. *Endocrinology*. Berkeley, Calif.: Kelsey St. Press, 1997.

Cappellazzo, Amy, and Elizabeth Licata, eds. *Robert Creeley's Collaborations*. Buffalo, N.Y.: Castellani Art Museum, 1999.

Castleman, Riva. *A Century of Artists Books*. New York: Museum of Modern Art, 1994.

Césaire, Aimé. *Lost Body (Corps perdu)*. Illustrations by Pablo Picasso. Introduction by Clayton Eshleman and Annette Smith. New York: G. Braziller, 1986.

Davenport, Guy. *A Balthus Notebook*. New York: Ecco Press. 1989.

Ewald, Wendy. *Secret Games: Collaborative Works with Children 1969–1999*. New York: Scalo, 2000.

Lewallen, Constance M., ed. *Joe Brainard: A Retrospective*. New York: Granary Books, 2001.

———. *Joe Brainard: A Retrospective*. Berkeley: University of California, Berkeley Art Museum; New York City: Granary Books in association with Mandeville Special Collections Library, University of California, San Diego, 2001.

Motherwell, Robert, ed. *The Dada Painters and Poets: An Anthology*. Cambridge, Mass.: Harvard University Press, 1981.

Yau, John. *Berlin Diptychon: Poems by John Yau; Photographs by Bill Barrette*. New York: Timken Publishers, 1995.

Online Art Resources

Artcyclopedia: This site features a comprehensive index of museum sites, image archives, and art headlines. artcyclopedia.com

ArtLex: This site provides a collection of more than 2,700 terms and definitions covering all aspects of art. artlex.com

Art Resource: This site features an extensive digital library of over 10,000 artists. artres.com

Arts Edge: This site provides information on arts standards, model programs, and curricula. artsedge.kennedy-center.org

The Arts Education Partnership: This site offers links to the National Endowment for the Arts and the results of the NAEP "The Nation's Report Card" Arts Assessment. aep-arts.org

ArtsEdNet: This site features art lesson plans and curriculum ideas, as well as numerous virtual exhibitions. artsednet.getty.edu

ArtsNet: This site offers links to general art resources, including grants, venues, and events. artsnet.org

The President's Committee on the Arts and the Humanities: This site contains a national study of arts education and its effects. pcah.gov

The Visual Knowledge Program: This site provides lesson plans and ideas for incorporating art into public school curricula. vkp.org

Notes on Contributors

Will Alexander is a poet, novelist, essayist, and educator who lives in Los Angeles. He has three works forthcoming: a trilogy of novels, *Sunrise and Armageddon*, from Spuyten Duyvil; a novella, *Alien Weaving*, from Green Integer; and a book of poems, *Sri Lankan Loxodrome*, from Canopic Press.

Pamela Freeze Beal teaches English at Lee County High School in Sanford, North Carolina. In addition to contributing essays to professional journals and books, she is an annual presenter at the North Carolina English Teachers' Association, which named her English Teacher of the Year in 1998. She has received National Board Certification in Adolescent and Young Adult/English and Language Arts. She enjoys writing poetry and fiction and sponsors local workshops for students who are interested in writing creatively.

Terry Blackhawk is founder and director of InsideOut, Detroit's writers-in-schools program, and is the author of a book of poems, *Body & Field*, from Michigan State University Press. Her workshops and classes for teachers on crossovers between writing and visual art are held annually at the Detroit Institute of Arts. She has published poems based on visual art in many journals, including *Poet Lore*, *US 1*, *Ekphrasis*, *Spoon River*, *Sow's Ear Poetry Review*, and *MacGuffin*.

Barbara Flug Colin, contributing editor of *Frigate*, an online literary magazine, has published articles in various magazines: *Arts, New York Art Journal, Art Now, M/E/A/N/I/N/G, Teachers & Writers,* and *New Observations*. She teaches a poetry-writing program that she initiated eleven years ago at the Henry Viscardi School, a state funded elementary and high school for physically challenged students, in Albertson, New York.

Kristin Dombek teaches composition at New York University and Barnard College. She is writing a book on composition pedagogy with Scott Herndon, and a dissertation on conservative evangelical Christian entertainment and retail culture.

Tonya Foster is a writer and a teacher. Her poetry and fiction have appeared in *Callaloo, DrumVoices, Western Humanities Review, The Hat, Gulf Coast, Lungfull,* and elsewhere. She teaches English at the City College of New York and poetry and writing at Cooper Union. She currently lives in Harlem and is completing "Money Talk," a piece on poetry, paranoia, patronage, and race.

Gary Hawkins approaches the questions of poetry as a poet, essayist, critic, teacher of both elementary-age children and undergraduates, and as a Ph.D. student. Mr. Hawkins currently lives in Houston, Texas, with his wife and their two dogs.

Scott Herndon is the co-author of *Brave New Voices: The Youth Speaks Guide to Spoken Word Poetry* (Heinemann, 2001). He is finishing his first novel, *Let It Fall Down*. He has been a teacher in New York University's Expository Writing Program for five years, and is completing his Ph.D. in the English Program.

bell hooks is the author of many books, including *All About Love, Outlaw Culture, Teaching to Transgress,* and *Art on My Mind*.

Susan Karwoska has taught writing in the classroom with Teachers & Writers Collaborative, in a drug rehab program for mothers with young children on the Lower East Side, and at Brown University, where she received her M.F.A. A previous essay of hers on teaching was published in *The Alphabet of the Trees* (T&W Books, 2000). She lives in Brooklyn with her husband and three children, and is currently working on a novel.

Holly Masturzo is Director of Teaching & Learning at Writers in the Schools (WITS), a nonprofit organization in Houston, Texas. An essay she wrote appeared in *The Alphabet of the Trees* (T&W Books, 2000). She has a Ph.D. from the University of Houston.

Rosalind Pace is Writer-in-Residence at Cape Cod Lighthouse Charter School in Orleans, Massachusetts. Her poems have appeared in *American Poetry Review*, *Denver Quarterly*, *Ontario Review*, *Ploughshares*, and other journals, and her collages have been exhibited in galleries and museums. She was a poet-in-the-schools in Pennsylvania and New Jersey for 25 years, and now lives in Truro, Massachusetts.

Kristin Prevallet is the author of two books of poetry, *Perturbation, My Sister* (First Intensity, 1997) and *Scratch Sides* (Skanky Possum Press, 2002), as well as numerous chapbooks. She co-edited the literary magazine *apex of the M*, and has edited a selection of poems and collages by Helen Adam (forthcoming from the National Poetry Foundation). Recent essays have appeared in the anthologies *Telling it Slant: Avant-Garde Poetics of the 1990s* (University of Alabama Press, 2002) and *Women Writing Beat* (Rutgers University Press, 2002). She currently lives in Brooklyn, where she teaches writing workshops at Pratt Institute and Cooper Union's Saturday Outreach Program.

Tina Rotenberg has been Director of Visual Arts/Langauge Arts (VALA) since 1995. She received her Ph.D. from UC Berkeley in Comparative Literature in 1986. Her primary commitments include writing prose and poetry, drawing and painting, and photography. She has lived in Berkeley since 1976.

John Rybicki's stories and poems have appeared in *Field*, *Ohio Review*, *Bomb*, *The North American Review*, and *The Quarterly*, as well as in numerous anthologies. His first book of poems, *Traveling at High Speeds*, was published by New Issues Press. He works for InsideOut, an organization that brings writers into inner-city schools in Detroit.

Julie Moulds Rybicki's first book of poems, *The Woman with a Cubed Head*, was published in 1998 by New Issues Press. She is currently collaborating with photographer Mary Whalen on a full-length poetry/photography manuscript inspired by the limericks of Edward Lear. She taught Children's Literature and Writing for the Elementary Teacher for seven years at Western Michigan University, and has led numerous writing and photography workshops with children at schools and community centers.

Ezra Shales works in New York City museums and schools and makes public art projects involving photography, sculpture, and memory. His permanent installation, *Measure to Scale* (2001), is on the facade of 92 Allen Street in New York City. (If you visit it, he suggests you bring a permanent marker to add to it.) Shales received an M.F.A. from Hunter College and is currently working toward a Ph.D. at the Bard Graduate Center for Studies in the Decorative Arts, Design, and Culture.

Marcia Simon was trained as an art historian and is also a writer and child therapist. She is the author of *A Special Gift* (Harcourt Brace, 1978), which was made into an ABC-TV "Afterschool Special" in 1979 and won a Peabody Award. She lives in West Nyack, New York, and Truro, Massachusetts.

Michael Theune is a Ph.D. student in Literature and Creative Writing at the University of Houston. He holds degrees from Hope College, Oxford University, and the University of Iowa. He has taught undergraduate poetry workshops at the University of Iowa and the University of Houston, and has worked for three years with Writers in the Schools in Houston, Texas. His work has appeared in a variety of publications, including *Verse*, *The Iowa Review*, and *The New Republic*.

Lee Upton's fourth book of poems, *Civilian Histories*, was published in 2000 by the University of Georgia Press. Her third book of literary criticism, *The Muse of Abandonment*, was published by Bucknell University Press.

Anne Waldman is a poet, performer, professor, editor, and cultural activist. She is the author of numerous books of poetry, including *Fast Speaking Woman*, *Kill or Cure*, and *Marriage: A Sentence*. *Vow to Poetry*, a book of essays, interviews, and manifestos, was published by Coffee House Press in 2001. She is the co-founder of the Jack Kerouac School of Disembodied Poetics at Naropa University and the Artistic Director of its Summer Writing Program.

Michele Wallace is Professor of English at the City College of New York and the CUNY Graduate Center. She is also author of *Black Macho and the Myth of the Superwoman* (Doubleday, 1980), *Invisibility Blues: From Pop to Theory* (Verso, 1990), and *Dark Designs: Race, Gender, and Visual Culture* (forthcoming from Duke University Press).

Kathy Walsh-Piper is an art historian who has specialized in interdisciplinary education. She was the first educator to be designated "Museum Educator of the Year" by the National Art Education Society, and has worked at several museums, including the Art Institute of Chicago and the National Gallery of Art. She is currently a museum planning consultant and writer in Dallas, Texas. Her book *Image to Word: Art and Creative Writing* is forthcoming from Scarecrow Press.

Marjorie Welish, a poet, painter, and art critic, is the author of *The Annotated "Here" and Selected Poems* (Coffee House Press, 2000) and *Begetting Textile* (Equipage, 2000). She has contributed to several volumes on contemporary criticism and theory, including *Writing the Image after Roland Barthes* and *Uncontrollable Beauty: Toward a New Aesthetics*. Her selected criticism appears in *Signifying Art: Essays on Art after 1960* (Cambridge University Press, 1999). As a painter, she is affiliated with the Baumgartner Gallery in New York.

Beth Zasloff is a fiction writer who currently teaches at New York University and with Teachers & Writers Collaborative. Her fiction has appeared in *Jane* magazine, and she has collaborated with puppeteers in performances and exhibitions in New York City at P.S. 1, Contemporary Art Center, Los Kabayitos puppet theater, and the Collective Unconscious. She taught at Saint Ann's School in Brooklyn, New York, from 1996 to 1998.